D1577415

What Price Bordeaux?

Also by Benjamin Lewin

Genes

Essential Genes

Cells

What Price Bordeaux?

Benjamin Lewin MW

Vendange Press
Dover
2009

Copyright © 2009 by Benjamin Lewin

All rights reserved. Published in the United States
by Vendange Press.

Library of Congress Cataloging-in-Publication Data
Lewin, Benjamin
What Price Bordeaux / by
Benjamin Lewin
Includes bibliographical references and index.

ISBN 978-1-934259-20-7

Library of Congress Control Number: 2009924566

Without limiting the rights under copyright reserved above, no part of
this publication may be reproduced, stored in or introduced into a
retrieval system, or transmitted, in any form or by any means (electronic,
mechanical, photocopying, recording or otherwise) without the prior
written permission of both the copyright owner and the above publisher
of the book.

All enquiries should be directed to contact@vendangepress.com.

Printed in China
1 2 3 4 5 6 7 8 9 10

For the Anima Figure

Contents

Preface

WE WERE ON ONE OF OUR RESEARCH VISITS TO BORDEAUX. The plane from London taxied slowly into the terminal. We disembarked and walked in a line of passengers to immigration. The immigration booths were locked up and abandoned; there was no way through into the deserted airport. My wife turned to me and said, "Now you've gone and done it." She had been saying for ages that my incessant requests to the French authorities as I tried to establish the real facts behind the Bordeaux wine industry would get me banned from France. Bordeaux is one of the greatest places on earth for producing fine wine; but it has a mystique based on centuries of obscurity about details, and the light of transparency is rarely welcome. The security alert that had closed the airport was a good metaphor.

All had seemed friendly when I started the project, but things changed quickly at any attempt to delve below the superficial. When the Conseil des Grands Crus Classés heard I was writing a book, they immediately offered assistance in finding documents or photographs. But when I raised the sensitive question of whether information could be found on the land holdings of the great châteaux when they were classified in 1855, the answer started with "Malheureusement." Another professional organization, the CIVB, were at first happy to provide general information about the economics of Bordeaux production, but clammed up when we got down to fine details about sales in individual sectors. (They would not even tell me the average price of a bottle of red Bordeaux in 2007!)

It has been an interesting expedition trawling among the records to establish what really goes on in Bordeaux. Putting it all together, I have wary respect for the success of the Bordelais in building a powerful wine industry whose top wines have unrivalled quality and fetch unprecedented prices, but despair at their inability to recognize long-term over short-term interests and to deal with the endemic problems of generic wines; admiration for the top wines but dismay at the inability to stop the more obvious abuses; and concern as to whether traditional Bordeaux will survive the flying winemakers and future global warming.

Bordeaux is a place like no other. The range of quality runs from plonk to the finest on earth; the classification system is uniquely based on price but differs from place to place; wine production is tightly regulated as elsewhere in France, but when it comes to naming a wine you could drive a trailer load of jeroboams through the loopholes. In this book I have tried to establish the underlying realities of Bordeaux. What really goes on in the glittering palaces of the Grand Cru Classés and the extensive *caves* of the negociants? And of course the basic running theme is what this means for the consumer, and how is it possible to determine before purchase what lies inside that expensive bottle of Bordeaux?

Picking up the wine list in a shop or restaurant, under the heading "Bordeaux" you may well be faced with a price range from less than $10 to more than $1000. Superficially there is little to distinguish these wines: all are described as Château Quelquechose. All the bottles bear a label stating "Appellation Contrôlée," accompanied by the name of a wine-growing region. Regional descriptions vary from "Bordeaux" for the cheapest to "Pomerol" for the most expensive, yet in each region there is a wide range of prices, so the description does not necessarily carry any obvious implication. A handful of wines may be picked out as having a classification such as "Grand Cru Classé," but this means different things in different parts of Bordeaux. None of the labels identify grape varieties, yet some wines will be made predominantly from the austere Cabernet Sauvignon and others from the lush Merlot. Without any systematic description, how are these wines to be distinguished? What does regional description mean in Bordeaux? Does classification have any significance? What is the relationship between quality and price? Here I analyze these questions, from the rich wine-growing history of Bordeaux to the problems of today.

Bordeaux is full of paradoxes. The entire system of wine production in France is based on the notion of the supremacy of *terroir*, the distinctive and unchangeable quality of each individual vineyard plot. Yet man created the terrain of the Médoc, the most famous part of the wine region, when Dutch engineers drained the marshes in the 17th century, affecting drainage all around. The international reputation of Bordeaux was established by the classification of its top properties in 1855; yet the landholdings of these *Grand Cru Classés* have changed extensively since then without their classification being in the least affected. The top wines of Bordeaux are in such worldwide demand that the best vintages can scarcely be had for love nor money; yet generic wines are being sent for distillation because they cannot be given away at any price. Faced with the challenge from the New World, some châteaux have turned to a more "international" style of wine production, standing on its head the original attempt of New World producers to make wines that would compete with Bordeaux; now Bordeaux is making wines more like those of Napa Valley in California.

After losing a battle with France, Mary Tudor, Queen of England, said that after her death, Calais would be found engraved on her heart.

Many have similar feelings about Bordeaux: we respect it for establishing a paradigm that at its best is rarely, if ever, equaled—but at the same time we are filled with rueful exasperation at the ways of the Bordelais and concerned at possible loss of its traditional character. There are all too many laments about the globalization of wine, not merely in Bordeaux for that matter, and the arguments are often full of fury but short on facts. Here my approach is more quantitative than has been common for a subject that is usually viewed somewhat subjectively. I have done my best to dig out the facts that underlie what actually goes into the bottle, which are not always easy to establish. From this starting point, it becomes possible to base the debate on reality and, perhaps, to see where Bordeaux is going.

Thanks are due to many châteaux proprietors for information gained in the form of fascinating exchanges by correspondence or by visits to the châteaux, and also to those negociants and courtiers who allowed me access to their records of prices on the Place de Bordeaux. Given the inflammatory nature of the process of classification in Bordeaux, the conclusions suggested by these prices are likely to be controversial, and I believe that people would prefer not to be thanked by name, but my heartfelt thanks anyway. I am also indebted to archivists in Bordeaux and elsewhere who dug out files on the 1855 classification and other matters that had been carefully buried in obscurity. Additional thanks are due to Bill Blatch, Jean-Michel Comme, and Peter Sichel for their helpful comments on all or part of the manuscript. And the work would never have been finished without the efforts of Ann, my wife and indefatigable tasting companion.

Benjamin Lewin MW

1

Terroir and Typicité

MAN HAS PRODUCED WINE FOR THOUSANDS OF YEARS. Pottery dating from before 5400 B.C. has traces of tartaric acid, a compound produced specifically by grapes, indicating that the pots had contained wine.[1] We have no means of knowing what this wine was like, but the first cultivation of the grapevine as an agricultural crop can be traced to Mesopotamia around 4000 B.C. The cultivated grapevines were from the species Vitis vinifera, and all the famous varieties of today—such as Cabernet Sauvignon, Pinot Noir, or Chardonnay—are their descendants. Viticulture and vinification became quite sophisticated in Egypt by 2700 B.C.; jars from that period have stoppers with hieroglyphs giving details of the wine, much like a label of today.

Wine was important in the cultures of ancient Greece and Rome, although it was somewhat different from what you find in today's bottle. The Romans usually added honey or spices and herbs to the wine, and diluted it with water: only Barbarians consumed wine undiluted! The lack of inert containers for storage had a big effect. Wines were stored in amphorae (clay jars), but the porous walls had to be sealed with compounds such as tree resins. Resins were also added to the wine for their preservative effect.[2] This must have had quite an effect on the taste. Resinated wine predominated until into the Common Era; the concept that wine should be the unadulterated product of the grape dates from early Western European culture. (You can get a sense of the difference by tasting Retsina, still made in Greece, where a little pine resin is mixed with white wine; it's definitely an acquired taste.)

The idea that wines can be distinguished according to where the grapes were grown goes back at least to Roman times. One of the most famous wines was Falernian, grown on Mount Falernus, near Naples, and distinguished according to whether it came from the upper, middle, or lower slopes (the middle slope was considered best, and the vintage of 121 B.C. was exceptionally fine). Around 70 C.E., Pliny compiled a list of the best regions for production of Roman wine, identifying more than 80 wines, in an approach somewhat equivalent to today's classifications.[3]

The importance of origin was honed into a key concept in wine production in the last century in France. The French have a single word to describe the potential of a plot of land for wine production: *terroir* implies that each vineyard has a unique combination of soil, aspect, and climatic features that determine what type and quality of wine it is capable of producing. The basic concept is pretty simple: other conditions being equal, one plot of land will always produce better wine than another, because its terroir is better. Things get more complicated when you try to define exactly what determines the terroir; no two people in the wine business have the same definition. Indeed, many people feel that "terroir" has a mystique in French viticulture that cannot be adequately translated into English.

Terroir dominates the view of wine in France with its implication that the ultimate quality of a vineyard is limited by predetermined factors beyond human control. French logic then demands that sites should be classified according to their terroir; those where the terroir is unsuitable cannot be used to cultivate grapes, those with ordinary terroir can make table wine, those with better terroir can make fine wine, and so on. This concept is at the heart of regulating production and describing wine in all of Europe. You see its results on the label of every bottle of European wine.

The Origins of Regulation

Wine production in France is more tightly regulated than anywhere else in the world. This is both a blessing and a curse. Protection against imitations is a benefit; the label on the bottle really means something. But it can get out of hand. You see trade protection at its most intense in Champagne, where the name is protected ferociously. You can't use the word "Champagne" in Europe in any context except on the label of a bottle of sparkling wine from the region.[4] The other side of the coin is that the system is equally fierce in enforcing regulations that are enshrined by history but that may stifle innovation. So it's illegal to grow grape varieties that aren't specifically allowed within the system; such restrictions contribute to the failure of French wines to compete with the New World.

France was the first country to set up a detailed classification system for its vineyards. The roots of the system go back to the first part of the 20th century when wine production in France was in dire straits. The vineyards had been decimated by an infestation of the insect phylloxera (which feeds on the roots of the vines), production and quality were further reduced by a series of poor vintages, and demand for wine was suppressed by a world recession. Fraud was rife, with wine from inferior sources routinely passed off as coming from Bordeaux or other quality regions.

Regulation was long overdue when the first attempts were made to protect defined geographical areas for wine production. The idea was straightforward: if a wine was labeled as "Bordeaux" it would really have to come from grapes grown in the Bordeaux region. The intervention of the First World War (not to mention a rearguard action by wine brokers who made their living by blending wine from different sources) delayed the introduction of effective legal restrictions until 1919. Further laws followed, until the national system of Appellation d'Origine Contrôlée (AOC) was introduced in 1935.

The name describes its purpose: wines in the system have controlled origins, which means they come from specific places that are named on the bottle. This is intended to protect the producer (and more incidentally the consumer) by ensuring authenticity. But the system goes far beyond describing origins into controlling many aspects of production on a region-by-region basis. The regulatory body in charge of the system developed into INAO, the Institut National des Appellations Contrôlées. Wine is only a part of the AOC system, which applies to a wide variety of agricultural products—there are AOCs for spirits, olive oils, cheeses, and chickens (such as the famous Poulets de Bresse).

Only the top wine-producing regions were included in the AOC. Other classification systems were introduced later to cover the remaining wines. Now all wine in France is classified into one of three categories. At the bottom, wine is simply described as Vin de Table. It is not allowed to have any geographical description or statement of vintage. The next level is Vin de Pays, introduced at the end of the 1970s; it usually comes from a broad area (declared on the bottle) and may state a vintage. The AOC remains the top level of classification.

The system has had an influence far beyond France. Details vary, but all countries of the European Union now have regulations based on the same principle: that wine is divided into three broad classes, where increasing restrictions on geographical origins are associated with higher quality. At the top level of equivalence to the AOC,[5] the name on the label should mean that the wine comes from a certain place and has a character reflecting the history of that place.

Location, Location, Location

Grapevines are amazingly hardy, and will grow anywhere they can get enough heat, light, and water. Practically speaking, this means wine can be made successfully from grapevines grown between the 30° and 50° lines of latitude. All but the most northern parts of France are to the south of the 50° line, and wine is grown in many parts of France (Figure 1). Champagne comes up close to the limit of latitude, and Alsace and the Loire also are regarded as "cool climates" for wine production. The rest of France has moderate or warm climates.

Every AOC wine in France has a place name on its label describing where it comes from. This is its *appellation*. Each region has a hierarchy of appellations of ascending quality. The details vary with the region, but the appellation contrôlée is generally like a pyramid, with a broad base of wines that can come from anywhere in the particular region, narrowing to a peak of top wines that can come only from more restricted areas. In ascending order, the hierarchy goes from region, to

Figure 1

France has about 475,000 hectares of AOC vineyards. The areas of vines in the major areas (in hectares) are:[6]

Alsace	*15,000*
Bordeaux	*120,000*
Burgundy	*29,000*
Beaujolais	*22,000*
Champagne	*30,000*
Languedoc	*60,000*
Loire	*50,000*
Provence	*29,000*
Rhône	*78,000*
Southwest	*20,000*

A hectare is 2.47 acres.

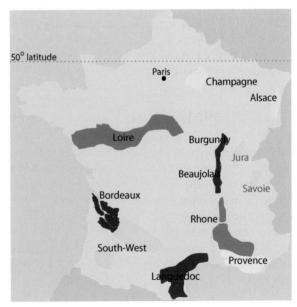

district, to commune, and finally to individual vineyards. (But not all levels are used in all regions.)

The lowest level of regional AOC wine typically is half or more of annual production, and is described with a broad geographical term, such as AOC Bordeaux or AOC Bourgogne (for Burgundy). The next step up, the district AOC, describes broad locations within each region, such as AOC Graves (a district of Bordeaux) or AOC Sancerre (a district of the Loire). When there are yet higher levels, the communes usually take the names of individual villages within a district.[7] Altogether, about two thirds of French vineyards have been assigned to a quality level in the AOC system.

The district names don't carry any immediate implications about quality unless you happen to know their reputation. There's a partially hidden code that can be helpful, though; some terms usually indicate areas of relatively large size and lower quality, such as "Côtes." Almost all appellations with Côtes in the name are only just one step up from the regional AOC. Examples are the Côtes de Bordeaux (which covers a wide swatch of Bordeaux) or Côtes du Rhône (which covers almost all of the Rhône).

Districts can vary significantly with size, but typically the smaller the size, the higher the quality. It is not necessarily obvious how to identify appellations of the highest quality in each region. This is particularly marked for those regions that make the very top wines: Bordeaux, Burgundy, and (to a lesser degree) the Rhône. Here the quality difference between the top wines and the bottom wines in the AOC is much greater than in the other AOC regions. The solution to distinguishing the top level takes a different form in each region.

The Appellation Contrôlée Pyramid

In Burgundy, terroir is the driving force, and the appellation is a direct indication of potential quality. Every individual plot of land has a level in a hierarchy— the epitome of classification by terroir. There may be up to five levels of hierarchy (Figure 2). Going up from the base levels of the regional and district AOCs, the first of the real quality levels, and the heart of the system, are individual communes, named for villages that have become famous, such as AOC Vosne Romanée. And then within each commune, the best vineyards are classified as Premier Cru or, at the very top, Grand Cru, and the label says "AOC" followed by the name of the Cru. A clue to quality is that in Burgundy, and in most of the AOC

Figure 2

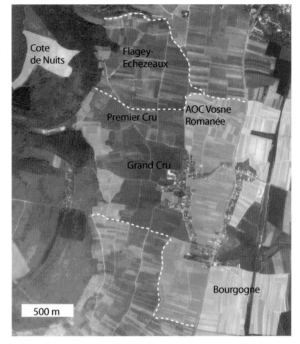

Vineyards around Vosne Romanée are classified into five levels of hierarchy. The white dashed lines mark the boundaries of the commune (and also show Flagey-Echezeaux to the north).[8] *In ascending order, the classification levels are:*

Region=
Bourgogone

District=
Cote de Nuits

Commune=
Vosne Romanée

Premier Cru

Grand Cru

(Individual Crus are not identified.)

system, the word "cru" indicates a top-level wine. Unfortunately, this is not universally true in Bordeaux.

Going up the hierarchy, the average sizes of the appellations decrease. Communes are not large, but the premier crus contained within them can be quite small, and the grand crus may be tiny, sometimes even just individual vineyards. The best vineyards in Burgundy occur in the Côte d'Or, a narrow escarpment that runs roughly south to north centered on the city of Beaune. Its 11,000 hectares (27,000 acres) are divided into 27 communes, varying mostly from 100 to 300 ha. They include 375 premier crus and 46 grand crus, mostly less than 10 ha each.

At the top levels, the label of a bottle of Burgundy can give a precise indication of its place of origin. A bottle that says "AOC Romanée-Conti" can come only from a tiny 1.8 ha vineyard in the heart of Burgundy. There's nothing comparable to this detailed mapping anywhere else in the AOC system. The roughly 500 different descriptions of land in the Côte d'Or form a relatively steep pyramid, steadily narrowing from the base of two thirds of regional AOCs (such as Bourgogne) to the 1% of grand crus at the peak (Figure 3, left).

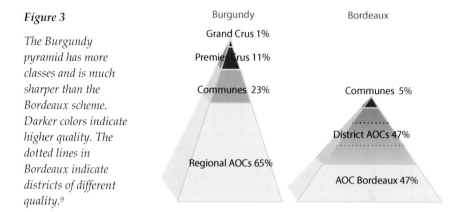

Figure 3

The Burgundy pyramid has more classes and is much sharper than the Bordeaux scheme. Darker colors indicate higher quality. The dotted lines in Bordeaux indicate districts of different quality.[9]

While the history of Burgundy resulted in a highly detailed classification of land according to its intrinsic quality, things took a different turn in Bordeaux, where the appellation system is relatively simple. Bordeaux has both a smaller number of layers and a much flatter distribution (Figure 3, right). The generic description AOC Bordeaux can be used for red and white wines made anywhere in the region. (The wine can be labeled as AOC Bordeaux Supérieur if it is made under slightly more restrictive conditions.[10]) One step up is a series of district appellations, each defining a relatively broad area. Altogether they occupy about the same area as generic Bordeaux. They are not put into a hierarchy, although as a practical matter they fall into roughly three groups of quality levels. The communes at the top represent only 5% of Bordeaux, compared with a much larger proportion in Burgundy. The lack of any significant hierarchy in the appellation system means Bordeaux must rely on other means to distinguish and classify its wines.

A Tale of Two Bordeaux

Goodness knows Bordeaux has enough appellations. In fact, it has by far the greatest number of appellations of any wine region in France. The Bordeaux AOC includes 57 of the total of 474 appellations in the system. But what does this mean?

The first thing to realize is that there are really two Bordeaux. The wine region is divided by the river Garonne and its estuary, the Gironde (which gives its name to the local political and administrative unit, the Departément de Gironde). The left bank lies to the west of the Garonne; the right bank lies to the east (Figure 4). The Dordogne river

Figure 4

The Gironde divides Bordeaux into the left bank and right bank.

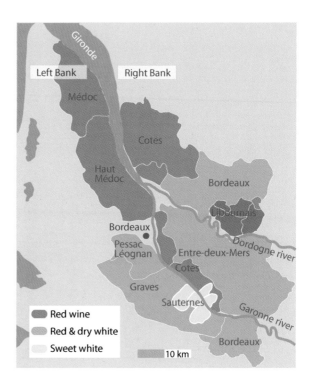

flows through the right bank. (The region between the Garonne and the Dordogne, downstream of where they fork off from the Gironde, is called Entre-deux-Mers, which literally means "between two seas.") Some parts of the Bordeaux region produce only red wine, some produce both red wine and dry white wine, and some small regions concentrate on sweet white wine.

About two thirds of the vineyards, and the greatest number of appellations lie on the right bank. The appellations have a very wide range of qualities. The right bank contains most of the areas that produce wine at the lowest level of AOC Bordeaux. This can be red or white. Much of the rest of the right bank is occupied by broad district appellations, consisting of the Côtes and Entre-deux-Mers. The most important areas of the right bank are a small group of appellations in the Libournais (which takes its name from the town of Libourne); St. Emilion and Pomerol are the best and best known, producing only red wine.

The appellations of the left bank extend both north and south of the city of Bordeaux itself. The Médoc is the peninsula to the north of the

Figure 5

On the left bank to the north of Bordeaux, wine is grown in a broad band parallel with the Gironde. The Médoc appellation lies to the north; the Haut-Médoc extends from just north of St. Estèphe to the outskirts of Bordeaux. Within the Haut-Médoc are the individual communes where the best growths are located.

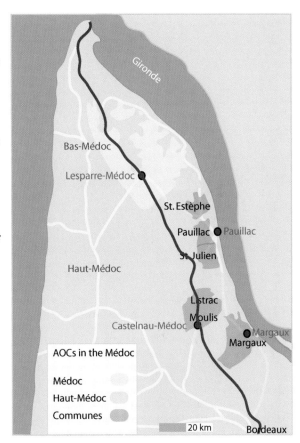

city, where the wine-producing regions are clustered in a band parallel with the Gironde. It is divided into the Bas–Médoc in the north and the Haut-Médoc in the south (Figure 5). (It may be counter-intuitive to look at the map and see the Bas-Médoc to the north of the Haut-Médoc, but the names reflect positions relative to the orientation of the river: Bas refers to territory lower down the river, Haut to territory farther from the sea.) Wine is produced throughout the Médoc, although all of the great wines come from the Haut-Médoc.

Wine from the Bas-Médoc has the Médoc AOC without any subdivisions. ("Bas" is not used in the name because it is felt to be demeaning.) The Haut-Médoc is the only part of Bordeaux that has any degree of hierarchical organization. Wine from the Haut-Médoc may be Haut-Médoc AOC, but within the Haut-Médoc are six communal appellations at the peak of the hierarchy. Their wines are labeled with

Figure 6

The vineyards of Haut Brion lie within the ring road for Bordeaux and are surrounded by suburban housing. The vineyards of Mission Haut Brion are just across the street.[11]

the names of the communes, including the famous appellations of St. Estèphe, Pauillac, St. Julien, and Margaux. The Médoc produces virtually entirely red wine.

The regions of Pessac-Léognan and Graves are close to the south of Bordeaux. In fact, the suburbs of Bordeaux now run into Pessac-Léognan, encroaching on the vineyards so far that the famous property of Haut Brion, which has made wine since the 16th century, is now entirely surrounded by suburban housing (Figure 6). To the south of the city most growers produce both red and dry white wine.

The sweet wine region of Sauternes lies towards the southern tip of the Graves (and is faced by some regions for sweet white wine production on the other side of the river). Farther south lie some undistinguished vineyards where only generic AOC Bordeaux can be produced.

Bordeaux is the local capital of the Département of the Gironde. Wine is by far the most important product of the Gironde. The Département extends over roughly one million hectares of land (10,000 square kilometers), half consisting of woods and a quarter agricultural. Approximately half of the agricultural land is given over to grapevines. The other major crop is maize, but in regions where vines are grown the crop is mostly a monoculture.

Standing on the bell tower in St. Emilion at the heart of the right bank, a view of the surrounding countryside gives nothing but a sea of grapevines, with a rabbit warren of winding roads making it impossible to distinguish one property from the next. On the other side of the

Gironde, driving up the left bank from Bordeaux along the Gironde, you pass a few fields of maize interspersed with vines, but then rapidly come into wine country where there are only vineyards. The only part of the region not dominated by vineyards is the western half of the Médoc.

Restricting the Yield

Rules of increasing rigor apply to wine production going up each appellation pyramid. One factor greatly influencing quality is the yield—the amount of wine produced from a given area—because when more grapes are produced, their juice is less concentrated. Yield is usually measured in hectoliters/hectare. (A hectoliter is about 11 cases of wine; a hectare is 2.47 acres.) Yields can be anywhere from 35 to 80 hl/ha in the AOC system, depending on the region. (An average production of 50 hl/ha would be equivalent to about 2700 bottles per acre. In a typical Bordeaux vineyard of 8000 vines per hectare, this is roughly equivalent to producing 1 bottle of wine from every vine.) By way of comparison, yields are usually limited to less than 90 hl/ha in Vin de Pays, and can be unlimited in Vin de Table.

Wines of better appellations ought to be more concentrated than wines of lower appellations. This belief is enshrined in the AOC regulations for each region (Figure 7). Returning to Burgundy, a simple Bourgogne at the base of the Burgundy pyramid can be made at a yield of 55 hl/ha, but grand crus can be harvested at no more than 35 hl/ha. The greater flatness of the appellation hierarchy in Bordeaux is reflected in a much smaller range of yield limitations between the generic AOC and the top communes. The principle of limiting yields is impeccable, but interpretation may make a mockery of the regulations: these stated levels are often increased by up to 20% for individual vintages.[13]

Figure 7

Yields in Bordeaux vary much less with appellation than in Burgundy.[12]

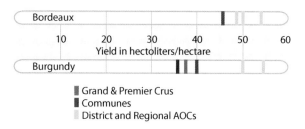

Bordeaux

10   20   30   40   50   60
Yield in hectoliters/hectare

Burgundy

▊ Grand & Premier Crus
▊ Communes
▊ District and Regional AOCs

Figure 8

Bordeaux appellations are shown in groups of similar quality. Darker color indicates higher quality. The numbers indicate the limitation on yield in hectoliters per hectare. Bordeaux and Bordeaux Supérieur come from the same regions, but have different quality levels as indicated by yields of 55 versus 50 hl/ha.

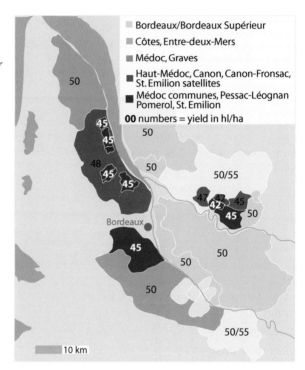

The highest quality levels in Bordeaux occupy only a relatively small part of the region (Figure 8). Taking the yield limitation as an indication of quality, the best appellations in Bordeaux should be the communes of the Haut-Médoc (St. Estèphe, Pauillac, St. Julien, Margaux, Moulis, Listrac), Pessac-Léognan, and the appellations in the Libournais (St. Emilion, Pomerol, Lalande-de-Pomerol, Canon-Fronsac). But this is not obvious from the label unless you happen to know the reputation of the individual AOC.

Typicité: Interplay of Terroir and Cépage

You can't just plant any old grape variety in any place. The terroir and climate of each region determine what grape varieties can be successfully grown there. The French argue that hundreds of years of experience have produced the perfect match in each region, giving the wine what they call *typicité*—a unique representation of the character of the region.

Black grapes require more heat to ripen than white grapes, so the cooler regions in the north of France focus on white wine. Even white grapes have some difficulty in ripening in the most northerly region, Champagne, but that little problem was overcome by the genius of producing a sparkling wine where addition of sugar counteracts any excess acidity. The relatively cool climates of Alsace and the Loire also produce mostly white wine.

Red wine becomes more prominent moving south, and grape varieties change as temperatures become warmer. Each grape variety (called a *cépage* in France) requires a certain temperature in order to ripen, but loses its character if the temperature rises too much. Going south, this dictates movement from the delicate Pinot Noir of Burgundy, to the sturdier Cabernet Sauvignon and Merlot of Bordeaux, the stronger Syrah of the Northern Rhône, and the positively lush Grenache of the Southern Rhône.

The level of regulation increases going up the quality scale. Stepping back, Vin de Table can be made from any grape varieties a producer chooses, Vin de Pays in each region can usually be made from a wide range of varieties, but AOC can be made only from a narrow range of specified varieties. Some AOCs are restricted to either red wines or to whites, but when both types of wine are permitted it's up to the producer to decide which varieties to plant in each vineyard, and in what proportions.

In Bordeaux, you can grow only six types of black grapes and six types of white grapes.[14] (Three black varieties, Cabernet Sauvignon, Cabernet Franc, and Merlot, actually account for more than 80% of all plantings.) Any of these grape varieties can be grown anywhere in the region, but further restrictions may apply within specific appellations. The appellations of Haut-Médoc and St. Emilion, for example, apply only to red wines. You can plant any combination you like of the permitted black grape varieties to make a red wine that carries the appellation label. But if you make a white wine, it can be labeled only as Bordeaux AOC, even though the grapes have been grown within the Haut-Médoc or St. Emilion appellation boundaries.

The concept of typicité is at the heart of the Appellation Contrôlée system. The regulations state that a wine must conform to "usages locaux, loyaux et constants," meaning that it must be faithful to local traditions. Typicité includes the character of the particular grape variety or varieties, but is influenced also by the terroir. So the adjacent communes of Pauillac and St. Julien in the Médoc each should express their own typicité. (Pauillac is more powerful, St. Julien is more elegant.)

Because typicité is bound up with place, the AOC system has not allowed grape varieties to be mentioned on the label (with the notable exception of Alsace). It's been considered to be an important part of the concept that the name of the AOC alone should convey the crucial indication of character of the wine; the authorities felt that the importance of the AOC would be undercut by naming the varieties. You might wonder whether there's an element of trade protection here, since Bordeaux wine can be produced only in Bordeaux, but Cabernet Sauvignon, for example, can be produced anywhere. If this is the intention, it has backfired, because the absence of identification for grape varieties has become a big problem in competing with the wines of the New World, which boldly list grape varieties on the label as a major selling point. But in 2005, INAO reversed itself and finally conceded that grape varieties could be named on AOC labels.

Each AOC reflects its history. Usually it codifies the grape varieties that were predominant when the regulations were promulgated. But change can still occur within the limits of the AOC regulations. In fact, Bordeaux has changed much more than people usually realize. As recently as 1970, red wine was in a minority. Today, red wine is almost 90% of production.[15]

Most French wine-growing regions are covered by both AOC and Vin de Pays. Most producers concentrate on either AOC or Vin de Pays wines, but some produce wines in both categories.[16] For the most part, Vin de Pays represent lower quality, using lesser grape varieties grown on inferior terroir. However, there are exceptions where a producer wants to make a high quality wine from grape varieties that are not permitted in the AOC, and as a result is forced (or for other reasons decides) to label the wine as a Vin de Pays or even a Vin de Table.[17]

The Bordeaux Blend

In Bordeaux, almost all wines are blended from a mix of different varieties. Certainly on the left bank it would be regarded as unsophisticated (and lacking in sufficient flavor interest) to produce a wine exclusively from Cabernet Sauvignon. The dependence on blending may be one reason for the difference in emphasis on land classification between Bordeaux and Burgundy. In Burgundy, each type of wine is produced exclusively from a single grape variety, white wine from the Chardonnay grape, and red wine from Pinot Noir. When you are making wine from just one variety, the quality of the terroir is the only distinguishing factor between one place and another. But when you are growing several grape varieties, different parts of a vineyard may be suited to different varieties; a plot that gives only average results with one variety may give excellent results with another.

So there is no single prescription for Bordeaux wine. There can be wide variation in the proportions of the different grape varieties. Usually the different varieties are harvested and fermented separately and then blended together at some stage before bottling to produce the final wine. The details of this *assemblage* depend on the vintage; because the success of each variety depends on the climatic conditions of the year, the assemblage is different every year.

The appellation rules nominally allow the same grape varieties to be grown anywhere in Bordeaux, but in fact there is a major difference between left bank and right bank. A blend of a majority of Cabernet Sauvignon with a minority of Merlot dominates the Médoc, whereas a majority of Merlot with a minority of Cabernet Franc forms the dominant blend on the right bank. Graves is somewhere in between, although it is usually grouped with the Médoc. The difference between the wines of the left bank and right bank is due to the different grape varieties as much as to the terroir itself.

Left bank wines are more austere, with more evident structure, and (at least at the top levels) can age for decades. They used to be rarely approachable when young, but a trend to warmer vintages, together with changes in viticulture and vinification, has greatly shortened the period before they can be enjoyed. All the same, there is no mistaking the contrast with the more forward, approachable, lush quality of wines from the best regions of the right bank.

The reputation of Bordeaux for producing great, long-lived wines has spurred competition from the New World. The concentration in the New World on specific grape varieties has led many producers to focus on wines made almost exclusively from Cabernet Sauvignon, but sometimes a wine is described as a "Bordeaux Blend." The Meritage category of wine in California is intended to imitate Bordeaux in this way.[18] But "Bordeaux blends" really might better be called "left bank blends," since they are almost always based on Cabernet Sauvignon as the main variety.

For white wines, it's not so much the geography as the type of wine you want to make that determines the blend. Bordeaux white wines are produced from Sauvignon Blanc and Sémillon, with the former comprising the majority of the blend for dry wines, and the proportions reversed for sweet wines.

Bordeaux from Top to Bottom

It's all very well to argue that Bordeaux has a typicité reflecting the unique match of terroir and grape varieties, but it has a split personality. "New 2005 Bordeaux wine prices may challenge records' said the Bloomberg news report in April 2006.[19] Yet just weeks later, the BBC reported "Bordeaux wine-makers in France face crisis distillation."[20]

With some 10,000 wine producers in the region, there is enormous variation between the best and the worst. At the very top, prices continue to rise vertiginously: the supply simply cannot satisfy world demand. At the bottom, approximately half of the production is generic AOC Bordeaux for which there is little demand; the wine simply cannot be sold at an economic price for the producer.

Not only generic Bordeaux, but also some of the districts, just cannot make wine that is competitive today. Part of the problem lies with the AOC system. A list of 57 different Appellation Contrôlées is too fragmented, and simply inappropriate for wines at the lower quality levels. The whole concept of terroir as reflected in the AOC presupposes that each appellation has a distinctive character: this is palpably not true for much of Bordeaux. The terroir is not good enough, and the climate is not reliable enough, for the minor regions to produce sufficiently characterful wines. Indeed, it is now generally acknowledged that the excessive number of appellations confuses consumers and prevents any but the best appellations from gaining sufficient recognition in the marketplace. Proposals to combine several of the lesser appellations on the right bank in order to simplify the system have taken years to gain approval in the slow-moving AOC system, but finally from 2008 several of the minor districts have been combined into a single appellation called "Côtes de Bordeaux."

Another problem has been the lack of a Vin de Pays to soak up lower quality wines. In regions where there are both Vin de Pays and Appellation Contrôlée, a producer can decide that the price for AOC wine is not high enough to justify the restrictions imposed by the appellation rules; then he can produce a Vin de Pays instead, where lower price is at least compensated by the ability to produce larger quantities. But Bordeaux has been unusual; there has been no Vin de Pays, and for the past twenty years, Bordeaux wine has been virtually synonymous with AOC.[21] In fact, for half a century the AOC has been steadily taking over all the production of Bordeaux; areas devoted to AOC wine were 53% in 1951, 75% in 1979, and 99% in 2005.[22] It's hard to believe the expansion produced an increase in the quality of the terroir used for AOC. But the only alternative classification was Vin de Table, not much of a choice. Although a Vin de Pays is now being introduced (it's called the Vin de Pays d'Atlantique, and includes the Departéments to the immediate north and east as well as the Gironde itself), it's not clear that this will be enough to solve the problem.

There is no denying that Bordeaux has had an enormous historical impact on red wine production. Indeed, its best appellations remain world leaders. But much of the wine at the generic level simply cannot attract today's consumers. Wide variations within each appellation mean that you need to look beyond the geographical description of the AOC name to understand quality. The role of the producer has become paramount, and indeed has been embedded into the classification system in a unique way (Chapter 3). Will this system help or hinder Bordeaux to maintain a position at the forefront of red wine production in the face of increasing competition?

2

A Sense of Place

IT MAY SOMETIMES SEEM THAT WINE PRODUCTION in Bordeaux has origins deep in antiquity, but in fact Bordeaux is a relatively recent addition to wine-growing regions. Wine was produced in more southern regions around the Mediterranean long before it reached Bordeaux. "The peoples of the Mediterranean began to emerge from barbarism when they learned to cultivate the olive and the vine," said the Greek historian Thucydides in the fifth century B.C. Wine production began in Bordeaux in late Roman times,[1] but became an important part of the economy only in the middle ages.

Bordeaux's first role in the wine trade was in export. When the Romans arrived in 56 B.C., Bordeaux was recognized as a center for commerce, and the city was already an active port. Bordeaux became a major wine exporter during the three centuries of English control of Aquitaine (1152-1453). King John of England (1199-1216) is supposed to have taken a particular liking to the wines of the region, purchasing them for his own consumption.[2] Following his reign, Bordeaux became the major supplier of wine to the English, shipping wine from the surrounding regions. Local production of wine came later, spreading out slowly from the city. By the 18th century Bordeaux had become an important producer as well as exporter.

Both local and foreign wines passed through the hands of the merchants, leading to the creation of the powerful class of negociants, who matured the wines to suit the palates of their customers. Blending of wines from different sources was common, so it was not until later that the wines of Bordeaux began to be appreciated in their own right. As wines became distinguished by their areas of origin, changing market conditions brought about shifts in which regions fetched the highest prices. The importance of the individual producer emerged during the 18th century; slowly the producer developed into the primary determinant of quality, and the characteristics of the wine became associated with the producer's location.

The Origins of Wine Production in Bordeaux

The earliest artifacts from Roman times suggest that the Bordelais then consumed wine produced in Gascony (to the south east). At the start of the Common Era, wine production had not penetrated as far north as Bordeaux; the Atlantic climate was thought to be unsuitable for viticulture.[3] But during the first century, new varieties of grapes became available that were capable of growing in more northerly regions. It may have been during this period that the principal grape varieties became established in Burgundy and Bordeaux.[4]

A variety called Allobrogica (after the Allobroges tribe) made its way north up the Rhône, extending the region of viticulture; possibly it may later have developed into what we now know as Pinot Noir. A vine called Biturica (named for the Bituriges tribe who lived on the left bank of the Gironde and founded the town of Burdigala, later to be known as Bordeaux) was imported into Bordeaux, where it was planted to establish the first vineyards.[5]

Biturica resisted the cool temperatures of the Atlantic region, and flowered successfully, whereas the varieties previously available had been too difficult to culture effectively.[6] Its exact origins are unclear, but the variety known in the region as Bidure or Vidure may be its descendent. Cabernet Sauvignon used to be known as Vidure-Sauvignonne or Petite-Vidure. Another variety, Carmenère used to be known as Grand Vidure. There have been speculations that Biturica may have been an ancestor of some of the modern varieties of Bordeaux, but no one really knows.[7]

Wine production had its ups and downs in the region. In a forecast of things to come, the Roman Emperor Domitian banned all new plantings in A.D. 92, and ordered that half of the vines in the provinces should be uprooted.[8] Ostensibly this was because of concern that there was insufficient land available for growing more important crops, specifically wheat; but possibly the real motive was to protect wine production in Italian regions. (Wine had become an important commodity and the wine trade was economically significant by this time.[9])

It's not clear how successful production was over the next century or so, but Bordeaux remained an important center for exports. However, exports (and possibly production) ground to a halt when the Roman Empire collapsed. After the third century, Bordeaux descended into relative inactivity for several hundred years.[10]

The English Takeover

When Eleanor of Aquitaine married Henry II of England in 1152, Bordeaux started three hundred years under English rule. The tight connection with England survives to this day in the wine trade, and you still its signs in various social ways, such as the presence of exclusive equestrian clubs. During this period, Bordeaux made the transition from exporting wine to producing it.

A major driving force in Bordeaux's rise to importance as a wine-producing center was England's need for wine.[11] After the English took over Aquitaine, Bordeaux became one of their major wine suppliers, although this did not happen immediately. At the start of King John's reign in 1199, Bordeaux was not among the principal suppliers; the wines of Poitou, exported from La Rochelle to the north, were more important.[12] But after La Rochelle capitulated to the French in 1224, Bordeaux stayed loyal to England, and became the major center for wine exports.

Because of problems with spoilage, wines were exported as soon as possible. Merchants demanded only the new, fresh wines. Most exports took place in an intensive period of 6-8 weeks relatively soon after the harvest.[13] The wines would arrive in England in time for Christmas.[14] Wine was exported from the port of Bordeaux itself and from ports all along the Garonne and Dordogne rivers.[15] After the town of Libourne was constructed on the Dordogne in 1270, its port acquired about 15% of exports; most of the rest went through Bordeaux. A fleet of up to 200 ships took wines to England, which accounted for about a quarter of the total exports.[16]

By the start of the 14th century, half of Bordeaux's exports went to England.[17] The exported wine came largely from Gascony, extending to sources as far away as Toulouse, almost 150 miles distant. Only about 15% of the wine came from the vicinity of Bordeaux itself.[18]

The demand for young wine made it important to get on the boat as soon as possible. When wine production become important around the city in the 13th century, a custom developed that local wines had priority over those of the southwest; later this was given legal force.[19] During the

14th century, various privileges accrued to the merchants of Bordeaux under the name of the "police des vins" (policies concerning wines).[20] It was forbidden to bring wines from the outlying regions into the city before Saint Martin's day (November 11); by then the major sales of the new vintage had already been accomplished. In 1373, Edward III extended the law to prevent foreign wines being brought into the city before Christmas.

A law of 1401 prevented wines of the Médoc from being exported from ports in the Gironde; they could be exported only via the port of Bordeaux.[21] The law stayed in effect until the 17th century.[22] (This may have been a factor in the relatively slow development of viticulture in the Médoc.) All these efforts helped to make Bordeaux a major port for export of wine. The trade grew while the English owned Bordeaux and was profitable for both parties. The loss of Bordeaux at the end of the Hundred Years War in 1453 was surely one of the major misfortunes in British foreign policy (Figure 9).

Following its reversion to France, Bordeaux suffered a decline in wine exports, but soon recovered its importance. The Bordelais were doughty in defending their interests. Almost immediately after taking control, in October 1453 Charles VII of France abolished the preference for local wines. But he was rapidly persuaded to change his mind, and restored the privilege the following April.[24] Although the wines of Bergerac,

Figure 9

A painting of the Battle of Castillon where the English lost the Hundred Years War shows the death of John Talbot, the English leader. Château Talbot in St. Julien (in the Médoc) is named after him.[23]

Cahors, and Gaillac to the southwest of Bordeaux had acquired a good reputation during the Middle Ages, their ability to compete with those of Bordeaux itself was impeded by such regulations until into the 18th century.[25]

Anglo-French Relations

As a major exporter, Bordeaux has always been buffeted by the effects of extraneous (and uncontrollable) events on its markets. Added to the intrinsic vagaries of climate and the vicissitudes of pests and diseases, war and taxation have been the most important extrinsic factors. Until the mid-nineteenth century, the state of war—most often with England—determined whose ships were able to come to Bordeaux to collect the wine. (Most exports seem to have been dispatched in the fleets of the purchasing nation rather than the French.) Besides determining the general prosperity of the region, the export market influenced what styles of wines were in demand.

During the 17th century, the Dutch took over the commercial roles that previously had been played by the English. According to Colbert (Minister of Finance for France) in 1669, "The Dutch come every year to the Garonne and Charente rivers with 3-4000 ships to transport wines during October, November, and December… They consume roughly a third [in Holland] and adjust and adulterate the other two thirds [for re-export]."[26] Because the wines were wanted more for export than for consumption, the Dutch had different priorities from the English, and this caused an important change in the market (page 29). The Dutch also introduced distillation as a means of producing eaux de vie.[27]

By the end of the 17th century, Bordeaux was in crisis because exports were prevented by the British naval blockade.[28] During this period, the English wine market was taken over by Spain and Portugal, especially by Port,[29] which was known as "black wine."[30] Even during this period, however, some wine from Bordeaux found its way to England in the form of prizes captured at sea by privateers. (Figure 14 shows an example of an advertisement for a sale.) Hugh Johnson has suggested that some of this may in fact have been a fig leaf to cover the continuation of trade with traditional suppliers.[31] Exports resumed from 1700, but with Holland established as the most important market.[32] Less than 5% of the exports were declared as intended for England.

The Methuen treaty signed in 1703 between England and Portugal reinforced the position that had been gained by Portuguese wines, which were taxed at only two thirds of the rate applicable to French wines.[33]

And general demand for wine was reduced by increases in the overall tax rate.[34] The tax was based on volume, and was the same for wines of all qualities, making it unprofitable for Bordeaux to export its cheaper wines to England. After trading with France was resumed, the English quickly became known for purchasing the best Bordeaux wines at high prices, making them an important export market.[35] With some ups and downs during subsequent periods of hostility, the relationship has continued until the present day.

The city of Bordeaux was at the center of the developing wine trade. It's a tribute to the power of the merchants in the city, and to the importance of the port as an export center, that wine from a widespread region extending far in all directions became known by the name of the city. Epitomizing the unique nature of its production and distribution system, "Bordeaux" stands for the generic description of the wine area, although elsewhere in France, descriptions take the name of the region (Burgundy, Rhône, Languedoc, Loire, Alsace, Champagne). Interestingly, other cases where a city has given its name to a wine region and style also owe their origins to the export trade with England: Port (from Oporto in Portugal), and Sherry (from Jerez in Spain).

The Growth of the Médoc

Until the 13th century, vineyards were still mostly confined to the regions immediately around the city. A Bordelais leaving the city by any exit would encounter vineyards extending into the distance. Vineyards were planted right up to the Garonne. By the late 15th century, an area surrounding the city up to about 3 km out was essentially a monoculture of vines.[36] Of course, the city then was confined to the small area encompassed by the old city walls; these former vineyard plots have now become part of the great urban sprawl of Bordeaux. Yet even by the start of the 18th century, when the city was beginning to expand, it was still surrounded by vineyards (Figure 10).

The early history of wine production in Bordeaux is basically the history of the left bank, where vineyards were established in the Graves to the south and in the Médoc to the north. One of the oldest vineyards in the Graves was the property of the Archbishop of Bordeaux. At the start of the 14th century, when he became Pope Clément V, he gave his private vineyard to the archdiocese; named after him, it still produces wine as Château Pape-Clément.

Figure 10

The map of Hippolyte Matis of 1716 shows vineyards all around the city.

 Vineyards

 Fields

Vineyards in the Médoc were established during the 13th and 14th centuries, especially in the infertile soils of the Haut-Médoc where few other crops could be grown successfully.[37] They were largely confined to a band running along the Gironde, extending from St Estèphe, through Pauillac, to Margaux, extending inland only at Lesparre-Médoc and Castelnau-Médoc. With less favorable terroir, and lying farther from the city of Bordeaux, the Bas-Médoc was not cultivated for viticulture until later.

Even by the 15th century, production of wine was of relatively small economic importance in the Médoc.[38] Certainly it was never more than a secondary culture. Vineyards established in the 16th century in the Haut-Médoc were largely local affairs. They were mostly based on rather small holdings, although there was some tendency to amalgamation of parcels held by the larger Seigneuries (the grand estates held by the local aristocracy or their equivalent).[39] Some of the important estates of today originated in this period. Steady growth turned viticulture into a major economic contributor by the end of the 17th century.

Things picked up after 1710, when there was a "fureur de planter" (rush of planting). This was triggered by the winter freeze of 1709 that killed many of the vines in the region, together with the end of the war with England that had suppressed trade. It created the first of many boom and bust cycles. Planting became so excessive that it sparked proposals to pull up many of the vines.[40] Interestingly, an exception was made for those planted on gravel soils, which were already recognized as being superior. As in many subsequent cases, proposals to remove vines went nowhere, but did in fact lead to a ban on all new plantings from 1725.[41]

Figure 11

Vineyards were developed on the left bank, but the right bank was less well developed, according to the map of Cassini of 1773.[42]

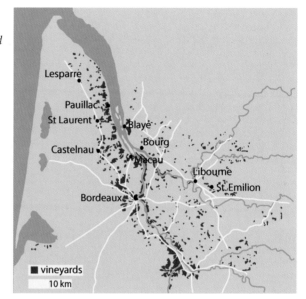

During the second half of the 18th century, viticulture became important on the left bank, where vineyards already occupied the areas that are cultivated today. By contrast, the right bank was more sparsely cultivated (Figure 11).

Changes in the Médoc during the 18th century are evident in comparing maps from the beginning and end of the century. A large-scale map of the Médoc was constructed by Claude Masse after 1700. A map of the Guyenne (which included Aquitaine) was drawn up by Pierre de Belleyme under royal instruction starting in 1766. Superimposing the two maps shows two notable features: the contraction of the marshes; and the expansion of the vineyards (Figure 12).

The Médoc was (and still in part is) a marshy area. Many of the marshes were drained in the 17th and 18th centuries (Chapter 5). Both the "palus" (alluvial regions closer to the river) and the "marais" (marshy areas farther inland) contracted during the century, creating new possibilities for planting vineyards or other crops. The narrow band of vineyards parallel with the Gironde at the start of the century extended considerably inland by the end of the century. Only 9 wine producers are marked on the map of Masse, but another 35 are included on the map of Belleyme.

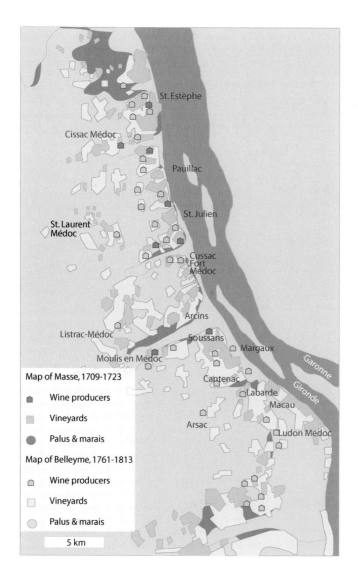

Figure 12 Comparison of the maps of Masse and Belleyme shows the growth of viticulture in the Haut-Médoc in the 18th century. Vineyards shown in Masse are in darker green; additional vineyards shown in Belleyme are in lighter green. Additional marshy areas shown only in Masse are in darker brown; they contracted during the century to the regions in lighter brown that correspond to those shown in Belleyme.[43]

At the start of the 18th century, vines were already planted on what are now recognized as the best terroirs for wine production, but nowhere was production of wine the dominant agricultural activity. By the middle of the century, most of the major wine estates of today had been established as working vineyards.[44] Some of the estates were established previously, and the first records of commercial vineyards often show up early in the century. By the end of the century, viticulture had become close to a monoculture in some parts of the Haut-Médoc.[45]

Vines have been the most important crop in the Haut-Médoc for the past century. Today, going north from Bordeaux into the Haut-Médoc, first you encounter some kilometers of agricultural land, mostly growing wheat and similar crops, up to Ludon-Médoc, where the first vineyards are found. The area through the communes of Margaux is largely devoted to vineyards. Then there is a substantial break where there are few vines and most crops are wheat or sunflowers, after which vineyards become a monoculture and run continuously from St. Julien through St. Estèphe. Vineyards are interrupted now and again by the small streams (*jalles*) that run from the west to empty into the Gironde.

The spread of viticulture through the Bas-Médoc is more a phenomenon of recent times. Vignerons of today can remember when "almost every farm practiced polyculture and wine was not considered any more important than wheat."[46] In fact, planting vines was considered to be less profitable.

From the Cru to the Château

The first thing you ask about most French wines is where the wine comes from: what is its appellation? But Bordeaux is different. The first thing you look at is the name of the château. The place of origin and the quality of the producer are all tied up in this one name. How did this happen?

Until the 16th century, little attention was paid to the exact origins of a wine. Wine imported into England in the 15th century was described for tax purposes simply as "Red Gascon" or "Red Rochelle."[47] Contracts for purchasing wine in barrels specified that it "should be good, sellable, not tart, without any rot, have no loss of color,"[48] rather than that it should come from any particular place. Those of some merchants were recognized as being worth a premium.[49] Distinctions between origins were being drawn on the local market by the 16th century, when wines from some places were recognized as having consistently better quality, and meriting higher prices.[50, 51]

During the 17th century, the main distinction was between the plateaus a little inland and the alluvial palus closer to the river. While the most important trade was with England, the inland regions were the most important, because the English wanted wines that would drink well in the immediate future. They therefore preferred the more refined wines produced in the inland regions.

 Things changed as the Dutch became dominant during the century. The Dutch needed wines that could be transported to their colonies; this gave a preference to heavier wines. They were not particularly concerned with quality, but used the wine as a basis for blending. As a result, they became important purchasers of "petits vins" (wines of lower quality), which previously had not been commercially important;[52] they blended them with wine from the Languedoc or the Rhône to increase their strength, or even added sugar or syrup.

The different priorities of the English and Dutch had their effects upon the marketplace. During the period of Dutch dominance, vineyards were extended into the palus, producing a heavier and coarser wine that transported better.[53] The relative price of wines originating from the palus increased by comparison with those from areas farther inland.[54] (There is a curious parallel with the effects of Prohibition in the United States in the 20th century, when producers turned to growing grapes with thick skins that could be better transported to consumers, as opposed to the grapes that had been used for fine wine production;[55] a similar price inversion resulted.[56])

Prices were set for each general region following the vintage; in fact, a regulation of 1635 called for this to be done at an annual assembly held before September 29. Records from 1647 show the classification made that year by the Bordeaux Jurade (a municipal council). The wines of the palus were at the top of the list, Sauternes and Barsac were next, and the "Graves and Médoc" were only in third place.[57] The high position obtained by the wines of the palus was only temporary. (Much later, at the time of phylloxera, the vines of the palus became useful again because their periodic inundation by water made them better able to resist the insect.)

Slowly individual communes, such as Margaux or Pauillac, came to be distinguished as having specific characters. By the mid 18th century, pricing had settled into a relationship between appellations that we would recognize today. The Médoc was at the top of the list. Within the Médoc, individual communes had much the same relationship as today, although Margaux was slightly ahead of the others. Graves was in second position after the Médoc. The palus were not far behind.[58] Prices for the right bank were not thought worth recording.

The wines of Pontac, later to be known as Ho Bryan and then Haut Brion, became specifically in demand in the early 17th century. A famous entry in Samuel Pepys's diary from April 10, 1663 notes he "drank a sort of French wine, called Ho Bryan, that hath a good and most particular taste that I never met with."[59] Haut Brion had a great success in London because Arnaud de Pontac, its proprietor, was unusually effective in marketing his wine. He established a restaurant in the City of London where Haut Brion was sold: "M. Pontack, the son of the President of Bordeaux, imported to England some of the most esteemed claret to establish a tavern with all the novelties of French cookery... He set up his father's head as a sign... and soon became noticed as the Pontack's Head."[60, 61] His clients included some of the most famous characters of the period—Daniel De Foe, Jonathan Swift, and the philosopher John Locke, among others.

In 1677, John Locke visited France and toured vineyards; as the result of a visit to Haut Brion, Locke perceptively summarized its advantages in terms anticipating modern concepts of terroir: "The vine de Pontac, so much esteemed in England, grows on a rising open to the west, in a white sand mixed with a little gravel, which one would think would bear nothing; but there is a such a particularity in the soil, that at Mr. Pontac's, near Bourdeaux the merchants assured me that the wine growing in the very next vineyards, where there was only a ditch between, and the soil, to appearance, perfectly the same, was by no means so good."[62] This description could scarcely be bettered today.[63]

The notion of the "cru" as representing a superior wine from a specific producer was first seen in documents from 1706, after which the proprietor became progressively more important.[64] At the start of the 18th century, the English were purchasing individually by name what were to be classified as first growths in 1855—Pontac (Haut Brion), Latour, Lafite, and Margaux. These were selling at 4-5 times the price of other wine from the Médoc.[65] This was the beginning of the establishment of the hierarchy of today. By the 1723 vintage, one English importer could write: "the four topping [superior] growths of La Tour, Lafite, Château Margaux and Pontac are exceeding good."[66]

As the market became more sophisticated, more refined distinctions were drawn between regions, and recognition of individual Crus increased. By 1740, a document from the chamber of commerce in Bordeaux described 19 separate subdivisions within the Médoc, and

Figure 13

At *Château Pontet Canet, the small building on the right was constructed at the start of the 18th century before prosperity became general; the larger building on the left was constructed in 1781. The connection between the two buildings was not made until the late 19th century.*

remarked how the qualities of certain Crus depended on the efforts of their proprietors.[67] By 1741, the Bordeaux broker Abraham Lawton had begun to classify the Crus; a list of his quotations for their prices between 1741 and 1774 shows many names that are recognizable today in the leading properties.[68]

The château at Pontet Canet nicely illustrates the growth of prosperity in the Médoc during the 18th century (Figure 13). The smaller building on the right was constructed before wine production became really profitable. The large building on the left was constructed later in the century as individual proprietors began to establish their reputations.

The first recorded use of "château" in the context of wine production was in the diary of Lord Hervey of Bristol, a connoisseur of his time, who mentioned "Château Margou Claret" in 1724.[69] The term came into more common use in the first half of the 19th century, but when the leading producers were classified in 1855, its significance was still more architectural than viticultural; only 4 of the 80 properties that were classified were described as "châteaux."

During the century, "château" became a successful marketing term implying a significant producer with a good reputation; the Cocks & Féret guide to the wines of Bordeaux of 1908 listed 1600 wine-producing "châteaux."[70] Images of imposing châteaux became more common on labels, and in fact many of the grand châteaux of the Médoc were constructed during this period. A cynic might see the way in which physical reality followed the marketing concept as a paradigm for Bordeaux, which, after all, routinely sells its wine two years before it is bottled.

The First "Clarets"

Old-fashioned English wine merchants still use "claret" to describe Bordeaux red wines.[71] Looking at the wines of today, you would never guess that the term probably originated from "clairet," meaning light-colored.[72]

Until the 18th century, wines were produced for immediate consumption. They were lightly colored and low in alcohol; the closest modern parallel would be a nouveau wine (like Beaujolais Nouveau). An old French proverb goes "the wine is drawn; it must be drunk," likely referring to the rapidity of spoilage.[73] Young wines were more valuable than older wines.[74] The exported wine was typically the "vin de l'année" of the last vintage. A "vin vieux" would be a wine of the previous vintage, considered less good, and sold off at less than half the price. None of these wines would have had the chance to acquire increased complexity with age—the feature for which they are famous today.

At the beginning of the 18th century, the term "New French Clarets" was first used in the English market in advertisements for wines seized at sea (Figure 14).[75] There's some controversy as to whether "New French Claret" actually referred to wines in a new style of higher quality (specifically Haut Brion, Margaux, Lafite, and Latour) or to the most recent vintage.[76, 77] But at all events, these were still young wines of the current vintage. In fact, the most important aspect of vintage at this time may have been the need to distinguish young wines from those that were effectively too old.

Aging first became an option during the early 18th century as the result of two key developments: preventing the wine from spoilage

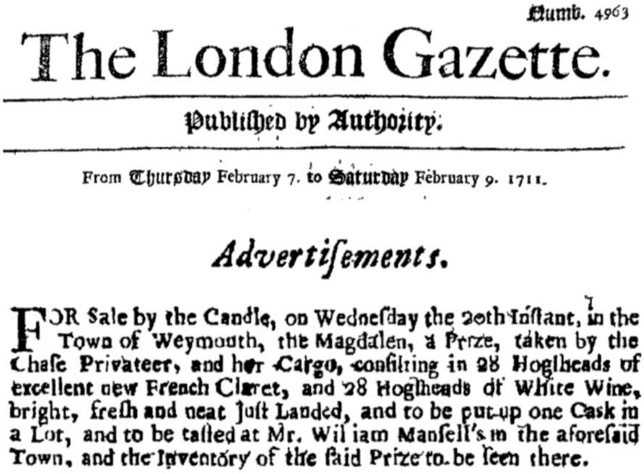
Numb. 4963

The London Gazette.

Publiſhed by Authority.

From Thurſday February 7. to Saturday February 9. 1711.

Advertiſements.

FOR Sale by the Candle, on Wedneſday the 20th Inſtant, in the Town of Weymouth, the Magdalen, a Prize, taken by the Chaſe Privateer, and her Cargo, conſiſting in 28 Hogſheads of excellent new French Claret, and 28 Hogſheads of White Wine, bright, freſh and neat Juſt Landed, and to be put-up one Cask in a Lot, and to be taſted at Mr. William Manſell's in the aforeſaid Town, and the Inventory of the ſaid Prize to be ſeen there.

Figure 14

An advertisement in The London Gazette of February 7, 1711 offered 28 hogsheads of new French Claret from a prize taken by a privateer.

while it was in barrel; and bottling it under conditions that prevented subsequent spoilage.

The introduction of sulfur as a preservative made it possible to keep wine in barriques for 2-4 years without spoilage. The technique was invented by the Dutch, in the form of burning a sulfur candle in a barrel before it was filled with wine, and so became known as the "allumette Hollandaise." It was used when barriques were initially filled and when wine was racked (moved) from one barrique to another. By the mid 18th century it was in common use.[78, 79]

Corks became available to use as stoppers soon after 1700. Between 1723 and 1751 several plants for producing bottles opened in Bordeaux; by the end of the century, production was up to 3 million bottles per year.[80] It was during this period that the idea originated of selling the wine in glass after it had been matured in wood. One further development was necessary before wine could be aged for any substantial period: by 1775 the production of bottles was standardized so they could lie flat, enabling the wine to stay in contact with the cork to prevent it from drying out.[81]

Distinctions begin to be made between wines on the basis of their potential longevity. Courtiers described wines as being "sèveux" (vigorous), meaning that they would age, as opposed to those described as "moins longue garde," which were appropriate for immediate consumption.[82] During the 18th century, the art of *élevage* became increasingly important. This meant maturing the wine after the vintage until it was ready to drink. The transition from selling young wine in cask to exporting older wine after maturation reinforced the importance of the merchants, because they had the capacity to undertake the extra work and to make the necessary investment. The vast bulk of wine continued to be sold in barrels.[83] But the existence of satisfactory bottles meant that the ultimate client would be able to age the wine.

A Spreading International Reputation

The hostilities between England and France at the start of the 18th century initiated England's decline in importance as an export market. During the second half of the 19th century, and through the 20th century, disruptions caused by war were more temporary, and taxation became more the driving force. French wine was to be eclipsed in England for a century and a half. A report to the French Minister of Commerce in 1858 complained that "French wines had been the British drink of choice in the seventeenth century, but that the preferential tariff treatment of Portugal and Spain and the British investment on the Continent that followed had led to the French wines being displaced. French exports to Britain had barely changed in the last hundred years; they were less in the mid-1840s than they had been in the late 1600s."[84]

Punitive taxation, in the form of discriminatory duties on French wine introduced in England, made the trade in ordinary wine unprofitable in the 18th century. The barrier was overcome by exporting premium wines, and it was during the first half of the 18th century that a demand for fine wines arose. The concept of "grand vins" first developed around 1690;[85, 86] they were distinguished by a higher quality that deserved higher prices relative to other wines. These were initially the first growths, followed by the development of a hierarchy.[87]

By the mid to late 18th century, appreciation for slightly older wines was developing. Thomas Jefferson, during his travels to wine country when he was the United States Ambassador to France, noted that "[Château Margau, La Tour de Segur, Hautbrion] are not in perfection till four years old; those of De la Fite, being somewhat lighter, are good at three years, that is, the crop of 1786 is good in the spring of 1789."[88] And more than one vintage became available on the market. In 1787, according to Jefferson, the 1783 vintage cost 2000 livres per tonneau, compared to the 1800 livres per tonneau of the 1785 and 1786.[89] This may be the first evidence for a premium paid for an older wine.[90]

By early in the 19th century, the reputation of Bordeaux was well established both in France and internationally. A major part of the total production of roughly 2 million hl was exported directly from the port of Bordeaux, with the exception of a catastrophic reduction to 10% of the normal figure brought about by the British blockade during the Napoleonic wars.[91]

Only the best wines were exported in bottles, increasing from roughly about 7% in the 1830s to about 10% by the end of the century.[92] Significant quantities of even the most important wines continued to be exported for bottling abroad until the mid twentieth century. Berry Bros in London, for example, were known for the quality of their bottling, which continued until 1966, and Van der Meulen in Belgium was also well regarded.[93]

Exports to the oldest market, Britain, greatly increased when the tax on French wine was cut to a tiny fraction of its former value following the Anglo-French "free-trade" treaty of 1860.[94] With Bordeaux at the forefront, by 1882 France had became the most important source of wines for Britain.[95] It remained so until 2000 (when it was overtaken by Australia).

Trade with the United States had become important in the 1840s, followed in the 1860s by Argentina. Most of this wine came from the Médoc or the Graves. Exports fluctuated considerably, but by the second half of the 19th century were generally around 1 million hl, out of a harvest most often in the range of 2-3 million hl.[96] Britain was once again (just) the most important export market.[97] By the end of the century, the major export markets had steadied as Britain, Germany, and Belgium; this remained the case for the first half of the twentieth century, although their relative orders of importance varied.[98] Today, Britain and the United States are the most important markets, followed by Belgium and Germany. One third of production is exported,[99] the vast majority in bottles.

Settlement of the Right Bank

Different regions developed wines of repute at roughly half-century intervals. Around 1660, Haut Brion in the Graves became the first property to attract a reputation by name, followed by the Médoc in the first decade of the 18th century. On the right bank, Canon-Fronsac became known around 1750-1760, with St. Emilion soon following suit, and becoming better known than its neighbor soon after the start of the 19th century. Pomerol did not become well planted until later in the century, but was set back when the phylloxera infection struck.

The major town of the right bank, Libourne, was probably founded on the site of the Roman town of Condat. It takes its present name from the foundation of the bastide Leyburnia in 1270. Located on the Dordogne river, its port was second in importance to Bordeaux. In the middle ages, wine (mostly from the Libournais or from Bergerac) was brought along the Dordogne to Libourne and then transported to England. This stopped at the end of the Hundred Years War, and did not resume until the 17th-18th centuries. The respite was fairly brief; today Libourne is essentially a port for pleasure vessels.

By the second half of the 18th century, wine was being made in a wide area of the right bank, although viticulture was far less important than on the left bank (Figure 11). As on the left bank, the vineyards occupied the palus as well as areas farther away from the river. In the region around Libourne, the palus were in fact better settled with vineyards than the areas that today are part of the appellation of Pomerol (Figure

Figure 15

*The Carte de Belleyme of
1785 for the region
around Libourne shows
vineyards in the region
that today is part of the
Pomerol appellation
(pink) concentrated less
densely than those in the
palus along the river
(green).*

15). The greatest concentration of vineyards was in the immediate
vicinity of the town of St. Emilion.

The wines of the right bank remained relatively unknown until quite
recently. In the mid 18th century, they were not well known in Bordeaux,
and were valued distinctly below those of the Médoc. (The best wines
were divided into premier and second crus but were valued below all
the crus of the Médoc.[100]) This situation continued for the next two
centuries, and it was not until after the Second World War that the wines
of the right bank became internationally known in their own right.

As in the Médoc, the distribution of vineyards has changed over time,
with the same emphasis on finer wines from better terroirs at the
expense of the palus. The best appellations are in the Libournais. At the
top are St. Emilion and Pomerol, with the surrounding regions, such as
Lalande-de-Pomerol and the satellites of St. Emilion, as well as Canon-
Fronsac, enjoying some repute. The palus have been relegated to broad
regional appellations or excluded altogether from the AOC system.

Place and Quality

The geographical pattern of wine-producing regions in Bordeaux was becoming established by the mid 19th century. According to Cocks & Féret of 1868, the Médoc, Graves, Libournais, Bourg and Blaye were all well cultivated; the largest area under cultivation was Entre-deux-Mers (but then as now getting low prices). [101] Maps of the period show the left bank in some detail, even naming some châteaux, but the right bank is much sketchier (Figure 16).

The largest change in cultivation today is the growth of the various areas, mostly on the right bank, where generic Bordeaux is produced. The most significant change in prices is the ability of the top wines of the Libournais to rival those of the Médoc.

Today the majority of producers are located on the right bank, with more than half making wines of the lowest level appellations, AOC Bordeaux and the Côtes (Figure 17). Just over a third are found in the higher quality appellations of the Libournais or Médoc and Graves. The left bank altogether has roughly a quarter of the producers.

Figure 16

A late 19th century map emphasizes the regions of the Left Bank.[102]

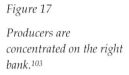

Figure 17

Producers are concentrated on the right bank.[103]

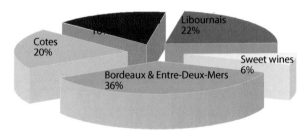

Almost all of the several thousand producers in Bordeaux are described as "Châteaux," but the name can be misleading with regards to their size and importance. Until 20 years ago, the average vineyard holding for the Gironde as a whole was only about 6 ha, which translates into roughly 3000 cases of annual production; a decline in the number of growers has brought the average up to 13 ha today (7000 cases annually).[104] So most producers are relatively small. The large estates of the left bank (where the use of "château" originated) are the exception.

On both the left and right bank, the view of the best terroirs for wine was determined by the commercial climate of the time. When heavier wines that transported well were in demand, the palus were preferred territory. When more refined premium wines were required, attention shifted to gravel-based soils in the Médoc and to clay-based areas away from the river in the Libournais. Slowly the present hierarchy emerged, with top wines made from the communes of the Haut-Médoc, Pessac-Léognan, St. Emilion, and Pomerol, other quality wines made from the Bas-Médoc, Graves, Canon-Fronsac, Lalande-Pomerol, and St. Emilion satellites; and rather more ordinary wine made elsewhere.

This hierarchy, of course, reflects the present view of what constitutes quality in wine. It has certainly changed over the past half century, even over the past couple of decades, and no doubt will continue to develop. It's an open question whether it will withstand the climatic changes that seem to be occurring today (Chapter 10).

3

The Importance of Being Classified

"INFIRM OF PURPOSE, GIVE ME THE DAGGER," said Lady Macbeth. Well Macbeth was positively resolute compared with the inconsistency of classification in Bordeaux. The lack of any significant hierarchy among appellations, together with a wide range of quality in most appellations, means that the appellation on the label conveys little direct information about quality. It's left to each appellation to decide how to classify its wines, and within the appellations, systems of classification vary widely.

At one extreme, Pomerol (the smallest appellation in Bordeaux) famously has no classification whatsoever, allowing Château Pétrus, selling at more than $1000 per bottle, to have the same description as generic Pomerol from Moueix (the proprietor of Pétrus) selling at $25 per bottle. At the other extreme, the Médoc has five levels of Grand Cru Classés, three levels of Cru Bourgeois, and Cru Artisan. Wow! you will say, recollecting the discussion in Chapter 1 about terroir and its classification in other regions, with 9 different levels of classification there must be an incredibly detailed definition of land. Well, no, actually there is no classification of land at all involved in this system. It is all done on the price of the wine. And, in fact, the whole thing is based on an accident.

In 1855 the Emperor Napoleon III organized a Universal Exposition in Paris. This was intended to provide a showcase for French products (and not incidentally to outshine the Great Exhibition that had been held at the Crystal Palace in London in 1851). The Bordeaux Chamber of Commerce was invited to display the wines of the Département of the Gironde as well as other regional products. The wines were to be submitted to a jury that would consider them for medals on the basis of tasting.

To accompany the display and to give some significance to the individual wines, the Chamber of Commerce commissioned a wine map of the Gironde. They asked the brokers who usually handled the wines in Bordeaux to provide a list of the leading châteaux, identified by class and commune, to accompany it.[1]

Over the following two weeks, a committee of brokers drew up a list of 57 red wines (all from the Médoc except for Haut Brion) and a list of 21 Sauternes. The intention was not to classify the wines of the Médoc as such, but the quality of wine produced on the right bank was generally considered lower, and its producers were less well known to the brokers, who naturally enough concentrated on where their business came from: the left bank.

A great deal of guff is talked about the basis for the classification; exaggerated claims have been made about the procedures the brokers went through to assess each château. But the speed with which the classification was drawn up precludes any idea that extensive tastings were organized or visits arranged.[2] The brokers cannot have had time to do more than consult their records before putting together a list representing received wisdom at the time. The main criterion for the classification lay strictly with the commercial basis of pricing in prior years, which the brokers would have been able to consult from their records. This lends little credence to fanciful comments suggesting that they made a detailed analysis of terroir or indeed took into account any factors other than price.

No one ever intended the classification to be more than a contemporary guide to display the wines at the exposition. The brokers would have been enormously surprised at its subsequent longevity. But the system has stuck. So unlike other regions in France, classification of the top wines in Bordeaux is performed not in terms of the land but in terms of the producers.

How Good was the Classification?

The brokers were in a good position to provide a classification on demand, because it had already become a routine tool of their trade, resulting from the practical need to set opening prices each year. Establishing a relative ranking of châteaux enabled them rapidly to set absolute prices in response to the quality of the particular vintage.

Roughly a century earlier, the first classifications had distinguished four wines, Châteaux Haut Brion, Margaux, Latour, and Lafite, as fetching the highest prices and comprising a group of first growths. By 1815, Guillaume Lawton, of the brokerage house Tastet & Lawton, had classified 65 châteaux into five levels of growths. Classifications from other commentators followed regularly, generally with very similar conclusions. Whereas brokers had made the first classifications as a utility for the marketplace, now classifications began to reach a wider audience, and were made public in books or magazines devoted to wine. In his book on the 1855 classification, Dewey Markham records no fewer than 25 different classifications (some of them revised several times) before 1855.[3]

Over the hundred years from the early classifications to the formalization of the 1855 classification, the group of first growths never changed. Movements among the other groups occurred, most often reflecting promotions. But the 1855 classification is generally quite similar to earlier classifications, suggesting there was significant stability in the price relationships between the groups of châteaux over the first half of the 19th century. The brokers therefore regarded the construction

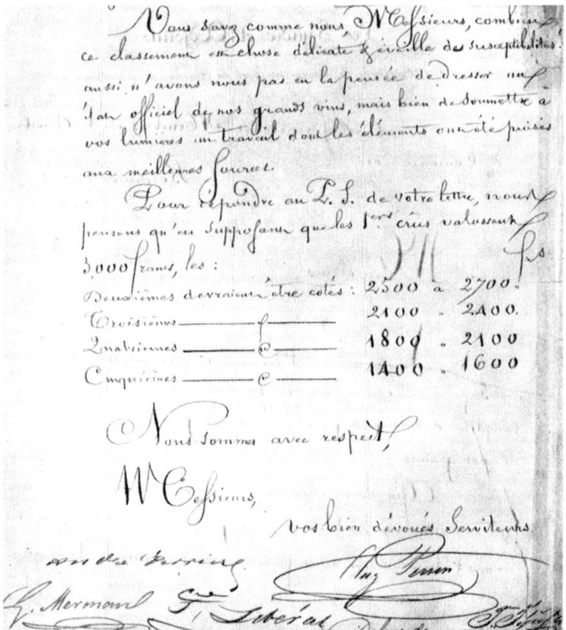

Vous savez comme nous, Messieurs, combien ce classement est chose délicate & éveille de susceptibilités; aussi n'avons nous pas eu la pensée de dresser un état officiel de nos grands vins, mais bien de soumettre à vos lumières un travail dont les éléments ont été puisés aux meilleures sources.

Pour répondre au P. S. de votre lettre, nous pensons qu'en supposant que les 1ers crûs valussent 3000 francs, les :

Deuxièmes devraient être cotés :	2500	à	2700.	
Troisièmes	—	2100	.	2400.
Quatrièmes	—	1800	.	2100
Cinquièmes	—	1400	.	1600

Nous sommes avec respect,

Messieurs,

vos bien dévoués Serviteurs

Figure 18

An extract from the brokers' reply of April 18, 1855 to the request to draw up a classification.[4]

of the classification as a fairly routine representation of commercial reality. However, they were conscious both of the need for fairness and of the transient nature of their work, as indicated in their reply to the request for classification: "We realize as you do that classification is a delicate matter, and we have not intended to make an official list of our great wines, but rather to submit to you the results of our work relying on our best sources" (Figure 18).

The classification divided the most important châteaux into a series of price bands. The first growths sold at 3,000 Francs/tonneau, the seconds at 2,500-2,700, the thirds at 2,100-2,400, the fourths at 1,800-2,100, and the fifths at 1,400-1,600. (A tonneau is a unit of 900 liters, amounting to four of the traditional barriques, or 100 cases.) The classification had an immediate self-reinforcing effect on prices, with the ratio of the price of first growths to fifth growths increasing in the next 10 and 20 years.

Available data on pricing suggest that the brokers' classification was in fact quite accurate. The range of prices for each group of classified growths between 1840 and 1854 shows that the first growths are quite clearly separated from the seconds (Figure 19). Where the division is drawn between each subsequent group is more arbitrary. The cut-off at the bottom is hard on those excluded, since the best Cru Bourgeois achieved very close prices. As Jullien remarked just previously in 1848, "[cru bourgeois] often acquire quality which makes them very difficult to distinguish from fifth growths".[6]

The decision of the brokers to concentrate on the Médoc was clearly justified by the pricing of the time. The second crus of the Graves and the premier crus of St. Emilion sold consistently below the level of the Médoc cru bourgeois (Figure 20).

Figure 19

The range of prices for the groups of classified growths is shown for the period preceding the 1855 classification. The average first growth price is set at 100 for each year.[5]

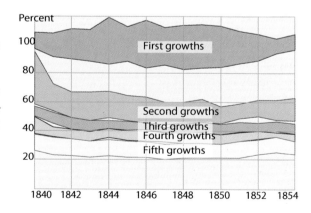

Figure 20

Prices for wines of the Médoc were far higher than for other regions in 1858, as seen on the export market in London.[7]

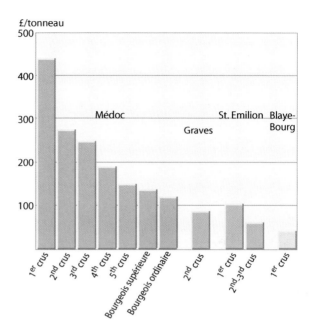

The original classification places the château in each class in order of a steady decline in average price (Table 1). Later there was an attempt to list each class alphabetically, but this is usually ignored. The fit between pricing and groups of growths is not perfect, but this could reflect the fact that the pricing data still available to us today may not be quite complete. Also, the brokers may have given less weight to more recent years. For example, the relatively high prices of Giscours and La Lagune in the third growths reflects a sharp rise in their prices in the five years immediately preceding the classification, which brought them into the range of the second growths, but preceding this period they were clearly in the third growths.

Some distortion in prices may have resulted from the fact that this was a difficult economic period. Production was hit by the infection of oïdium. Some wines were sold by subscription; in order to ensure a steady cash flow, certain châteaux had been forced to sell their production at set prices for a period of years in advance, irrespective of the quality of the vintages.[8] All this has to be taken into account in comparing the raw price data with the brokers' assessment. Looking at the relative prices over the period immediately preceding the 1855 classification, there seems little to quarrel with in the brokers' judgment.

Table 1 *Average prices of the classed growths during the period 1840-1854.*

Firsts				Fourths	
Lafite Rothschild	104%				
Margaux	103%				
Latour	93%				
Seconds				Branaire	45%
Mouton Rothschild	67%			Talbot	45%
Lascombes	65%			St. Pierre Roulet	44%
Durfort Vivens	64%			Lafon Rochet	44%
Pichon Baron	61%			Saint Pierre Bontemps	43%
Léoville Poyferré	61%			Tour-Carnet	43%
Léoville Las Cases	60%			Prieuré Lichine	43%
Rauzan-Gassies	59%			Pouget-Lassalle	41%
Rauzan-Ségla	59%			Duhart Milon	41%
Brane Cantenac	57%			Beychevelle	39%
Ducru Beaucaillou	57%			Pouget	38%
Gruaud Larose	56%			Marquis de Terme	34%
Cos d'Estournel	56%			**Fifths**	
Léoville Barton	55%			Haut-Bages Liberal	35%
Montrose	54%			Grand Puy Ducasse	35%
Thirds				Lynch Bages	34%
Lagrange	49%			Pontet Canet	34%
Giscours	56%			Belgrave	33%
La Lagune	53%			Grand Puy Lacoste	33%
Malescot St. Exupéry	48%			d'Armailhac	33%
d'Issan	48%			Lynch Moussas	33%
Ferrière	47%			Batailley/Haut Batailley	32%
Marquis d'Alesme	46%			Pedésclaux	32%
Kirwan	46%			Camensac	31%
Boyd Cantenac Brown	46%			Cos Labory	31%
Desmirail	45%			Dauzac	31%
Palmer	43%			Croizet Bages	31%
Langoa Barton	39%			du Tertre	31%
Calon Ségur	38%			Clerc Milon	28%

Prices are relative to an average first growth price of 100.[9]

The wine map of the Gironde, accompanied by the classified list of châteaux, was duly presented at the Universal Exposition in April 1855. The fact that the classification was so widely accepted with little controversy suggests there was general agreement on which wines belonged in each class. There was no thought at the time that the classification would have any permanence, and there were only a handful of protests from individual proprietors. The only one of these to be successful concerned Château Cantemerle, whose proprietor complained directly to the brokers, with the result that Cantemerle was added to the list of fifth growths in September of 1855.[10]

Occasional allegations of partiality on the part of the brokers do not gain much support from the price data, but still surface even today. In recent catalogs for their wine auctions in New York, Christies stated: "Château Mouton-Rothschild stands alone in its feat of being the only Château of the 1855 Médoc classification to change status. While this classification purported to consider only market prices in its framework, the exclusion of Mouton from the ranks of the four other Premier Grand Cru Classé reeked of bias."[11] But in fact it did not at all seem that way in 1855. As was widely acknowledged at the time, Mouton Rothschild was clearly at the head of the second growths but did not reach first growth prices. Things have changed since then, and no one successfully disputed the case for Mouton's promotion to first growth in 1973 (Chapter 13).

It All Depends What You Mean by "Official"

Even today there is a great deal of misunderstanding (some inadvertent, some less so) about the basis for the 1855 classification, in particular whether it had or has "official" status. The most common misapprehension is that the classification was born with official status. The Mairie of the town of Pauillac still claims that "C'est en 1855 que Napoleon III officialisa le classement des plus grands vins du Bordelais."[12] "Officialisa" is a bit strong considering that the classification was produced purely as a temporary device to display the wines at the exposition in Paris. Sylvain Boivert, Directeur of the Conseil des Grand Cru Classés says that "C'est un Classement officiel et c'est même le premier classement officiel de vins au monde."[13] (It is an official classification, and even the first official classification of wines in the world). But by what authority is the classification "official"?

To be sure, the 1855 classification almost immediately superseded all other attempts at classification. In each edition of his book, *Traité sur les vins du Médoc*, from 1824 to 1853, William Franck presented his own classification. But in the 1864 edition, he instead reproduced the brokers' classification. Indeed, the classification became routinely used by authors of books on the wines of Bordeaux, avoiding the need for (and possible controversy created by) making individual classifications. The central role of the classification was reinforced when it was reproduced for the Universal Expositions in London and Paris of 1862 and 1867.

But the classification still had no official status. A court case brought in 1869 by Arnaud Roux, the proprietor at Château Peyrabon, against Franck's publisher on grounds of damage resulting from Peyrabon's failure to be included in list of classed growths was dismissed: "There is nothing official about the classification of the Médoc's wines, nor is it definitive and irrevocable; it changes according to the opinions of the wines' relative quality as formed by the brokers, those who sell the wine, and those who consume it; [the classification] always leaves open the hope for all proprietors or a new and higher standing for their wines."[14] Clearly enough, the classification was regarded as no more than a snapshot of the brokers' commercial opinions at this particular point in time.

The first implication of any "official" status appeared in the publication of the second edition of Cocks & Féret's *Bordeaux et ses vins*. Cocks & Féret was to become the bible of Bordeaux, presenting comprehensive and frequently updated information on all the châteaux of Bordeaux. It is now in its 18th edition (published in 2007). In the second edition of 1868, Edouard Féret stated that "for the five categories of grand crus we have followed the text of the last official document established by the Union of Brokers in 1855."[15]

The status of the Grand Crus was reinforced by the formation of the Union of Crus Classés of the Médoc in 1901. The classed growths of Sauternes later formed a similar association. However, the first legal recognition of the term was when legislation in 1949 offered protection for the use of *Cru Classé* as a description (Figure 21).[16]

The law of 1949 limited use of "cru classé" to two circumstances: wines officially classified by INAO; or wines classified in 1855. But the distinction seems clear: "official" applies specifically to INAO's activity. Subsequent modifications of the law in 1964 and 1988 effectively restricted "cru classé" to be used exclusively for Bordeaux.[17, 18]

So what does this actually mean for the status of the Grand Cru Classés? There are sometimes claims that the 1949 decree gave legal status to the 1855 classification.[19] But the law was concerned with the repression of fraud. Its purpose was to make sure that the label did not make exaggerated claims for the wine.

Does this constitute an incorporation of the 1855 classification into French law? Or is the recognition of the 1855 classification more like acknowledgement of a trademark, if you will, than an official ratification of the classification itself? Remember that the brokers themselves denied any official significance for their list (Figure 18).

Official or not, the classification is recognized in French law at least to the extent of affecting the tax status of the château. Markham points out that châteaux classified in 1855 got a higher tax credit on potential assets than other châteaux.[20] To them that have, shall be given.

JOURNAL OFFICIEL DE LA REPUBLIQUE FRANÇAISE   5 Octobre 1949

MINISTÈRE DE L'AGRICULTURE

Décret n° 49-1349 du 30 septembre 1949 modifiant les décrets des 19 août 1921 et 31 janvier 1930 portant règlement d'administration publique pour l'application de la loi du 1er août 1905 sur la répression des fraudes dans la vente des marchandises et des falsifications des denrées alimentaires et des produits agricoles en ce qui concerne les vins, vins mousseux et eaux-de-vie, les vins de liqueur, les vermouths et les apéritifs à base de vin.

« Art. 13. — Est interdit, en toute circonstance et sous quelque forme que ce soit, notamment:

« Sur les récipients et emballages;

« Sur les étiquettes, capsules, bouchons, cachets ou tout autre appareil de fermeture;

« Dans les papiers de commerce, factures, catalogues, prospectus, prix-courants, enseignes, affiches, tableaux-réclames, annonces ou tout autre moyen de publicité,

l'emploi, en ce qui concerne les vins, vins mousseux et eaux-de-vie:

« 1° De toute indication, de tout mode de présentation (dessin, illustration, image ou signe quelconque) susceptible de créer une confusion dans l'esprit de l'acheteur sur la nature, l'origine, les qualités substantielles, la composition des produits, ou la capacité des récipients les contenant;

« 2° Des mots: « premier cru », sauf lorsqu'un décret pris en application de l'article 21 du décret du 30 juillet 1935 a prévu leur emploi;

« 3° Des mots: « cru classé », sauf lorsqu'il s'agit de vins provenant des domaines ayant fait l'objet d'un classement officiel homologué par l'institut national des appellations d'origine ou de vins de Bordeaux bénéficiant du classement de 1855;

Figure 21 Clause 3 of article 13 of the décret of 1949 states that it is forbidden to use the words "cru classé" except for wines that have been officially classified by INAO or for wines of Bordeaux that were classified in 1855.

Commercial Classifications Define the Médoc

The 1855 classification covers 61 châteaux, 60 in the Médoc, with the
addition of Château Haut Brion in Pessac-Léognan. (Actually a total of
57 châteaux were classified in 1855, but since then some have been
divided, increasing the total number of classified growths to 61.) The
next step down in the Médoc is the Cru Bourgeois classification, which
applies to châteaux in the Médoc that missed out in 1855. It classifies 247
châteaux into the ascending levels of Cru Bourgeois, Cru Bourgeois
Supérieur, and Cru Bourgeois Exceptionnel.[21] Another classification, Cru
Artisan, has been introduced for smaller producers.[22]

The locations of the châteaux that are classified as Grand Crus or as
Cru Bourgeois indicate the relative importance of the areas of the Médoc

Figure 22

*Almost all of the classified
growths are found in the
communes of St. Estèphe,
Pauillac, St. Julien, and
Margaux, with five in the
Haut-Médoc. Most of the
Cru Bourgeois
Exceptionnel and
Supérieur are found in
Listrac, Moulis, and the
Haut-Médoc, whereas Cru
Bourgeois predominate in
the Bas-Médoc.*

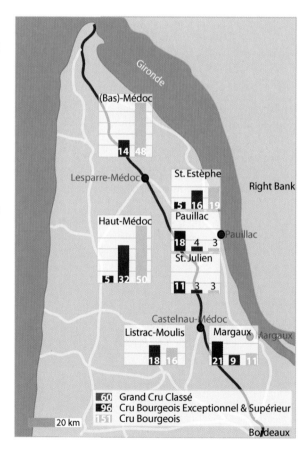

(Figure 22). In first place, with almost all of the Grand Cru Classés are the appellations of Margaux, St. Julien, Pauillac, and St. Estèphe. A handful of Grand Cru Classés are found in the Haut-Médoc, but there are none in the Bas-Médoc. The Cru Bourgeois Exceptionnel follow a similar pattern of distribution, although there is one (Château Potensac) in the Bas-Médoc. The greater importance of the Haut-Médoc compared to the Bas-Médoc is evident from the Cru Bourgeois classification. Cru Bourgeois Supérieur are concentrated in the Haut-Médoc, while the lower level of Cru Bourgeois is concentrated in the Bas-Médoc.

The 1855 classification preceded the establishment of the AOC system by the best part of a century. When the AOC system was initially described for Bordeaux, in 1936, the communes of the Médoc were distinguished from the Haut-Médoc and Bas-Médoc. Châteaux in Pauillac, for example, state "Appellation Pauillac Contrôlée" on the label.[23]

Châteaux that were classified in 1855 can include their classified status on the label. After the Second World War, when wine began to penetrate the consumer market more directly, it became common to state "Grand Cru Classé du Médoc" as an imprimatur. The first growths may state "Premier Grand Cru Classé," but other châteaux soon ceased stating their exact level in the hierarchy, and simply say "Grand Cru Classé du Médoc en 1855."

However, this does not make the classification system part of the Appellation Contrôlée; in fact the two systems remain independent.

The classification system far exceeds the appellation in terms of importance. This is evident on the labels. When the classification is included it usually features larger than the AOC (Figure 23).

Being a first or second growth has much greater effect on a château's reputation than its commune. Although with five levels of hierarchy the classification system is reminiscent of angels dancing on the head of a

Figure 23

Château Margaux states "Premier Grand Cru Classé" in much larger letters than "Appellation Margaux Contrôlée."

pin, it's really only at the top levels of the first or second growths that the hierarchy is determinative: much less distinction is made between the third, fourth, and fifth growths.

There are no regulations relating to the status of the Grand Cru Classés comparable to those for appellations. Progressive restriction on yields is one of the key means by which the AOC system imposes higher quality production on better terroirs, but there are no regulations enforcing differences between the different levels of Grand Cru Classés. Each château is limited simply by the regulations of its commune. The status of 1855 confers license without obligation on the château.

Other Classifications Imitate 1855

The long life of the 1855 classification, in spite of its deficiencies, is a tribute to its effectiveness. As a result, it has been imitated (with various modifications) in all subsequent classifications in Bordeaux.

As part of the 1855 classification, the châteaux producing sweet wine in Sauternes were classified into three tiers, with Château d'Yquem at their head as Premier Cru Supérieur, and the others as Premier Cru Classés and Deuxième Cru Classés. Like the classification of the Grand Crus of the Médoc, this has never been changed. The classification has actually held up quite well, although currently the unclassified Châteaux de Fargues and Raymond Lafon fetch prices at the premier cru level.

Other regions were not classified until the 1950s. Classification could have followed the AOC system that had by then been established for the rest of France on the basis of terroir. However, the producers were the driving force for classification, and perhaps unsurprisingly it was

Figure 24

Classified châteaux in the Graves can state both the classification (Cru Classé de Graves) and the AOC (Pessac-Léognan) on the label. Haut Brion is unusual in also being classified as a Premier Grand Cru Classé in 1855.

therefore once again the châteaux that were classified. So the model of the Médoc has been more or less followed as other areas have introduced classifications, but with the difference that INAO was responsible for each classification, which therefore became part of the AOC system.

In 1953 the châteaux of the Graves were classified (Figure 24). The classification system simply picked out the better châteaux to be described as Cru Classés on the basis of their production of red wine.[24] The classification was modified in 1959 to give Cru Classé status to some châteaux for their white wine.[25] The classification has no hierarchy and has never been changed.

Also organized by INAO at the instigation of the producers, the classification of St. Emilion was undertaken on a slightly different basis. First published in 1955, it classified the châteaux as Premier Grand Cru Classé (A) (2 châteaux), Premier Grand Cru Classé (B) (11 châteaux), and Grand Cru Classé (55 Châteaux). As the classification is part of the AOC, a wine is described as "Appellation St. Emilion Premier Grand Cru Classé" or "Appellation St. Emilion Grand Cru Classé." It may not be a coincidence that the St. Emilion classification was first published exactly one hundred years after the classification of the Médoc, but uses the same terms, and therefore could be confused with the original classification by the uninitiated (Figure 25).

In addition, roughly 600 châteaux can describe themselves as St. Emilion Grand Cru (a term which basically has little significance except to undermine completely the concept of "Grand Cru"). There is a world of difference between a Grand Cru Classé, which is classified, and a Grand Cru, which has no classification at all. And just to confound (intentionally or not?), the term "St. Emilion Grand Cru" is likely to appear on the labels of both. If you're looking for a château that is really part of the classification, you have to be sure the label also says "Grand

Figure 25

The St Emilion classification uses the same term, "Premier Grand Cru Classé" as in the Médoc, but it has a different significance.

Figure 26

Both unclassified and classified wines of St. Emilion can state "Saint Emilion

Grand Cru" on the label, and you have to look carefully for "Grand Cru Classé" to see whether a château is actually classified (right).

Cru Classé" (Figure 26).

Unlike the other classification systems, the châteaux of St. Emilion are reclassified every decade (most recently in 2006). Also, INAO has the right to approve or disapprove of transfers of land that affect the terroir of a château.

Each region has imposed its own idiosyncrasies on the classification system, and Table 2 (at the end of this chapter) summarizes the systems for anyone who is interested in the details.

Bordeaux is the only place in France (or for that matter in Europe) where it's the producer that is classified. However, this is really a feature only of the top châteaux in the top appellations: châteaux are classified in the Médoc and Haut-Médoc, Pessac-Léognan, St. Emilion, and in Sauternes and Barsac. The Pomerol appellation is the only one to offer wines at the top level without any classification system. In the other (lower quality) appellations, there is no classification aside from that of belonging to the appellation itself. The classified châteaux are the icing on the cake, but what a thin layer this is: fewer than 500 châteaux are classified out of the total of more than 10,000 in Bordeaux.

Classifications and the Law

So we are left with a dilemma concerning the curious question of legal basis for the 1855 classification. Over the years, there have been various legal cases involving the 1855 classification, usually concerning the right of an individual château to describe itself as a Grand Cru Classé after a change of ownership. The courts have accepted the existence of the classification as a fact and issued rulings on the right to belong to it.[26] But its lack of official status was confirmed by court decisions immediately following its appearance.[27] If it had none in 1855, when and how did it acquire it?

In 1973, a government edict promoted Château Mouton Rothschild from second growth to first growth (Chapter 13). Not everyone was happy about this. The Syndicat des Grand Crus had a court action going on the grounds that proper procedure had not been followed, but this failed.[28] This left standing an implication that the government had the authority to change the classification. Yet nowhere between 1855 and 1973 is there any declaration in French law giving legal status to the classification. The only legal change is tangential, in the form of the decrees of 1949 and 1964 restricting use of the term *Cru Classé* to Bordeaux, where it is used for both the five levels of the Médoc classification and the two top levels of St. Emilion. We are left scratching our heads as to how the classification made the transition from a commercial tool, drawn up by brokers to characterize the wines for the Great Exposition of 1855, into an official part of the French state.

The subsequent classifications of other regions undertaken by INAO have a secure legal basis. The regulations are published by INAO and given force in the form of décrets (decrees) that are published in the Journal Officiel of the Republique Français. Even the authority of INAO, however, is insufficient to ensure that everyone regards the classification as fair and impartial.

As part of the regular legal system, these new classifications have been subjected to challenges in the court system. In fact, the classification systems for the Cru Bourgeois of the Médoc and for St. Emilion were overthrown by court orders in March 2007 (the challenges were based on accusations of unfair practices when the classifications were drawn up). This placed the producers on the horns of dilemma, since it was unclear whether they would be able to use the terms Cru Bourgeois or Grand Cru Classé on their labels—no small matter with a vintage about to be bottled. From 2007, Cru Bourgeois does not exist as a classification, but there are plans to restore the classification from 2009.

The situation for St. Emilion is unsettled, since the decision in July 2008 suspended the classification, and restored the 1996 classification for three years, or until all court appeals are finished or a new classification is made (Chapter 9).

The Myth of the Classification

The 1855 classification defies the usual reliance on terroir. The vineyards of a château today are not necessarily the same as those it held in 1855. Châteaux can (and often do) change their terroirs by trading land (Chapter 5). Yet this does not affect their classification. The château is in effect a brand name, and the proprietor can change the terroir from which it is produced without affecting its classification. This is unique to the Médoc.

Many leading châteaux in Bordeaux now produce more than one wine from their vineyards, the Grand Vin being the château named in the classification, and the second wine being sold under a different name at a lower price (Chapter 11). It's entirely within their discretion which vineyard plots are used for each wine, further reducing the connection between the terroir owned by the château and the wine it produces.

There is no particular reason to suppose that all châteaux are performing equally at any particular moment in time. No doubt it is true that the potential of each château is influenced by the quality of the vineyards that it holds at that moment, but some may be under-performing due to lack of interest or resources, while others possibly are over-performing due to larger investments or attention than the others. The snapshot of the châteaux' relative positions in the 1855 classification is no more than that: a freeze-frame of performance over the period leading up to the moment of classification. What is the basis for supposing that 1855 was a magical moment when the reputation of each château could be set in stone?

If great wines come only from great terroir, why should the classification remain valid where there have been changes in the quantity or quality of the vineyards? How can the persistence of a classification based on price in 1855 be reconciled with the view that terroir determines quality? Yet after 150 years the 1855 classification remains the only authorized hierarchy of the leading Médoc châteaux. Irrespective of its "official" or other status, it has undoubtedly proved to be one of the most effective marketing tools ever used for wine—or for that matter, anything else: how many marketing campaigns last 150 years? Never mind the quality, feel the width, as they used to say in the rag trade!

Table 2 Classification systems for Bordeaux châteaux			
Region/Date	Status	Type of Classification	Hierarchy
Médoc 1855	Unofficial	Never revised	4 Premier Grand Cru Classé 15 Deuxième Grand Cru Classé 14 Troisième Grand Cru Classé 10 Quatrième Grand Cru Classé 18 Cinquième Grand Cru Classé
Sauternes 1855	Unofficial	Never revised	1 Premier Cru Supérieur (Yquem) 11 Premier Cru Classé 14 Deuxième Cru Classé
Médoc 1932	Unofficial	Replaced by classification of 2003	9 Cru Bourgeois Supérieur Exceptionnel 99 Cru Bourgeois Supérieur 339 Cru Bourgeois
Médoc 2003	INAO (AOC)	Currently suspended	9 Cru Bourgeois Exceptionnel 87 Cru Bourgeois Supérieur 151 Cru Bourgeois
Graves 1953 Graves 1959	INAO (AOC)	Never revised	13 Cru Classé (red) 10 Cru Classé (white)
St. Emilion 1954	INAO (AOC)	Revised periodically; 2006 revision suspended and 1996 restored	2 Premier Grand Cru Classé (A) 11 Premier Grand Cru Classé (B) 55 Grand Cru Classé
Médoc 2006	INAO (AOC)	Revised every 10 years	44 Cru Artisan

4

Wine in the Time of Classification

A VIGNERON OF 1855 WOULD RECOGNIZE LITTLE in a modern vineyard apart from the vines themselves. But he would be amazed by their orderly nature. In 1855, vines were growing on their own roots, whereas today they are grafted on to rootstocks. They were planted higgledy-piggledy (the technical term is en foule, the French for "in a crowd," meaning that new vines were propagated adjacent to old ones by sticking shoots in the ground). This gave up to 14,000 vines per hectare, whereas today they are planted in neatly aligned rows, each vine independent of, and separated from, the next, with a density rarely more than 8000 per hectare (Figure 27). And different grape varieties were interspersed in the same vineyard (this is called complantation in France); planting each variety in a separate block is a relatively modern development.

Figure 27 *Vines were crowded and disorganized in vineyards of the past, but are planted in tidy rows today.*

Figure 28 *An old basket press seems crude compared with the gleaming stainless steel of a modern fermentation facility.*

The whole process of converting grape juice into wine was completely mysterious in the first half of the 19th century. In 1855, it was not even known how alcohol was generated! It was not until almost a decade later, in 1863, that Pasteur discovered fermentation is catalyzed by yeasts, which change the sugar of the grapes into alcohol. And production has changed entirely: from an artisan process, in which every step was manual, to a highly technological process often controlled by a computer center (Figure 28).

Another big difference was that with relatively little capacity to manage the vines, yields were much lower in 1855 than today, about 18 hectoliters per hectare.[1] Today intervention is required to keep yields down to the appellation limits, typically 45-50 hl/ha.

So what was wine like at the time of the classification and how did it compare with the wine of today?

The Negociant's Skill

A major factor in wine production of the 18th and 19th centuries in Bordeaux was that the wine was relatively weak; it was rarely sold to the consumer as such. Part and parcel of the system in Bordeaux was that wine would be sold by the châteaux to negociants, who would then mature it. Sometimes they would sell it in bulk; sometimes they would bottle it first. Whoever performed the bottling almost inevitably "improved" the wine by blending it with stronger wine from foreign sources.

When the wines passing through the negociant's barrels were adjusted, part of the skill was the selection of the additional wines, as well as deciding on the proportions required. One negociant noted, probably in the late 18th century, "We blend according to the quality of the wine. When the wines are good, we use less foreign wine than when they are poor. The best wines to use for blending with the premier and second crus are those of Hermitage, Benicarlo, and a little Alicante."[2] (Hermitage is farther south, in the Rhône; Benicarlo and Alicante wines were imported from Spain.) In good years, a mixture from all three sources amounting to about 15% of total volume might be added to premier or second crus.[3] For wines of lower quality, more of the foreign wines would be added in order to give body and texture.

Blending may have originated with the purchaser and later have been taken over by the negociants. When the "New French Clarets" became popular in London in the early 18th century, the wines of the Médoc, and in particular the first growths, were sent to London in barriques, where they were mixed with wine from Benicarlo or Hermitage. Even when this form of blending was commonplace in Bordeaux, later in the century, barriques of wine from the Médoc were sent to London to be blended there for local consumption.

The producers were well aware of the need for blending. Lamothe, the régisseur (manager) at Château Latour, noted in 1810 that the vintage was ordinary but the wine was "agreeable and the help from old Hermitage that we propose to give it should compensate for the small deficiency in body."[4] Perhaps because blending may have originated in London, perhaps because of traditional Anglo-French rivalry, blending with foreign wines was commonly called the "travail à l'anglaise."

The effects of the changes in the wine are evident in comparing wine at source in Bordeaux with wine as sold in London in the early 1860s.[5, 6] All the first growths produced wine with alcohol levels just below 10%. By contrast, in London the level was usually in the range 15-17%, indicating a significant degree of fortification since the wine had left the châteaux.[7] Color, and tannin also, had been significantly "improved" by the addition of foreign wine.

As late as 1865, wines sold by one negociant were divided into two classes: roughly three quarters were "vins coupés" (blended), and only one quarter was "vins pur."[8] The blended wines included first growths and second growths.

Were there in fact any consumers who knew the taste of the unadulterated wines of the Médoc when the châteaux were classified in 1855?[9]

A Pale Imitation

Wines produced at the châteaux in 1855 were literally a pale imitation of their counterparts today: lighter in color, lower in alcohol, much lower in tannin, as well as reflecting different cépage usage and oak treatment.

The records of the first growths show how much individual wines produced in the 19th century differed from those of today (Table 3).[10] Many of the differences stem from the fact that the grapes were much less ripe.

Sugar levels at harvest were significantly lower, giving typical alcohol levels of 10%, compared with today's common 13% or more. Chaptalization (the addition of sugar to the grape juice before fermentation in order to increase the level of alcohol), which was routine in the second part of the 20th century, does not appear to have been practiced in Bordeaux in 1855.

Combined with the more limited possibilities that existed then for extraction from the skins, the wines would almost certainly have been much lighter in color. Overall levels of tannin in fact appear to have been only about 20% of the levels of today. Tannins give a wine the structure needed for aging, so this would have been partly responsible for the much shorter life of the wines, typically less than 10 years in the mid 18th century.

Although Cabernet Sauvignon was the dominant grape planted at the top châteaux of the Médoc in 1855 as it is today, the rest of the cépage mix was different. Merlot had begun to be planted only at the beginning of the 19th century, and was still a relatively small component. Malbec

Table 3 *Comparison of properties of the Médoc first growths in 1855 with 2005.*

	1855	2005
Color	Red	Purple
Alcohol	<10%	>13%
Tannin	1 g/l	>6 g/l
Oak	new Baltic oak[11]	new French oak
Duration of fermentation	< 1 week	~ 3 weeks
Grapes (in order of importance)	Cabernet Sauvignon Cabernet Franc Malbec	Cabernet Sauvignon Merlot Cabernet Franc Petit Verdot
Age to Drink	3-7 years	>10 years

Figure 29

Grape varieties planted at Château Latour in 1855 and today.

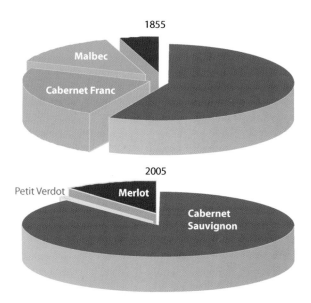

was considered to be of high quality, and remained important until the phylloxera epidemic at the end of the century. Cabernet Franc was planted then as it is now.

Grape varieties were not planted in blocks but were mixed with one another at this period, making it difficult to get a measure of exact numbers. Records of plantings at Château Latour[12] show that since 1855, Cabernet Sauvignon has increased, Cabernet Franc has decreased, and Malbec has been replaced by Merlot (Figure 29). These changes are typical of those in the Haut-Médoc generally, although proportions vary with the château. It appears also that the use of barrels made from local (French) oak may not have been common until some time after the 1855 classification, and this must have affected flavor.

And of course the wines were consumed much younger than they are today. Should the hierarchy established then retain validity in the very different conditions of today?

Contraction and Expansion

The châteaux that were classified as the Grand Cru Classés have been the most important in the Médoc in terms both of their land area and their overall economic impact since at least the 18th century (admitting some changes in the membership of the group from time to time).

Figure 30

The Grand Cru Classés have almost doubled their vineyard areas since 1960. The dashed line estimates the decline in the first half of the century.[14]

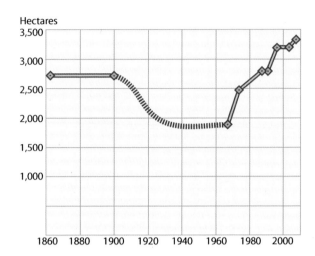

Contemporary information at the time of classification was mostly devoted to production levels rather than to area cultivated, but it seems that the total vineyard area of the Grand Cru Classés in 1855 occupied about 2650 hectares.[13]

In the depression of the first half of the 20th century the cultivated area declined significantly: it is not clear exactly how much. By the 1960s, it was increasing again (Figure 30). In 1967 the total area was still below the level of 1855, at about 1,946 hectares.[15] Around 1970 it was restored to roughly 2,500 ha, close to the level of 1855.[16] Today the area is about 3,380 hectares, an increase of about one third since the classification.[17] This is not nearly as great as the increase in production, which of course largely represents improvements in viticulture and vinification.

The extent of change at individual châteaux varies enormously.[18] Most have significantly increased the sizes of their vineyards since 1855 (Figure 31). Most of the expansion has been in the last fifty years. Sometimes it has resulted from occasional purchases, sometimes from a determined effort by a proprietor. Prieuré-Lichine increased from 11 ha in 1855 to 69 ha today, largely as the result of the growth undertaken by Alexis Lichine in the 1960s. The process continues: Pichon Baron increased from 30 ha in 1967 to 70 ha in 2004. In certain cases, additional land has been used to produce a second wine rather than to augment the grand vin.

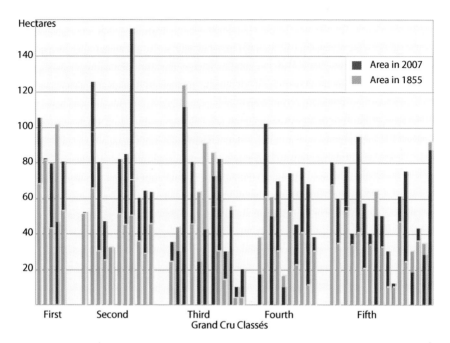

Figure 31 *The average classed growth has one third more vineyard land now than in 1855, but some châteaux have more than doubled in area while others have not increased.[19] The peak of the red column shows hectares in 2007, the peak of the green column shows hectares in 1855.*

A few châteaux still occupy roughly the same land area now as in 1855, notably Margaux, Durfort-Vivens, Ducru Beaucaillou, but even where there have not been overall changes in size, there have usually been changes in the details of the landholdings. One feature of the organization of vineyards in 1855 was its extremely broken up nature.[20] Châteaux had many individual small plots, sometimes indeed as small as a single row of vines. One of the smallest, Château Marquis d'Alesme Becker, had 4 ha divided into 36 separate parcels. Cos d'Estournel, which had been painstakingly assembled by more than 80 individual land purchases between 1820 and 1848, consisted of 55.3 ha divided into 120 parcels. Continuous trading and exchange of land has rationalized these arrangements, although in large part only after 1945. (One incentive for rationalization was introduction of mechanized equipment that could be used in large areas, compared with manual treatment of an individual row of vines.)

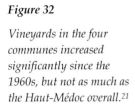

Figure 32

Vineyards in the four communes increased significantly since the 1960s, but not as much as the Haut-Médoc overall.[21]

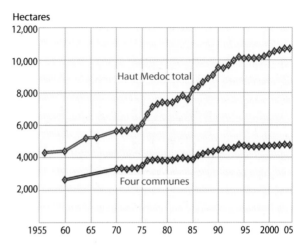

General economic expansion in the Médoc in the past half-century has seen a significant growth in vineyard area in the recent period. Between 1970 and the present, for example, vineyards in the peninsula more than doubled from 7,253 ha to 16,380 ha.[22] Most of this increase was in the Bas-Médoc and Haut-Médoc appellations. Comparison of the Haut-Médoc overall with the four communes (St. Estèphe, Pauillac, St. Julien, Margaux) demonstrates steady expansion of plantings over a half century. Soon after 1990, plantings reached something of a plateau in the four communes, where of course the best terroirs had long since been planted, although it continued to increase in the Haut-Médoc (Figure 32).

The Grand Cru Classés form the major part of the four communes. They have not expanded as much as the unclassified châteaux, so their relative proportion of area and production has fallen from just over a third of the Haut-Médoc in 1970 to just over 20% today.

The sharp increase of the 1960s was a mixed bag. Some of the replanting consisted of reclaiming vineyards that had fallen into disuse during the 1930s. But some consisted of planting land that had not previously been deemed suitable for cultivating vines. Pijassou observed sadly that he had observed land clearing that could only lower the quality of the wines.[23] The combined effect of contraction and expansion, together with continuous trading in land between châteaux, means that very few of the Grand Cru Classés occupy terroir today that is exactly comparable to that of 1855.

And 150 Years Later…

One of the major changes since 1855 is the sheer quantity of wine produced by each château, in conjunction with expansion of their vineyards.

In the period before the 1855 classification, production was fairly stable at the Grand Cru Classés. Allowing for the ups and downs of vintage variation, there is not much difference in the annual production figures for the first growths cited by Thomas Jefferson[24] in 1787 with those given by Cocks & Féret in 1868. After the classification, however, there was an accelerating pace of change.

Production at the Grand Cru Classés has increased enormously since 1855. Some of it is diverted to a second wine, and does not appear under the name of the château itself (Chapter 11), but even with this in mind, they still produce vastly more wine now than then (Figure 33). Total production has increased almost 5-fold, from roughly 375,000 cases in 1855 to 1.75 million cases today.

A common feature between 1855 and today is the economic concentration of a small number of leading châteaux. The Grand Cru Classés are the smallest group of châteaux in the Médoc, but have by far the most economic importance. They are relatively large estates, with an

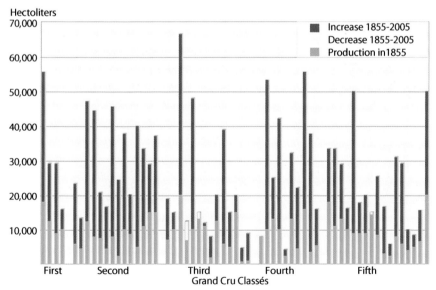

Figure 33 *Production has increased greatly since 1855 at almost all châteaux.[25]*

Figure 34

Relative prices show that many châteaux have changed positions in the hierarchy since 1855. Prices are relative to the average of the first growths. Color reflects position in the 1855 classification.[26]

This figure includes only the classified growths. See Figure 115 for a recent hierarchy that also shows the positions of other wines.

Relative prices 1835-1855	Relative prices 1982-2005
Lafite Rothschild	Margaux
Margaux	Latour
Latour	Mouton Rothschild
Haut Brion	Lafite Rothschild
	Haut Brion
Mouton Rothschild	Léoville Lascases
Lascombes	Palmer
Durfort Vivens	Pichon Lalande
Pichon Baron	Ducru Beaucaillou
Pichon Lalande	Cos d'Estournel
Léoville Poyferré	Pichon Baron
Léoville Lascases	Montrose
Rauzan-Gassies	Lynch Bages
Rausan-Segla	Rauzan-Ségla
Brane Cantenac	Léoville Barton
Ducru Beaucaillou	Léoville Poyferré
Gruaud Larose	Beychevelle
Cos d'Estournel	Calon Ségur
Léoville Barton	Grand Puy Lacoste
Montrose	
Lagrange	Brane-Cantenac
Giscours	Gruaud Larose
La Lagune	Saint Pierre
Malescot St. Exupéry	Lascombes
d'Issan	Langoa Barton
Ferrière	Branaire Ducru
Marquis d'Alesme	Pontet-Canet
Kirwan	Duhart Milon Rothschild
Boyd Cantenac Brown	Clerc Milon
Desmirail	Prieuré Lichine
Palmer	Giscours
Langoa Barton	La Lagune
Calon Segur	Malescot St. Exupéry
Branaire	Lagrange
Talbot	d'Issan
St Pierre Roulet	Marquis-d'Alesme-Becker
Lafon Rochet	Talbot
St Pierre Bontemps	Rauzan Gassies
Tour-Carnet	Haut Batailley
Prieuré Lichine	Dauzac
Pouget-Lassalle	du Tertre
Duhart Milon	Cos Labory
Beychevelle	Cantenac Brown
Pouget	Marquis de Terme
Marquis Terme	Ferrière
Haut Bages Libéral	Lafon Rochet
Grand Puy Ducasse	Haut Bages Libéral
Lynch Bages	Cantemerle
Pontet Canet	d'Armailhac
Belgrave	Kirwan
Grand Puy Lacoste	Durfort Vivens
d'Armailhac	Grand Puy Ducasse
Lynch Moussas	Croizet-Bages
Batailley - Haut Batailley	Lynch Moussas
Pédesclaux	Camensac
Camensac	Tour-Carnet
Cos Labory	Desmirail
Dauzac	Boyd Cantenac
Croizet Bages	Pédesclaux
du Tertre	Batailley
Clerc Milon	Belgrave
Cantemerle	Pouget

Table 4 *An economic breakdown of the Médoc*[28]

Category	Number	Land area	Production	Revenue
Grand Cru Classés	60	3,380 ha	1.6 million cases	€450 million
Cru Bourgeois	238	7,200 ha	3.2 million cases	€300 million
Others	893	5,800 ha	3.1 million cases	€150 million
Total	1191	16,380 ha	7.9 million cases	€900 million

average vineyard of 55 ha (135 acres) and an annual production of 300,000 bottles. Other châteaux tend to be smaller, and there are many small growers who send their grapes to cooperatives.[27] Although the classed growths have about 20% of the planted vineyards and production, they account for at least twice that proportion of revenue (Table 4).

Ranking the Grand Cru Classés on the basis of their prices of the past twenty years shows major changes from the order of the 1855 classification (Figure 34). The first growths easily retain their place at the top, joined by Mouton Rothschild, which has moved from its position at the head of the second growths. The second growths have mostly retained their positions, the most notable changes being the addition of Châteaux Palmer and Lynch Bages. Many of the fifth growths are still in the bottom group. But in between there have been substantial movements; almost none of the third growth châteaux would still be in the same group. Dividing the châteaux into groups of the same size as those of 1855, only 28 of the 61 châteaux would still remain in their original price groups.

What are the forces determining the position of each château? Do some châteaux have better terroir, or is their position in the classification self-reinforcing, giving them greater resources because they can claim higher prices? When châteaux decline due to neglect, can they be resurrected by new investment? And how can châteaux originally lower down in the hierarchy fight their way up?

The classification of Grand Cru Classé is a powerful imprimatur, at least at the top level. No one goes to a wine store crying "I want a fifth growth," but the reputation of the first growths, and also of a group of second growths known as the super-seconds, stands as a powerful brand, both collectively and individually. Many of the châteaux in the fourth and fifth groups, however, now obtain prices no better than, and often significantly less than, unclassified châteaux.

With the châteaux now producing far more wine from larger vineyards than those of 1855, what significance does the classification have today? Can we trace the determinative events at the châteaux and relate them to changing positions in the hierarchy?

5

The Land and the Brand

"I FORGET THE NAME OF THE PLACE, I forget the name of the girl, but the wine … was Chambertin," Hilaire Belloc once said, dreamily recalling an evening in his youth. Great wine has character that speaks of its origins, of the terroir where it was made. It is unforgettable. At its ultimate, you smell and taste a great wine and know that it could come from nowhere else than one specific plot of land.

Terroir is not an easy concept to define and a great deal of nonsense is talked about it. Basically it focuses on the idea that the features of a particular plot of land will determine (perhaps more precisely one might say will limit) the quality of wine made from that land. Given the same viticulture and vinification, the wines made from any two plots of land, even those adjacent to one another, will differ according to the terroir, as seen most clearly in the exquisitely detailed mapping of Burgundy.

Terroir has a perfectly rational explanation in terms of the underlying properties of the vineyard. But often enough mystical forces are invoked. Consider this flowery description: "The intervention of man, as effective as it may be in the domains of viticulture and vinification, is absolutely incapable of modifying, even in the most minute way, the nature and characters of the terroir that are expressed in the inimitable properties of a Bordeaux, a Burgundy, or a Champagne."[1] Ah! the glories of France.

In reality, the characteristic nature of the wine—what in France would be called the typicité—can be changed quite significantly, whether for good or bad, by human intervention. And this capacity has increased enormously in recent years. All the same, terroir makes an important contribution to typicité, even if some views of its role are so extreme as to be risible.

No two people agree on exactly what constitutes terroir, but factors involved are the physical and chemical composition of the soil, the aspect of the land, and climatic effects such as wind and rain. Insofar as there is a consensus, drainage appears to be the most important single factor. The amount of water reaching the roots has the largest influence on how much energy vines put into vegetative growth (putting out shoots and leaves, and so on) as opposed to developing the fruit. This determines the quantity and quality of the grapes. The composition of the soil, including its mineral content, may also be important (although this has yet to be proved in any scientific manner). And aspect (exposure to the sun), rainfall, and other climatic effects naturally have an important impact on vine growth and berry ripening.

Terroir is a feature of small areas. The Chambertin so fondly remembered by Hilaire Belloc could only have come from a plot of 12.9 hectares in the heart of Burgundy's Côte d'Or. But Bordeaux is much larger than Burgundy, and many châteaux in Bordeaux have extensive vineyards, covering far more diversity of terroir than any Burgundian premier or grand cru. So what is the significance of terroir for production in Bordeaux?

The land is different on the left bank and right bank. The left bank is generally rather flat and its best soils are gravelly. The right bank has more slopes, and its soils have more diversity; generally there is more clay, but there are gravelly terraces in St. Emilion, and iron in the soil in Pomerol. And the role of man in the origins of terroir is very different. The right bank has not changed greatly over the past five centuries, but the left bank is another story.

The concept that terroir is intrinsic and immutable has its limitations. New World vineyards have been created by terraforming; the summits of hills have been removed and reconfigured to generate top vineyards in the Napa valley, for example. But we do not need to look only at the modern era to see that terroir can be changed. Until the 17th century, the Médoc was a bucolic hinterland of marshes, but then was drained by Dutch engineers. They had little idea they were affecting the terroir of what would become one of the most famous wine regions in the world. Is this so different from what has happened more recently in the New World? Indeed, has any other example of terroir modification had such broad or long lasting effects?

Whether the terroir is natural or made by man, the basic question is: how far are the great wines of Bordeaux driven by terroir? Do they provide unique representations of conditions that can be found only in their specific vineyards? Or are they brands, representing commercial marques where the underlying quality depends on changing methods and sources of production?

Creating the Terroir

The terrain of the Médoc that we know today originated in the 17th century. Before then, the marshes were so extensive in the Bas-Médoc that conditions there for human habitation were regarded as marginal. The wetlands of the Médoc are usually divided into palus and marais. Palus (originally called paluds) are the alluvial lands at the edge of the river, and marais are the marshy areas farther inland, but the two terms are often used together, with frequent references made to the "palus and marais" of the Médoc.[2] The modern terrain results from a progressive draining of the marshes over the past four centuries. While the results are most dramatic in the Bas-Médoc, marais have been drained throughout the Médoc, extending right to the city of Bordeaux. Today the remaining marais are preserved wetlands (Figure 35).

The reconstruction of the Médoc started with the edict of Henri IV in 1599: "All the palus and marais of the royal domain… situated along rivers or elsewhere are to be drained and dried by Sieur Bradley and his associates, or by the proprietors, and rendered appropriate for cultivation." The work on the Médoc was undertaken by Dutch engineers led by Conrad Gaussen. Basically this involved constructing a dike around each marais with a canal to drain out the water. During the 17th century, three major marais were drained in the Bas-Médoc, reclaiming more than 5000 ha. The work continued over the next two hundred years (Figure 36).[3]

Figure 35

A palu is a marshy area criss-crossed by many small streams and typical wetlands vegetation. (Photo of the Reserve Naturelle de Bruges; see also Figure 37).

Figure 36

The marais of the Bas-Médoc were drained progressively starting in the 16th century.[4]

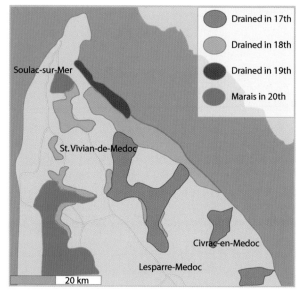

The work was mostly financed by the Dutch, although in some cases there was also local finance, typically involving a consortium of proprietors, who in due course recouped their expenses by charging rent when the land became fit for cultivation.[5] You might think that draining the marshes would be universally approved, but in some cases the work had to contend with opposition from those who had benefited from the previous state of the marshes, such as fishermen.[6]

Palus and marais occupy a smaller proportion of the Haut-Médoc than the Bas-Médoc. As a result of the successive drainage projects (Figure 12), what remain in the Haut-Médoc today are mostly the palus extending out immediately from the river. Drainage of the large marais to the south of Beychevelle, and of the region to the immediate north of Bordeaux (known as the Palu de Bordeaux), altogether represented the reclamation of more than 4000 ha, and made the most substantial change in the terroir of the Haut-Médoc.

There was a surprising amount of cultivation in the area of the palus before they were drained. The Palu de Bordeaux originally occupied the area between the old city of Bordeaux and the region of Bruges.[7] More than half of it was cultivated, for the most part with crops grown on meadows, but with a large area of vines at the southern tip.[8] All of this area now forms part of the suburbs of Bordeaux. All that remains of the Palu today is a small swampy area (preserved as the Reserve Naturelle de Bruges) just to the north of Bruges (Figure 37). Running from the west past the Reserve Naturelle de Bruges to empty out into the Gironde is

Figure 37

The area around Bruges used to be the Palu de Bordeaux, but now this is part of the suburbs of Bordeaux, and only the Reserve Naturelle de Bruges remains.[9]

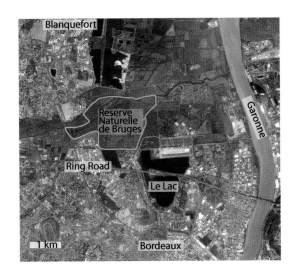

the stream of the Jalle de Blanquefort, the limit of Gaussen's drainage, which forms the boundary between the appellation of the Médoc to its north and Graves to its south.

Water, Water, Everywhere

The Médoc is superficially surprising as top terroir for wine because it is so flat and marshy. Most good wine-producing areas are relatively hilly, with slopes and angles that give good drainage. The highest point in the Médoc is only just above sea level (43 meters at Listrac-Médoc). Some areas are in fact below the level of the tide, with immediate consequences for the terrain.

Water both above and below ground is one of the major factors influencing wine production. Rainfall is crucial: with some rare exceptions, the problem in the Médoc is not usually lack of sufficient rainfall (remember that irrigation is not allowed), but too much rain, or, more often, rain at the wrong time. Typically it rains around the equinox of September 21, just coming up to harvest; in fact, only two harvests in the past twenty years have been completely without rain.

At ground level, the river is an omnipresent influence in the Médoc, not merely for its moderating effect on the climate, but for all the little streams (jalles) that run from the west to drain into the Garonne,

Figure 38

*Drainage is necessary
because rain accumulates
in the rows between the
vines.*

including many canals that drain marshy areas. The saying "vines hate wet feet" describes the need for good drainage, so that the roots are exposed to water, but not to too much. The best results for grapevines are found where the soil is poor, forcing the roots to go deep, with the water table close to root level. This stresses the vine, restricting vegetative growth in favor of developing berries. Accordingly, drainage systems are common in the vineyards to stop the accumulation of rainfall near the surface (Figure 38).

The AOC system has a schizophrenic attitude to water. It all depends on whether the water is above or below ground level. Any change in water provision above ground is strictly *verboten*. Woe betides a producer who tries to protect his vines from excess rain. When tarpaulins were used at Château Valandraud in 2000 to run excess rain into drainage ditches and keep it from reaching the vines, the authorities refused to allow the wine to be labeled as AOC St. Emilion. With characteristic insouciance, it was put into a separate bottling labeled Interdit de Valandraud and classified as a Vin de Table (Figure 39). Both wines sell for about the same ($200 per bottle) making a mockery of the appellation system.

On the other hand, management of water below ground is fine. Led by the Grand Cru Classés, drainage systems have been installed to handle the persistent problem of excess water in the Haut-Médoc. This made a major change to the terroir during the 19th century.[10] At first, pine logs were used to create simple channels for running off water, then bricks were used, later replaced by pottery drainage pipes buried at 1-2 meters. Today, PVC is used. Château Latour, always ahead of the game, installed the first drainage systems in wood in 1817, adding stone drains in 1835.[11] Several of the top vineyards in the Médoc installed drainage systems following the recognition afforded by the 1855 classification; those on the right bank generally did not have the resources to do so until after 1945. To the south, Château d'Yquem installed 100 km of

Figure 39

Château
Valandraud is
AOC St. Emilion
Grand Cru
(right), but wine

made in 2000 from part of the vineyard where vines
were protected from the rain, had to be labeled
separately as a Vin de Table, with no vintage or
geographical description (left).

drainage to improve its vineyards in the 19th century; the system is regularly replaced as individual vineyard plots are replanted.[12]

So not only has the entire terrain been changed by major drainage projects, but individual vineyards are drained as necessary. Where does this leave the claim that the terroir of the Médoc should be protected from human intervention because it is uniquely suited to produce the greatest wines?

And just to confound further any possibility of consistency, the use of reverse osmosis machines to directly extract water from the grape juice before fermentation is perfectly legal: even Alice in Wonderland might have been confused by a system that says it's illegal to prevent water from reaching the grapes from the sky, but perfectly legal to remove it from the wine by physical manipulation.

The Gravel Mounds

It's often said the terroir of the Médoc was created by the drainage of the marais, and that the famous areas for wine production would not otherwise exist. This is not entirely true. In the Bas-Médoc, drainage greatly changed the terroir by creating large new areas of cultivable land, but the spread of viticulture is more recent. In the Haut-Médoc, change was less drastic, although effects on the vineyards could be profound, if sometimes indirect.

Immediately adjacent to the river, the soil is alluvial, consisting of "black sand" with high water reserves; this is less favored terroir. Away from the river, all the best wines of the Médoc are grown on ancient gravel-based soils. The gravel beds date from the Günzienne glaciation during the Quaternary (Pleistocene) period. Carried from the Pyrenées

Figure 40

Gravel mounds provide the best terroir in the Médoc, forcing vines to develop deep roots.[13]

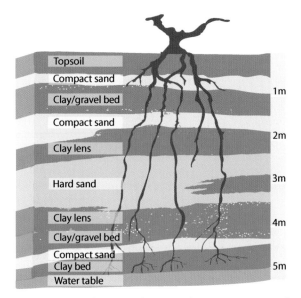

by the Garonne river, the Günz gravel covers layers of coarser material that were laid down during the previous (Tertiary) period.

Running closely parallel with the river are the famous "gravel mounds" that provide the best terroir (sometimes called the "Graves de Bordeaux"). A little farther inland, roughly 10 km from the river, soils are also gravel-based, but here the mix also includes more sand and clay on a limestone plateau.

A gravel mound consists of topsoil on compact sand, sitting on top of a gravel bed that can range from a few centimeters to 2 or 3 meters in depth. Below that are alternating layers of compact sand and clay lens (Figure 40). Grapevines can establish deep roots on the gravelly soil, which has good drainage and a low water table. The gravel mounds are ideal terroir for Cabernet Sauvignon.

The gravel mounds are slightly elevated, and so were not subject to flooding, although in some cases they were surrounded by marais. The second growth of Château Léoville Las Cases provides a famous example: its vineyards sit atop a gravel mound that was surrounded by marshes that flooded at high tide until the marais were drained. This illustrates one of the important effects of draining the marais: not only was the swamped land released for agricultural use, but the lowering of the water table on the adjacent gravel terraces improved their potential for quality wine production.

The extension of vineyards into the palus when heavier wines (temporarily) became fashionable in the 17th century, however, was the most direct consequence of the conversion of the palus into cultivable

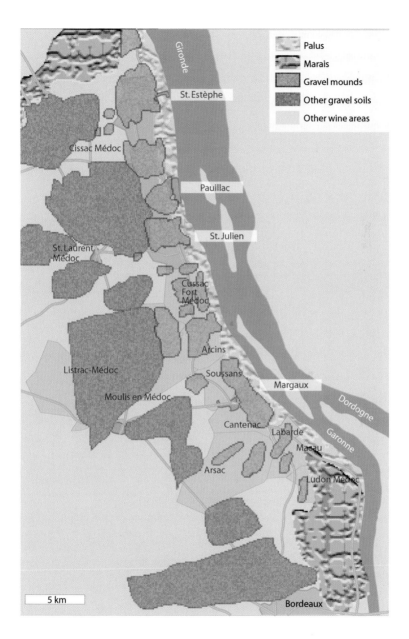

Figure 41 *The terroir of the Haut-Médoc. Palus run along the river and marais are found farther inland. The gravel mounds lie in a line parallel with the river; other gravel soils are farther inland.*

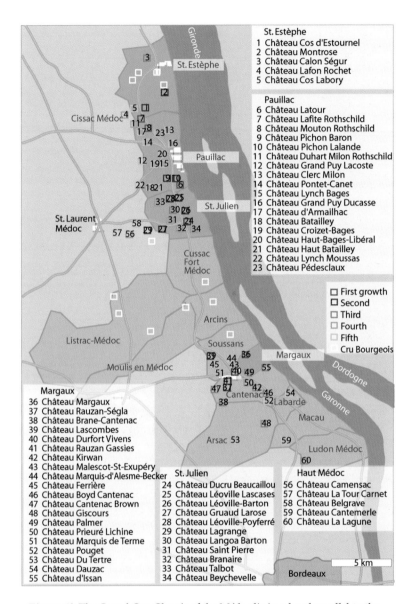

Figure 42 *The Grand Cru Classés of the Médoc lie in a band parallel to the Gironde, and are mostly located in the appellations of St. Estèphe, Pauillac, St. Julien, and Margaux.*

Figure 43

The lake near Château de Reignac was constructed to protect the vineyards against winter freezes.[14]

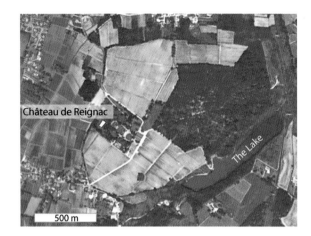

Château de Reignac

The Lake

500 m

land. By and large, the effects of the reclamation of the marais on the terroir of the vineyards were indirect rather than direct.

The gravel mounds form a line of outcrops more or less parallel with the river, all the way from Graves to St. Estèphe. Château Haut Brion is located on one of the largest of the gravel mounds, then there is a break in the line until Margaux is reached. The largest of the gravel mounds in the Médoc run through St. Julien, Pauillac, and St Estèphe (Figure 41).

Virtually all the classified growths (as well as some other châteaux) are located on the gravel mounds (Figure 42). That is not to say, of course, that all terroirs on the gravel mounds are equivalent. In fact, there is considerable heterogeneity in the details of the terroir.

The Bordeaux climate is maritime, and the proximity of the vineyards to the rivers further dampens climatic extremes. But sometimes this is not enough. When Yves and Stéphanie Vatelot bought Château de Reignac in 1990, damage to the vines from winter freezes was a constant problem. The vineyards occupy a block of 80 ha on a plateau at the high point (about 30 m) at Saint-Loubès, towards the northern tip of Entre-deux-Mers. So in 1993 the Vatelots constructed a lake just to the east of the vineyards (Figure 43). About 1000 m long and 100 m wide, it provides a heat sink that combats the freeze and protects the vineyards. Sometimes the terroir needs a little human help. It's legal when it's not in the vineyards themselves.

The Answer Lies in the Soil

Terroir becomes increasingly significant as the size of the vineyard decreases. Perhaps one of the reasons it is paid much less attention in the New World (if not actually disdained) is the much larger size of the vineyards compared to Europe. Even in the classic French wine regions there is a big difference between Bordeaux and Burgundy. The average size of a classed growth in the Médoc is 55 hectares. In Burgundy's Cote d'Or, the land of detailed terroir mapping, not a single premier cru or grand cru is this large; the average cru is 14 hectares, half of the crus are less than 10 hectares, and some are less than a hectare. Assigning quality to terroir is really a matter of hectares rather than tens of hectares.

The relative scales of production in Burgundy and Bordeaux show why there is a difference in emphasis on terroir. The commune of Chambolle Musigny, with some 180 ha, is just a little larger than the vineyards of Châteaux Lafite Rothschild and Mouton Rothschild combined (Figure 44). But just over half of Chambolle Musigny is classified for village wine (Chambolle Musigny AOC), 60 ha are mapped into 23 individual Premier Crus, and 2 Grand Crus cover 26 ha. That's what they mean by terroir!

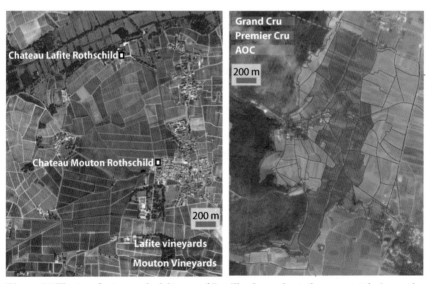

Figure 44 *The two first growth châteaux of Pauillac have about the same total vineyard area as the appellation of Chambolle Musigny, which has 25 separate Crus.*[15]

With two châteaux in Bordeaux occupying the same area as 25 separate definitions of terroir in Burgundy, terroir is a broader concept in Bordeaux. But even with sizes of the order of 1000 ha each, the four major communes of the Médoc are usually felt to have distinctive terroirs: Margaux the most feminine and elegant, St. Julien showing restrained precision, Pauillac the most powerful, and St. Estèphe the tightest. Yet the 1855 classification cuts across these individual terroirs, since first growths should be more intense than seconds, seconds more than thirds, and so on. How does the precise assessment of quality into five levels of hierarchy relate to terroir?

Two features are crucial to understanding the relationships of Bordeaux châteaux to the land. The holdings of individual châteaux are rarely in single, contiguous blocks; often they are interspersed with the holdings of other châteaux. And there is significant heterogeneity in the details of the underlying terrain in the Médoc, which can change quite rapidly over short distances. The large sizes of the vineyard holdings mean there is often significant variation within the terroir of a single château.

In the context of scale, "gravel mound" is perhaps deceptive as a description of the underlying terrain. A mound is a sizeable geological structure that may extend for 5 km with a width of 1-2 km.[16] The gravel mound running through Pauillac and St. Estèphe includes several first growths and other classed growth châteaux. Cross-sections running along the north-south and west-east axes give an idea of its size (Figure 45).

Château Lafite Rothschild is immediately adjacent to three other châteaux. To its south is Château Mouton Rothschild. Both are first growths in Pauillac, but their styles are famously different, Lafite tending to elegance, Mouton more powerful. Note, however, that some of Lafite's vineyards cut right into those of Mouton (Figure 44). To the north of Lafite, separated from it only by the stream of the Chenal de Breuil, is Cos d'Estournel. But Lafite and Cos d'Estournel are at different elevations, and Cos d'Estournel has more of the underlying clay typifying St. Estèphe as compared to Pauillac. Cos d'Estournel is a very distinguished super-second, but even so does not aspire to the same breed as Lafite. And to the west, no more than a stream separates Château Lafite from the adjacent fourth growth of Château Duhart Milon (which is actually owned by Lafite Rothschild, but never produces anywhere near the same quality).

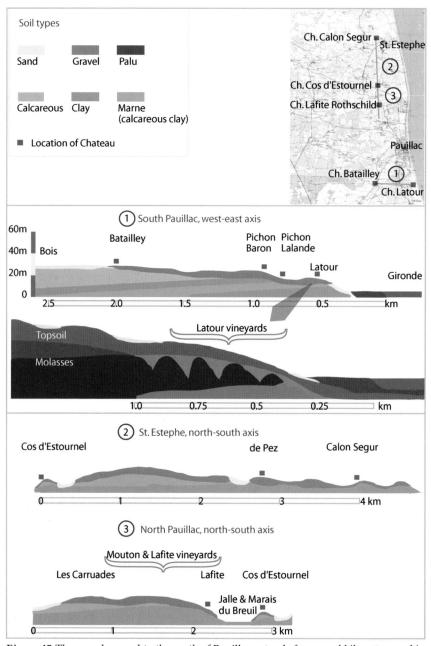

Figure 45 The gravel mound to the north of Pauillac extends for several kilometers and is 2 km wide.[17]

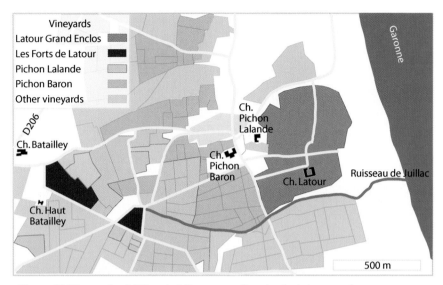

Figure 46 *Vineyards of different châteaux are often closely interspersed.*

Within Pauillac, the underlying strata change significantly on the east-west axis going from first growth Château Latour to fifth growth Château Batailley. Between them, the vineyards of Pichon Baron and Pichon Lalande are partly interspersed (Figure 46). The Pichons were at one time a single estate, but had separated by 1855 when both were classified as second growths. The stream of the Ruisseau de Juillac, just south of Château Latour, marks the boundary between Pauillac to the north and St. Julien to the south, so some of the vineyards of Pichon Lalande are actually located in St. Julien.

Château Latour has two blocks of vineyards. At the east are the main vineyards, known as the Grand Enclos. Even within these vineyards there are significant variations in the depths of the beds of gravel. To the west are more vineyards, but these are used to produce its second wine, Les Forts de Latour (usually considered to be the equivalent of a second growth).

So to what extent was terroir responsible for the original classification? The best vineyards in the Médoc are the most elevated, associated with thicker gravel mounds and better drainage. To a casual eye, the terrain looks quite flat, and you would never suspect there was a significant difference, but even a small elevation is enough to lift the land

Figure 47

*Through the famous
gatehouse at Château
Léoville Las Cases, the river
Gironde can just been seen in
the distance.*

significantly higher above the water table. The importance of drainage is emphasized by the old Médocain saying "the best vines can see the river," meaning that the vineyards are located on slopes draining into the Gironde (or sometimes into one of the streams running into it). The vineyards of Château Léoville Las Cases, for example, run from the road to the river, which can just be seen through its famous entrance (Figure 47).

The key vineyards of the first growths are on the best terroir, with deep gravel mounds of up to 9 meters and a relatively low water table.[18] The only one not to conform completely is Château Margaux, where some of the vineyards are on bedrock rather than gravel (and some people consider that in fact this makes it the best terroir in the Médoc).[19]

Although the châteaux of the 1855 classification mostly lie along the band of the gravel mounds (Figure 42 earlier), terroir varies significantly among them, even between adjacent châteaux. With the exception of the first growths, there is not really any geological evidence to support a hierarchy among them, or necessarily to distinguish them from other châteaux close by, given the extent and diversity of their vineyards.[20] This is not to decry the importance of terroir, or of making the best matches between grape varieties and individual vineyard parcels, but other factors, including restriction of yield and the assignment of lots to the grand vin and second wine, are equally important in establishing the brand of each château.

The Free Trade in Land

Sales and purchases of land by the classed growth châteaux is an extremely delicate issue in Bordeaux. "The châteaux communicate with reluctance on this sensitive subject," Louis Bergès, President of the Conseil Général of the Gironde, informed me.[21] Indeed, in the course of writing this book, I asked every Grand Cru Classé how its vineyards differed today from those when the château was classified in 1855; only one responded.

The classification may be static, but change has been continuous since 1855. The area of vineyards under cultivation at the Grand Cru Classés has gone down and then up again since 1855 (Chapter 4). While a few châteaux still have pretty much the same total area, others have increased significantly, often as much as doubling, implying that the terroir of today cannot be the same as in 1855. If it is true that the best sites were planted originally, it seems unlikely that the Grand Crus could have found new terroir equivalent to the quality of their holdings in 1855.

These bare statistics disguise much greater changes, since land has often changed hands between châteaux, sometimes associated with changes in ownership, sometimes under the impetus of rationalizing piecemeal holdings. Even the number of classified châteaux has changed. Although 57 châteaux were classified in 1855, now there are 61. Actually this underestimates the extent of change, because since 1855 there have been both splits and combinations.

When a château has been split, typically both of the new châteaux have inherited the right to classification, without any consideration of which part of the land went with which château. In one case the split actually occurred before the 1855 classification,[22] in some there seems to have been no argument about the rights to the classification of the progeny château,[23] but in other cases it has taken lawsuits to determine who had the right to be classified.[24] Classification does not necessarily go with the château that has the greater part of the land.[25] Sometimes the châteaux were later recombined.[26]

Assessing the terroir of the Grand Cru Classés is complicated by the fact that not all the wine goes into the grand vin that bears the name of the château; these days a substantial proportion is often used for a second wine. In some cases, much or even all of the second wine comes from specific parcels that are not considered good enough for the grand vin (Chapter 11). One demonstration of the freedom that châteaux have to change the underlying terroir was the large extension of the vineyards of Pichon Longueville Baron under its former owners. Many of the new holdings were not at the quality level of the original vineyards of the second growth. Now most of these plots are devoted to the second wine rather than to the grand vin. So the full land holdings of a château may not be a good guide to the terroir of the grand vin (although legally they could all be used for the grand vin).

Château Gloria is a brilliant example of the disconnect between the classification and the trade in land. Now some 50 ha in size, this property did not exist at the time of the 1855 classification; in fact it came into being only in 1942 when Henri Martin (later to become the Mayor of St. Julien) bought 6 ha of vineyards in the appellation. These vineyards were not part of any classified growth, but in the following years parcels were bought, one at a time, from most of the classified growths in St. Julien, including Beychevelle, Léoville Poyferré, Gruaud-Larose, Léoville Barton, St Pierre, Lagrange, Ducru Beaucaillou, Talbot, Pichon Baron, and Duhart Milon (consisting of a plot this Pauillac château owned in St. Julien).[27]

Château Gloria today owns a patchwork quilt of vineyards, still largely formed from land that was formerly part of the classified growths (and many of them deuxième crus at that). The actual château stands where there used to be a shed on the land of Château Saint Pierre Bontemps, which Henri Martin's father (Alfred) used as a barrel room. In fact, at one time Alfred Martin briefly owned the Saint Pierre Bontemps name; if he had not sold it, the vineyards that are now Château Gloria could have been called Saint Pierre Bontemps and the very same wine would be a Quatrième Grand Cru Classé!

No doubt the châteaux did not sell their best parcels to Henri Martin, but if the 1855 classification to any degree reflects the underlying terroir, it's hard to argue that Château Gloria should not be a classified growth. As it is, Château Gloria is not part of any classification (having disdained to be considered for the recent Cru Bourgeois classification). (And in 1982, Henri Martin actually purchased Château Saint Pierre; as another example of trade in land, he sold off some plots to Ducru Beaucaillou and to Gruaud Larose, but the rest is vinified as Saint Pierre.)

What's in a Name?

Other dramatic examples of change in the underlying land holdings come from châteaux that became all but derelict. During the 1940s and 1950s, Châteaux d'Issan and Malescot St. Exupéry were each reduced to not much more than 2 hectares, La Lagune declined to 4 hectares,[28] and

Prieuré was reduced to 11 hectares, just to cite the most extreme cases. The story of how Alexis Lichine bought the derelict property of Prieuré (for the knockdown price of £8000!), renamed it Prieuré-Lichine, and rebuilt it parcel by parcel (to a size of 57 ha, almost three times its original 20 ha) is well known.[29] The other formerly derelict châteaux also have been steadily expanded, and this pattern of contraction and expansion is by no means unusual.

Château Desmirail is an interesting example of the pulling power of the classification. It disappeared completely when it was incorporated into Château Palmer in 1957. The name was used for a second wine that accounted for much of the production of Château Palmer in the terrible vintage of 1963, but otherwise it disappeared from use. (The corollary, of course, is that Château Desmirail 1963 was in fact made from vineyards that mostly had no historical connection with the château, but this was perfectly legitimate in terms of the classification system.)

Lucien Lurton was making wine from some plots that had been part of the original Château Desmirail, but without any classification was selling it as ordinary wine of the appellation. In 1981, he bought the rights to the name from Château Palmer, and began to reconstitute Desmirail. The château presently consists of vineyards of about the same overall size as those classified in 1855, roughly 30 ha, with plots in Arsac and Cantenac that were part of the original holding, and also another plot in Soussans.[30] The same transactions could have been used to construct a château with a new name, along the lines of Château Gloria, but obviously M. Lurton felt that the cachet of a troisième Grand Cru Classé had something to add. Denis Lurton, who took over from his father in 1992, says that the status of the Grand Cru Classé is crucial in maintaining the price.[31]

It's also interesting to contrast the facility with which the original holdings of Desmirail were traced, and the pride with which Château Gloria identifies its vineyard plots with former grand cru classé holdings, with the blank response when the Grand Cru Classés are asked for information about their holdings in 1855!

The Value of Classification

The inherent contradiction in the classification system is captured by Madame Rambeau, who sells her grapes to the Pauillac Cooperative: "There are two hectares of my property that come within 80 centimeters (less than 3 feet) of Château Latour. Château Latour has requested many times to buy this property. I've always said no. But what I ask those people, if some day I sell to Château Latour, say they sell my wine. I sell my wine under Haut Pauillac. And overnight it will be sold under the label of Château Latour, but not at the same price. When you see that it sells at 800 to 900 francs per bottle, then that my wine sells at an average of 35 francs. That is a large difference. Yes, the difference is the transformation of genre. Me, I do not understand how one can pay just for a label."[32]

Land values are affected both by the classification of the château and the name of the appellation. There's always been grumbling about classification given the high stakes, but the process has become much more fraught and litigious in recent years. For the most part, the appellation boundaries established in the 1930s have stood the test of time, but of course now there is much more detailed understanding about the underlying terroir. With this in mind, some twenty years ago, Philippe Raoux, the new owner of Château d'Arsac, located just outside the Margaux appellation, asked the growers' syndicat to extend the AOC Margaux to include his vineyards. (Other châteaux in Arsac were included, but not Château d'Arsac, because at the time of the original classification the land was used only for raising chickens.) Following the authorities' refusal, he performed a detailed study of soils in Margaux, showing that his terroir was similar to classified land in Margaux, and went to court. In 1995, he won his case before the supreme administrative court in France, Le Conseil d'Etat.[33] INAO appealed against the decision, which was upheld by the appeals court in March 2007.[34] In fact, an exact value was put on the loss that had been caused by requiring the wine to be labeled Haut-Médoc instead of Margaux. INAO was required to pay damages of €877,000.

As a result of all this action, the Margaux Syndicat asked INAO to redefine the boundaries for the AOC Margaux. Demonstrating the dangers in such a process, while INAO decided to add 140 ha of land that it concluded had been incorrectly excluded from the appellation, it also removed roughly an equivalent amount of land where the terroir was felt to be inferior. Wine produced on this land can continue to be described as AOC Margaux for the next 20 years, but there is an absolute cutoff in 2030 after which it becomes Haut-Médoc.[35] This involves a significant potential loss for the proprietors who, of course, in the best new fashion, are now going to court.

Just as important as the potential reduction in the price of the wine is the potential loss in the capital value of the land. Higher prices for the land of classified growths reflect their ability to gain better prices for their wine in the marketplace. In Saint Emilion, where reclassification has been prevented by court order (Chapter 10), there is a huge effect on the value of a property. The vineyards of classified châteaux sell for about three times the value of unclassified châteaux, so with peak prices reaching €1 million per hectare, millions of euros could be at stake for a property of several hectares.[36]

Back in the Médoc, the steady expansion of Bordeaux means that land classified as Haut-Médoc rather than Margaux might well fetch more for housing development than for wine production, so an incidental result may be further expansion of the suburbs around the vineyards. Sadly, there are precedents for even good quality vineyards making way for housing. Eight vineyards were destroyed in order to construct the Merignac airport to the west of the city of Bordeaux, although admittedly this was not the best terroir. Within the town of Libourne, several classified growths of St. Emilion exist in small enclaves surrounded by housing; one can only speculate how long it will be before housing prices make it too great a financial sacrifice to run a vineyard.[37] The most famous example of encroachment is at the first growth, Haut Brion, which together with its sister property Mission Haut Brion, is entirely surrounded by suburbs (Figure 6). Fortunately, most of the wine-producing regions of the Médoc are too far north of Bordeaux for this to be an issue.

The Terroir and the Marque

"Bordeaux is about marques dressed up as terroir," said an American importer being shown round Bordeaux. Perhaps that is a little harsh, but certainly there is at the least considerable confusion between the land and the brand. On the one hand, there is ever increasing knowledge of the terroir, with more precise understanding of subsoils and drainage leading to better matching of vineyard plots to individual cépages. On the other hand, most top châteaux have at least some plots that habitually do not produce high enough quality juice to include in the wine that carries their name. Usually this is put into a second wine, but this further reduces the direct link between the total landholding and the classification. If terroir were classified directly, most châteaux would find some of their holdings excluded.

And as became evident in Margaux, the appellation boundaries drawn up in the 1930s are not completely reliable with regards to the quality of the land. Margaux is more spread out and heterogeneous than the other communes of the Médoc, but no one would claim, for example, that all Pauillac has the same quality of terroir—especially not its immediate neighbors, like Mme. Rambeau.

The contribution of terroir to the character and quality of the wines of the Médoc is immeasurable. The peak terroir of the gravel mounds, where the best results are obtained with Cabernet Sauvignon, is certainly a crucial aspect of the dominance of the Premier Grand Cru Classés. But it is not necessarily true that a detailed mapping of the terroir of the Médoc would correspond exactly with the reputations of the other châteaux.

To understand Bordeaux, it's necessary to realize the lack of direct connection between classification and terroir. There's nothing wrong with a classification system based on price, but it should be clear that what this represents is the relative success or failure of each château during the period of assessment. Success may depend on the intrinsic quality of the terroir, but it also reflects the quality of viticulture and vinification. And of course the terroir itself may change as a château sells or buys land. Present reputation is no more and no less than a snapshot of how successful a château has been in exploiting its terroir of the moment.

6

Crisis and Prosperity

MR. MICAWBER WOULD HAVE RECOGNIZED the underlying problem in Bordeaux. As he cheerfully observed

"Annual income twenty pounds, annual expenditure nineteen nineteen six, result happiness.

"Annual income twenty pounds, annual expenditure twenty pounds ought and six, result misery."

The same narrow line divides crisis from prosperity in Bordeaux. And it all hangs on something no one can control: the weather.

The basic problem in wine production is that quality is impacted by factors unrelated to the underlying costs. Income is not reliably related to expenses, so you can't markup the price to ensure a consistent profit margin. The costs of running a vineyard are more or less fixed: in fact, they may be greater in a difficult vintage, when more treatments of the vines are required. Yet the quality (and also the quantity) are determined by the caprice of annual weather conditions. A great vintage might have low costs and a poor vintage might have high costs. But demand may far outstrip supply for a great vintage, whereas there may be no demand for a poor vintage. Proprietors feel they are entitled to charge prices that bear no relation to cost in great vintages in order to compensate for the expenses incurred without adequate return in poor vintages.

Crisis is the rule rather than the exception in the world of wine. Problems arise at every stage from growing grapes to selling wine. Pests and diseases can damage the crop or even destroy the grapevines. Weather problems can obliterate a harvest without warning. Contamination can easily turn wine to vinegar or make it undrinkable in other ways. Yet despair can swiftly turn to jubilation when everything goes right and there is a great vintage.

Pests and diseases tormented vintages at the end of the 19th century, when the phylloxera infestation all but wiped out European grapevines. The humid climate of Bordeaux has made mildew a perennial problem, from the disasters of the 1850s to the difficulties of 2007. Climatic variation can be wild: an unprecedented freeze killed almost half the vines in Bordeaux in 1956; but in 2003 the vines were desiccated by extreme summer heat. In the past century, there have rarely been more than two or three good vintages per decade.[1]

When things go well, especially when there is a run of good vintages, prosperity can spread rapidly. During the mid 19th century, the trade in wine brought general affluence, as evidenced by the buildings constructed then on the Quai des Chartrons in Bordeaux, where the negociants and courtiers had their headquarters. And the splendid run of recent vintages is bringing another age of prosperity, as can be seen from the lavish reconstruction of chais and other facilities at the Grand Cru Classés of the Médoc (Figure 48), and by the gentrification of St. Emilion, which has turned over the past decade or so from a fairly run-down wine town to a chic spot listed by UNESCO as a World Heritage site.

Since wine is not an essential product, it is particularly susceptible to fluctuations of the general economy. Especially at the top end, wine is a discretionary purchase. The economic crisis of the Great Depression had a devastating effect on prices in the twenties and into the thirties, and Bordeaux was crunched again by the oil crisis in the seventies. As Bordeaux has lurched between crisis and prosperity over the past century, the effects on the châteaux are reflected by the history of the Grand Cru Classés.

Figure 48

Extensive renovation by a new proprietor in 2008 turned Château Cos d'Estournel into a building site.

Records of the châteaux show that more is at stake than the price of the wine itself. A run of poor vintages when expenses cannot be recouped has often led to the sale of a château at distressed price to a new proprietor with deeper pockets. Alternatively, the elevation of prices resulting from a run of good vintages can increase the value of châteaux to a level at which only the super-rich can become proprietors.

Plague and Pestilence

A fungus and a louse all but decimated the vineyards of Europe in the late 19th century. The fungus, oïdium, caused a short-term disruption of production, but a solution was soon found in the form of treatment with sulfur. The louse phylloxera almost destroyed wine production for several years, and the solution, grafting European vines on to the roots of American vines, changed the face of viticulture.

When oïdium arrived in Bordeaux in 1852, it reduced production to record low levels for the rest of the decade. The fungus causes a powdery mildew that spreads rapidly over the vine; when it reaches the grape skins, unpleasant odors ruin the wine. But by the end of the decade, it had been discovered that dusting the vines with sulfur powder killed the fungus, and production returned to normal.

Phylloxera arrived in France in 1868. This louse has an enormously complicated life cycle, but the crucial point is that its larval form lives underground and chews the roots of certain types of grapevine. It is lethal to the species Vitis vinifera, which includes all of the varieties from which wine is made. It is endemic in the United States and was carried to France inadvertently with some grapevine cuttings. (Its original name, Phylloxera vastatrix, means Phylloxera the destroyer.)

First phylloxera destroyed the wines of the Midi, and then it chomped its way through the rest of France and Europe. Ten years after its arrival in Europe, it reached Bordeaux (in 1879).[2] By then, experiments to kill the louse or at least to inhibit its spread, had failed everywhere. However, some of these measures brought temporary respite, and by the end of the 1880s a permanent solution was being widely employed, as the French Vitis vinifera vines were grafted on to rootstocks of American species of Vitis, such as Vitis riparia, which are naturally resistant to phylloxera. Viticulture was changed forever; with rare exceptions, wine-producing grapevines all over the world now are grafted on to foreign rootstocks.

The combination of temporary measures with replanting on new rootstocks allowed Bordeaux to resume normal production. (Replanting was not so rapid as sometimes thought, but most areas were substantially replanted before the end of the 19th century, although it was not until 1919, for example, that Graves was completely replanted.[3] The first growths continued to make wine from the original ungrafted vines for longer than most, since they had greater resources to continue combating phylloxera.)

Immediately following the phylloxera infestation, (downy) mildew (another fungal infection) appeared in 1882, and during the 1880s caused even greater losses in production than phylloxera, until the discovery that it could be prevented with copper. (The story goes that grapevines along the edge of the vineyards at Château Ducru Beaucaillou were immune to the disease. The vines had been painted with a solution of lime and copper sulfate to stop passers-by from taking the grapes. This was then developed into a mixture to treat the disease that became known as "Bouillie Bordelaise" or Bordeaux mixture in English.[4] It was used until the last factory producing it in Bordeaux closed in 2004.)

The Roots of Modern Viticulture

The various insults to the grapevine dented production quite seriously in the 1850s and then again in the 1880s (Figure 49). The low point of 320,000 hl was reached at the peak of the oïdium infection in 1854. From the 1880s, production showed an irregular progression, with a fairly steady increase in production interrupted periodically by runs of poor vintages, until reaching its present annual level of about 6 million hectoliters (66 million cases).

Bordeaux remained in transition from the discovery of phylloxera until the turn of the century. Before phylloxera struck, the area of vineyards had been increasing, and reached about 160,000 hectares. By 1882, a third of the vineyards had been destroyed by the insect, and the remaining two thirds were already infected, but the total vineyard area did not decrease that much, as the result of new plantings. A significant amount of planting of French vines (on their own roots) took place in the palus, where the periodic flooding killed phylloxera.[5] This was only transient as the longer tem switch took place to grafted vines.

Figure 49

Production in the Gironde has increased steadily, although with periods of decline due to vine diseases or other problems. The histogram shows average production for each decade.[6]

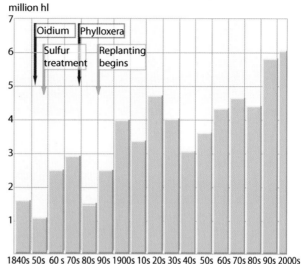

million hl

1840s 50s 60 s 70s 80s 90s 1900s 10s 20s 30s 40s 50s 60s 70s 80s 90s 2000s

The planted area stabilized around 135,000 hectares at the start of the 20th century (Figure 50). After the second world war, it declined fairly steadily to a minimum just below 100,000 hectares, and then recovered through the 1980s. It now stands around 120,000 hectares.

Grafting on to rootstocks began the move to modern viticulture. One reason why production recovered fairly rapidly was that vines are more productive on rootstocks than on their own roots. But this was only the start of a steady increase in yields (Figure 51). From a level in the teens at

Figure 50

The area of vineyards in the Gironde declined after phylloxera and dipped after the second world war.[7]

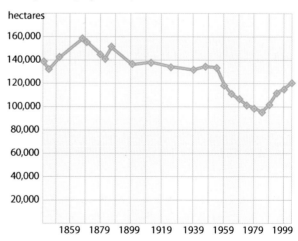

hectares

1859   1879   1899   1919   1939   1959   1979   1999

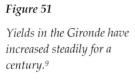

Figure 51

Yields in the Gironde have increased steadily for a century.[9]

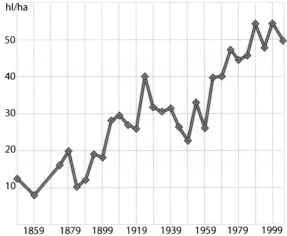

the time of the 1855 classification, yields increased to 30 hl/ha during the first part of the 20th century, and then to 40 hl/ha during the 1960s, and 50 hl/ha from the 1980s.[8] So Bordeaux has 20% less vineyards than a century ago, but 50% more production. With vintage variation reduced somewhat by modern viticulture, production has been steady for some years around 6 million hectoliters.

Ups and Downs of the Market

The fluctuations of the market for almost two centuries can be tracked by the price of Château Latour (Figures 52-54). Until very recently, when the first growths simply pulled away from everything else, relative changes in its price were a good reflection of general vintage conditions.

The first half of the 19th century was a difficult period for Bordeaux. At the time of the 1855 classification, recovery was about to begin from a run of poor vintages that had put financial pressure on the châteaux. Some successful decades followed, and the period of 1854-1885 was known as the belle époque, but then at the start of the 20th century prices more or less returned to where they had been a hundred years earlier. Extreme fluctuations from year to year reflected the changing quality of each vintage (Figure 52): not very comfortable for the proprietors in terms of predicting cash flow.

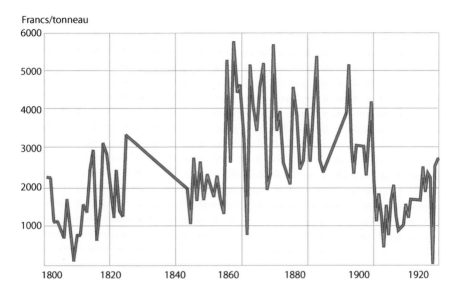

Figure 52 *Prices over a century at Château Latour showed wide vintage variation but little overall progress.*[10]

Repeating history, the first half of the 20th century was a dreadful period for Bordeaux. The combination of some terrible vintages with worldwide depression made it difficult or impossible to sell wine, even at the top levels. Prosperity did not really return until the 1950s; then things began to look better (Figure 53), although the sixties and seventies by and large are not remembered fondly in Bordeaux. The Bordelais made a terrible mistake in selling poor vintages at high price, leading to a crash in 1974, from which it took the best part of a decade to recover.

The modern era is generally reckoned to start from 1982, the first of a new style of vintage, when grapes reached unprecedented ripeness. What the good weather did naturally in 1982 has since been taken further with the aid of advances in viticulture and vinification. Prices became steadier for a period after 1982, until reaching the pattern for the 2000s, where good vintages seem to pull prices up to exaggerated levels, as seen in 2000 and 2003 (and in 2005, which goes right off the chart) (Figure 54).

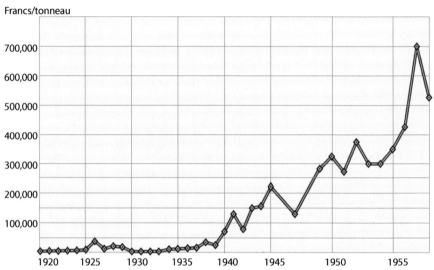

Figure 53 *Prices at Château Latour were static for the first half of the twentieth century but then began a steady rise.*[11]

Figure 54

Prices for Château Latour have increased since 1959 from €1 per bottle to more than €100 per bottle.[12]

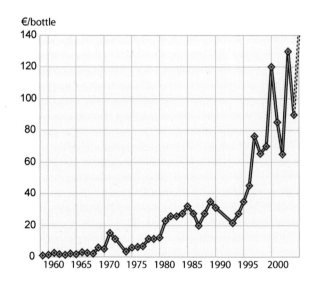

Aristocrats and Bourgeoisie

From the middle ages until the Revolution of 1789, much of the Médoc was occupied by *Seigneuries*. The seigneur was not necessarily an aristocrat (although many were), and the Seigneuries could be bought and sold. The system originated in the Middle Ages, when the seigneur owed loyalty to the King, and in return for ownership of the land, was obliged to provide various services, including numbers of fighting men. There was a sizeable contrast between the large landholdings assembled by the local Seigneurs and the small holdings of the peasants. (The gap tended to widen because the seigneurs had a right of first refusal on the sale of land and also were able to seize land in lieu of unpaid taxes by their tenants.[13]) Many of the Grand Cru Classés originated in the seigneuries, and even today tend to be much larger enterprises than the other châteaux.

Especially among the large estates, the local aristocracy predominated as owners during the 17th and 18th centuries. The upper middle classes, known as "parlementaires" were often involved in buying and building up the estates. By the mid-eighteenth century, vines had become the major crop in the large estates,[14] and revenue from wine had become the landholders' major source of income.[15] The seigneuries accounted for about 15% of total wine production, but obtained the highest prices for their wine because the quality was better than that produced by the bourgeoisie or peasants.[16]

Although most proprietors were originally local, the inheritance of large estates did not necessarily pass to local relatives, so in some cases the estates were run by local managers (régisseurs) on behalf of the owners. (Some of our best knowledge of the period comes from the extensive correspondence of the régisseurs with their proprietors.) Merchants from Bordeaux, especially those involved in the business of wine, including both negociants and courtiers, also purchased estates. By contrast, in the Libournais (on the right bank) the estates were smaller (as they remain today) and tended to be owned more by peasants.

Many of the Grand Crus originated in a few large estates that were later divided, often under the impetus of dealing with inheritance or providing dowries (Table 5). One of the largest seigneuries was the Ségur estate, founded by the Marquis de Ségur, who owned properties extending from Margaux to St. Estèphe. The Ségur estate at one time included Châteaux Lafite, Latour, d'Issan, du Tertre, Calon Ségur, and (briefly) what is now Mouton Rothschild. The most notable châteaux originating after this period are Cos d'Estournel and Montrose, which date from the second decade of the 19th century.

The Châteaux in the 19th Century

As the 18th century turned to the 19th, Bordeaux, and indeed all of France, was in turmoil. The decade of the French Revolution (1789-1799) brought disaster to the grand châteaux of Bordeaux. As members of the local aristocracy or wealthy landowners, the proprietors of the châteaux were particularly vulnerable. Many lost their heads; the proprietors of three of the leading four Crus (Lafite, Margaux, Haut Brion) went to the guillotine; only the owners of Latour escaped. Many estates were seized by the state. By the time affairs stabilized under Napoleon, however, many of the estates were back in the hands of their original owners.

Half of the classed growths changed ownership in the first half of the 19th century, but the overall pattern of ownership remained generally similar. A large number of châteaux were in aristocratic hands,

Table 5 *Large estates owned by local seigneurs through the 18th century included many of the Grand Cru Classés.*

Estate owner	Date	Region	Châteaux included in the estate
Marquis de Ségur	17th century	St. Estèphe – Margaux	Calon-Ségur, Lafite Rothschild, Latour, d'Issan, du Tertre, Mouton Rothschild (only briefly)
Seigneur de Léoville	1638	Seigneurie de Léoville	Léoville Las Cases, Barton, Poyferré
Duc d'Epernon	1587	Château du Médoc (Beychevelle estate)	Ducru Beaucaillou, Branaire
Durfort de Duras	14th century	Seigneurie de Duras	Lascombes, Durfort Vivens
Pierre des Mesures de Rauzan	1661	Rauzan estate	Rauzan-Gassies, Rauzan-Ségla, Desmirail, Marquis des Terme
"	1686	Pichon Longueville	Pichon Longueville Baron, Pichon Comtesse de Lalande
Bertrand Dejean	18th century	Grand Puy Estate	Lynch Bages, Grand Puy Lacoste, Grand Puy Ducasse

sometimes inherited by owners who were quite distant from Bordeaux. An almost equal number was owned by local merchants involved in the wine trade, typically negociants or courtiers, again often living off-site, typically in Bordeaux, with a régisseur running the property. Their knowledge of the local wine business no doubt placed them in a good position to take advantage when a château was for sale. A few châteaux were purchased by bankers or other local businessmen.

Given the international nature of the wine trade in Bordeaux, there has always been some influx of foreign merchants to the city, and on occasion they have purchased châteaux and sometimes assimilated into the local wine aristocracy. However, the vast majority of Grand Cru Classés have always been under French ownership.

At the time of the 1855 classification, seven of the classed growths were in foreign hands.[17] The most important was Mouton Rothschild. When Mouton was promoted from second to first growth status in 1973, Baron Philippe Rothschild was asked at a press conference why Mouton had not been given premier cru status in 1855. He pointed out that his great grandfather, who lived in London, had just purchased the property, and dryly joked "do you think a French jury at that time would have given a premier cru to a British neophyte?"[18]

Who Owns the Châteaux?

Owning a grand château is not for the fainthearted. Dependence on the vagaries of vintage makes for inevitable economic fluctuations, and there have been long periods when the few good years did not generate enough income to pay for expenses during the many poor years. Economic crisis is not a distant memory in the Médoc.

Profitability is extremely variable. In 2004, after a run of vintages that mostly sold well, most major châteaux were showing a decent profit on the current account, that is, on sales of the current vintage and any prior stock over the past year.[19] Typically the profit margins seem to be in the range of 10-30%. But some were saddled with debt from loans raised for capital improvements; the interest payments brought them into deficits up to 30% or so on the year.[20] Wine prices increased sharply in the 2005 vintage,[21] bringing a rapid improvement in the balance sheet.[22] Châteaux showed very high increases in profits, typically more than double the previous year.[23] No doubt the situation will reverse as the 2008 vintage hits the market in depressed conditions.

Figure 55

Sales of classed growth châteaux have occurred steadily since the classification, with a dip in the 1870s-1880s and a peak in the 1980s.

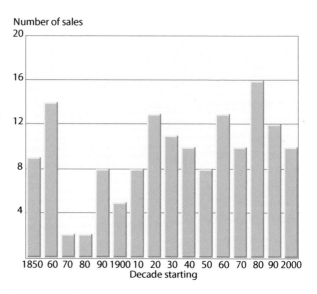

Such swings over short periods are common. The typical finances of a château allow profits to be made during a reasonable run of vintages; but (until recently) the profits were rarely high enough to support the level of investment required to make the improvements necessary for future growth. Perhaps for this reason, there is a long history of châteaux being purchased by people who have the resources to plough the necessary funds into improving the property. Although sometimes they are Bordelais, more often they are people who have made their money elsewhere, usually outside of the wine business.

Châteaux actually have sold at a fairly steady rate over the past century or so. With the exception of the 1870s and 1880s, when Bordeaux

Figure 56

Individuals whose business is wine still form the major group of château proprietors.[24, 25]

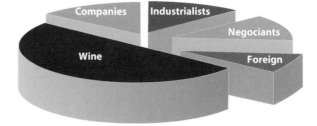

was ravaged by one disease after another, usually about 8-12 châteaux change hands each decade—roughly one per year (Figure 55). To be sure, some châteaux have changed hands many times, sometimes with several proprietors in rapid succession, while others have remained in the same family for long periods, with the only change coming by inheritance.

Complaints about ownership escaping from local hands have been common since the 18th century (when the target was the foreigners from Paris!), but for all this, the pattern of ownership remains largely in the hands of proprietors (or companies) whose principal activity is with the production of wine (Figure 56). The overall proportion of foreign owners has not changed in any very significant way over the past two centuries, although the list of châteaux with foreign proprietors has changed. There is not much evidence to support any concern that the Grand Cru Classés are in danger of falling into foreign hands as such.

The 1855 classification has conferred a mythic status on the Grand Cru Classés. They are viewed not merely as important economic interests, but as part of the patrimony of France. Indeed, when the negociant firm of Ginestet ran into trouble in the 1970s and was forced to sell Château Margaux, the French government banned the sale to the highest bidder (the American firm National Distiller) because it was foreign. They demanded that a French purchaser should be found.

Table 6 Grand Cru Classés owned by negociants and wine merchants

Château	Acquired	Owners	
Kirwan	1900	Schröder & Schÿler	Schröder Schÿler
Palmer	1938	Sichel/Ginestet/Mialhe/ Mähler-Besse	MAISON SICHEL PROPRIETAIRE · VINIFICATEUR · ELEVEUR
Belgrave	1979	Dourthe	Vins et Vignobles DOURTHE
Haut-Bages Libéral Gruaud Larose Ferrière Camensac	1983 1997 1992 2007	Taillan Group	TAILLAN
La Tour-Carnet	1999	Bernard Magrez Group	

Figure 57

The last date of sale of each Grand Cru Classé shows that about half have remained under the same ownership (excluding changes resulting from inheritance) for more than 40 years.

Château	Last Sale	Total in period
Langoa Barton	1821	
Léoville Barton	1826	5 in
Mouton Rothschild	1853	19th century
Lafite Rothschild	1866	
Calon Ségur	1894	
Kirwan	1900	
Léoville Lascases	1900	
Pouget	1906	
Talbot	1917	
Lynch Moussas	1919	
Léoville Poyferré	1920	
Brane Cantenac	1925	
Boyd Cantenac	1932	18 in
d'Armailhac	1933	1900-1945
Haut Brion	1934	
Marquis de Terme	1935	
Palmer	1938	
Lynch Bages	1939	
Ducru Beaucaillou	1941	
Haut Batailley	1942	
Croizet Bages	1942	
Batailley	1942	
d'Issan	1945	
Rauzan Gassies	1946	
Pédesclaux	1950	
Malescot St Exupéry	1955	
Cos Labory	1958	
Lafon Rochet	1959	
Clerc Milon	1960	
Durfort Vivens	1961	11 in
Duhart Milon Rothschild	1962	1945-1979
Clerc Milon	1970	
Pontet Canet	1975	
Belgrave	1979	
Desmirail	1981	
Cantemerle	1981	
Saint Pierre	1982	
Lagrange	1983	
Haut Bages Libéral	1983	
Grand Puy Lacoste	1987	
Pichon Baron	1987	
Branaire	1988	
Dauzac	1988	
Beychevelle	1989	18 in
Giscours	1990	1980-1999
Ferrière	1992	
Latour	1993	
Rauzan Ségla	1994	
Du Tertre	1995	
Gruaud Larose	1997	
La Tour Carnet	1999	
Prieuré Lichine	1999	
La Lagune	2000	
Cos d'Estournel	2000	
Lascombes	2001	
Margaux	2003	
Grand Puy Ducasse	2004	
Marquis d'Alesme Becker	2006	10 in 2000s
Montrose	2006	
Pichon Lalande	2006	
Cantenac Brown	2006	
Camensac	2007	

50% of châteaux have changed hands since 1970

The major group of proprietors, those whose principal activity is wine production, ranges from individuals who own a single château to families that have long been involved in wine production, sometimes owning multiple châteaux, and to corporations whose business is wine. Sometimes overlapping with this group are negociants who deal in the production of wine from growers in Bordeaux or elsewhere. It's usually the larger negociants, some relatively new, who also own châteaux; the old negociants of the Quai des Chartrons, who from time to time bought châteaux as good opportunities arose, have mostly been forced to sell.[26]

Usually 5-10 châteaux have been owned by the negociants at any moment during the past century. Château Kirwan has been in the hands of the old house Schröder & Schÿler for more than a century. Château Palmer has been owned by an association of negociants (with some changes in constitution) for more than half a century (Table 6). Others have been purchased more recently by successful negociants. A steady flow of purchases by the Taillan group has made them the owners of the greatest number of classified growths.

Only two of the families owning châteaux classified in 1855 are still in possession (at Mouton Rothschild and at Léoville Barton and Langoa Barton), but this over-estimates the rate of change. In fact, more than half of the châteaux are under the same ownership (or descendants of the same owners) as they were 40 years ago (Figure 57). In the past half century, two of the first growths have changed hands, and eight of the second growths have new owners. It's probably fair to say that new owners have tended to invest in the properties, so that a disproportionate number of the under performing properties are those where ownership has been static.

Indeed, more than half the Grand Cru Classés remain in the hands of the local wine families. Many of these families have been involved in wine in Bordeaux for many decades; on average they have been in the Bordeaux wine business since the 1920s (Table 7). In almost all of these cases, a member of the family is on the spot, running the château, sometimes actually making the wine. However, in many cases, they own multiple châteaux; it's one measure of the move towards concentration of the châteaux in fewer and fewer hands that very few (less than 10) of the Grand Cru Classés now are owned by individual proprietors who own no other châteaux.

Table 7 *More than half of the Grand Cru Classés are owned by local families.*

Château	Proprietor	Since
Château Léoville Barton Château Langoa Barton	Famille Barton	1820s
Château Mouton Rothschild Château Clerc Milon Château d'Armailhac	Baron Philippe de Rothschild	1850s
Château Lafite Rothschild Château Duhart Milon Rothschild	Domaines Barons de Rothschild	1860s
Château d'Issan	Emmanuel Cruse	1860s
Château Calon Ségur	Famille Gasqueton	1890s
Château Pouget Château Boyd Cantenac	Famille Guillemet	1900s
Château Talbot	Famille Cordier	1910s
Château Brane-Cantenac	Henri Lurton	1920s
Château Desmirail	Lucien Lurton	1920s
Château Léoville Poyferré	Didier Cuvelier	1920s
Château Lynch Bages	Famille Cazes	1930s
Château Marquis de Terme	Pierre Sénéclauze	1930s
Château Ducru Beaucaillou Château Grand Puy Lacoste Château Haut Batailley	Famille Borie	1940s
Château Batailley Château Lynch Moussas	Famille Castéja	1940s
Château Croizet-Bages Château Rauzan Gassies	Famille Quié	1940s
Château Léoville Las Cases	Famille Delon	1940s
Château Saint Pierre	Famille Martin	1940s
Château Pontet-Canet Château Lafon Rochet	Guy Tesseron	1950s
Château Malescot-St-Exupéry	Famille Zuger	1950s
Château Pédesclaux	Famille Jugla	1950s
Château Cos Labory	Famille Audoy	1950s
Château Branaire	Patrick Maroteaux	1980s

The right column indicates how long the family has been involved in wine in Bordeaux (not when they bought the particular châteaux).

The Conglomerates Arrive

The major change in ownership today compared with 1855 is the replacement of large individual landholders by international conglomerates. In 1855, many vineyards were part of large landholdings much of which was devoted to (agricultural) purposes other than viticulture. As the large landholdings were broken up (often due to inheritance laws), and as grape growing became more of a monoculture, this class of owners declined, effectively being eliminated during the 20th century (Figure 58). During the past half century, they have been replaced by very rich industrialists or large companies. The companies are often conglomerates for which wine production is one of many investment interests.

It's certainly not new for industrialists who have made money to purchase châteaux. There has long been a tradition of bankers or industrialists buying châteaux, investing in improvements, but finally being forced to give up as the costs became too great—the history of the Grand Cru Classés is replete with purchases and subsequent forced sales. At any given time, there are usually some 5-10 châteaux owned as investments by rich outsiders, but the relative steadiness of the number disguises a good deal of change in individual properties. Some of these individuals are foreign, as are some of the companies that are now investing in châteaux.

Figure 58

Trends in ownership of the Grand Cru Classés between 1855 and the present.

The key indicates the principal activity of the owner, although there is overlap between categories, so the number in each group is only approximate.

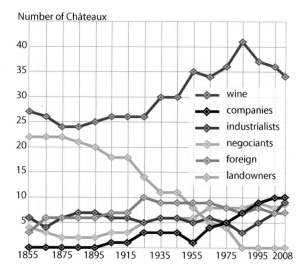

Table 8 Grand Cru Classés owned by industrialists or large companies.

Château	Proprietor	Source of funds	
Industrialists			
Château Margaux	Corinne Mentzelopoulos	Supermarkets	Félix Potin
Château Latour	Francois Pinault	Luxury goods	GUCCI
Château Montrose	Martin & Olivier Bouygues	Construction	Bouygues Telecom
Château Cantenac Brown	Simon Halabi	Property development	
Château Marquis-d'Alesme-Becker	Hubert Perrodo	Oil	PERENCO
Château Du Tertre Château Giscours	Eric Albada Jelgersma	Supermarkets	LAURUS
Château Cos d'Estournel	Michel Reybier	Petroleum	PEBERCAN
Château La Lagune	Famille Frey	Financial	FREY INVEST
Major Companies			
Château Pichon-Baron	AXA	Insurance	AXA redefining/standards
Château Pichon- Lalande	Roederer	Champagne	LOUIS ROEDERER CHAMPAGNE
Château Rauzan-Ségla	Chanel	Luxury goods	CHANEL
Château Lascombes	Colony Capital/ Yves Vatelot	Financial	
Château Prieuré Lichine	Ballande Group	Mining	BALLANDE
Château Lagrange	Suntory	Drinks business	SUNTORY
Château Beychevelle	GMF/Suntory	Pension/ Fund/Drinks	GMF
Château Dauzac	MAIF/Lurton	Insurance	MAIF ASSUREUR MILITANT
Château Cantemerle	SMABTP	Insurance	GROUPE SMABTP
Château Grand Puy Ducasse	Crédit Agricole	Financial	CA

The last twenty years has seen the usual stream of purchases by industrialists. Usually the proprietors are quite distant and appoint local managers, but they are enthusiasts about wine production. Often they have bought châteaux in need of renovation and have made significant investments. The châteaux have benefited from an influx of money made in finance, real estate, property development, oil, and the foods business (Table 8).

The new development of the past decade or so is the purchase of châteaux as investments by large (sometimes multinational) companies. Sometimes the purchasers have connections with winemaking in other regions, such as Champagne Roederer, or other aspects of the drinks business, such as Suntory; more often their other interests are completely different, such as insurance or other financial matters. This is now the fastest growing class of new owners.

Large firms do not usually purchase châteaux as an enthusiasm, but for their potential to generate a return on investment. Most often, the purchase is a long-term project, with company resources sometimes putting in more than comes out in the short term, but building up a property with a much greater long-term capital value. In some cases, the companies are engaged in building a portfolio of châteaux.

Altogether, almost a third of the Grand Cru Classés are owned by rich individuals or companies. This trend goes along with an increasing concentration of châteaux in fewer hands. Châteaux are often run as part of a larger wine business. Most individual proprietors of multiple châteaux stick either to the left bank or the right bank, but some span both. Large companies tend to be more catholic in their interests, often extending to other countries as well as to the Bordeaux region.

Fame and Fortune

There used to be a standard joke in the wine industry: "How do you make a small fortune in wine?" Answer: "Start with a large one." There's no doubt that fortunes have been spent creating cult wines or rescuing famous but derelict wine properties. But the fantastic increase in the price of wine at the top end now has generated a class of multi-millionaires who actually have made their fortunes in wine.

In the latest list of the top 500 fortunes in France, no fewer than 33 own wine businesses or châteaux (Table 9).[27] About a quarter of these are champagne houses, which are by far the largest businesses in wine, and often long established. Another quarter represent rich industrialists who have purchased châteaux in Bordeaux. But close to half are people

Table 9 *Many of the 500 richest people in France own properties producing wine.*

Rank	Name	Fortune	Company	Business
7	François Pinault	€7329	Printemps	Luxury goods
10	Alain Wertheimer	€5000	Chanel	Luxury goods
15	Pierre Castel	€3200	Castel Frères	Drinks
18	Martin Bouygues	€2913	Bouygues	Construction
19	Benjamin de Rothschild	€2900	Edmond De Rothschild	Finance
49	Chandon & Hennessy	€883	LVMH	Luxury goods
88	Jean-Jacques Frey	€426	Financière Frey	Financial
99	Michel Reybier	€400	Domaines Reybier	Oil
100	Jean-Claude Rouzaud	€400	Louis Roederer	Champagne
103	François Faiveley	€386	Faiveley	Construction
112	Bernard Magrez	€360	Groupe Magrez	Wine
141	Corinne Mentzélopoulos	€300	Château Margaux	Wine
148	Eric de Rothschild	€284	Lafite Rothschild	Wine
161	Pierre-Emmanuel Taittinger	€240	Champagne Taittinger	Champagne
177	Paul-François Vranken	€210	Vranken Pommery	Champagne
185	Philippe Cuvelier	€200	Clos Fourtet	Distribution
192	Denis Merlaut	€200	Bernard Taillan	Wine
194	Christian Moueix	€200	Jean-Pierre Moueix	Wine
217	Bruno Paillard	€165	Boizel Chanoine	Champagne
218	Bollinger family	€160	Champagne Bollinger	Champagne
240	Philippine de Rothschild	€150	Philippe De Rothschild	Wine
328	André Lurton	€100	André Lurton Vignobles	Wine
350	Daniel Cathiard	€90	Go-Sport	Sports
352	Carol Duval-Leroy	€90	Duval Leroy	Champagne
357	Luc Montaudon	€90	Champagne Montaudon	Champagne
394	Jean-Hubert Delon	€75	Léoville Las Cases	Wine
398	Gérard Perse	€75	Château Pavie	Wine
399	Christian Pol-Roger	€75	Champagne Pol-Roger	Champagne
411	Bruno Borie	€70	Jean Eugene Borie	Wine
412	Jean-Michel Cazes	€70	Château Lynch-Bages	Wine
424	Leroy & Villaine families	€70	Romanée-Conti	Wine
443	Roques-Boizel	€67	Boizel Chanoine	Champagne
475	Marcel Guigal	€61	Guigal	Wine

Rank shows position in the top 500 as of 2007. Fortunes are in millions. Non French nationals who would otherwise be in the list include Simon Halabi (wealth €2,500 M) and Eric Albada Jelgersma.

who have made money in wine, and among them are owners of several of the top châteaux of Bordeaux, including no less than 17 of the Grand Cru Classés of the Médoc.

Bordeaux dominates the list of people whose money comes from wine. The Rothschild estates naturally are prominent in the lists, but the estates of several super-seconds (the group of châteaux just below the first growths) also figure large, including most notably the Delons at Léoville Las Cases, the Bories at Ducru Beaucaillou, and the Cazes at Lynch-Bages. Of course, in addition there are families that have sold their châteaux to the newcomers, such as the Charmolües, who obtained €140 million when they sold Château Montrose to the Bouygues brothers. Corresponding with the larger size of the estates, most of the money is on the left bank, but the right bank is represented by Moueix, owner of Château Pétrus and other important châteaux, as well as an extremely successful negociant business. Outside of Bordeaux, Burgundy is represented by its top producer, Romanée-Conti, and the Rhône is represented by Marcel Guigal.

The rapid rise in prices of châteaux has been driven by the stratospheric increase in the price of top wines since 2005 on both left and right banks. When a château of 70 ha sells at a price of €2 million per hectare, only a conglomerate or a person in the top 500 list can afford to buy it. As individual proprietors are compelled to sell for inheritance or other reasons, no doubt there will be an accelerating concentration of châteaux in the hands of the rich and powerful.

The Ultimate Luxury Item

The wine writer Hugh Johnson has a scale for rating wine whose highest category is "buy the château." These days, not many people can afford to do that. With increasing wine prices, the value of land in the top areas has gone up and up, to around 1 million euros per hectare in the Médoc, 2 million in St Emilion, and possibly 3 million in Pomerol. Some of the expensive purchases of the past look like bargains now.

Is a château the ultimate luxury item? Certainly the proprietors gain social cachet: François Pinault, who owns the PPR luxury good company (including Gucci), Christies auction house, and Château Latour, is reputed to have said that no one paid him any attention outside the business world until he bought Château Latour, when suddenly he became a celebrity.

In addition to cachet, châteaux can be good investments. Consider Château Latour, bought by Allied Lyons in 1962 for 13 million Francs, and sold to M. Pinault in 1993 for 755 million Francs. The 58-fold increase compares pretty favorably with inflation over the period (about 7-fold). Or think about Château Margaux, bought by André Mentzelopoulos for €10.9 million in 1979, and after some reorganizations of ownership, bought by his daughter, Corinne, in 2003 for €300 million. The 27-fold increase beats the rate of inflation of 2.6-fold over the period by more than 10 times.

Of course, such dramatic gains reflect the recent period of great vintages and the increasing success of the first growth châteaux as luxury items, as well as the advantages of buying a property with great terroir in dilapidated condition. There are plenty of records to the contrary in less successful periods in the past where investors needed outside resources in order to prop up their châteaux.

The prosperity brought by increasing prices is now apparent everywhere, from the latest technological wizardry in very expensive newly built vinification facilities on the left bank, to the gentrification of the town of St. Emilion on the right bank. The trickle-down effect took quite a while to develop; even a few years ago, the town of Pauillac was really shabby, compared with the marble fittings of the Grand Cru Classés. But will prosperity ever reach the critical mass of small producers who make up the bulk of production in Bordeaux?

7

Winners and Losers

"BORDEAUX IS IN ITS WORST CRISIS FOR THIRTY YEARS," reported the local newspaper Sud Ouest in December 2005.[1] Two centuries of mistrust between château proprietors and negociants had once again broken out into open warfare. "Selling our wine below €1000/tonneau [$1 per bottle] is not only suicidal for our producers but also destroys the image of Bordeaux and our reputation," said Alain Vironneau, President of the Syndicat of Bordeaux and Bordeaux Supérieur (the union of small producers).[2] "In a world market, you cannot impose prices. Consumers, and the law of supply and demand, fix the price," retorted Francis Cruse, Director of the Union des Maisons de Bordeaux (the union of the negociants).[3]

In most wine regions, producers are happy to sell to wholesalers, retailers, and often enough directly to consumers: anyone who has the money is welcome to buy. But Bordeaux is different. Wine is traded only among professionals. A château is introduced by a courtier (essentially a broker) to a negociant. The negociant buys the wine and then sells it on to distributors in France or importers in foreign countries. This arcane system is called the *Place de Bordeaux*.

When the system developed in the 19th century, the negociants played an important role in the later stages of wine production. Having purchased the wine in barrels from the château, they would be responsible for its élevage (maturation). Ultimately they would sell it on, either still in barrel or after bottling. Effectively they controlled the market at the expense of the proprietors.

That's still true at the lowest levels. More than half the production of Bordeaux is generic wine (Bordeaux or Bordeaux Supérieur); a large part of this is purchased from the proprietors of small châteaux and incorporated into brands. Here the negociants are playing their traditional role of buying the wine and adjusting it to suit the marketplace. The recent fight between the small producers and the negociants reflected the producers' suspicion that the negociants were paying an artificially low price. In fact, it led to a boycott in which the producers refused to sell their wine, threatening to withhold the best vintage for many years from the market. They decided instead to send it for distillation!

But for the crème de la crème at the top, the situation is very different. Here the châteaux are firmly in the driving seat, setting prices and controlling allocations to negociants, whose role has basically been reduced to that of traders buying and selling finished wine. The general tide of rising prices has created enough prosperity to spread around all the players, and at least superficially to suppress the traditional antagonism.

Swimming in the Wine Lake

Bordeaux is a paradox between success at the top level; and failure at the bottom. During the en primeur campaign for the 2005 vintage, the Grand Cru Classés and other leading châteaux sold their fermented grape juice at unprecedented prices, in some cases reaching more than $10,000 per case paid in advance for delivery in 2007. At the same time, producers of generic Bordeaux were unable to sell their crop, and the CIVB (the organization representing châteaux and negociants in the Bordeaux AOC) appealed for excess wine to be removed by distillation.

While the grand châteaux have been changing hands for tens of millions of dollars, the price of AOC Bordeaux land crashed from $22,000 to $11,000 per acre over the past few years. According to Frederic Dubois, of the Lazard investment bank, "prices at the top end have been heavily increasing over the past 24 to 36 months…[but] the bottom price currently for an AOC Bordeaux property is the *prime d'arrachage*" (a payment from the government for pulling up the vines).[4] With small producers going bust, forced repossessions have made the French bank Crédit Agricole (a semi-cooperative that focuses on agriculture) the biggest landowner of vineyards in Bordeaux today.[5]

Never has there been a greater gap between the successful and unsuccessful.

Bordeaux has two personalities: Jekyll represents the top châteaux that fly off the shelf at any price (if indeed they ever reach the shelf),

Figure 59

Bordeaux had steady production (red) with growth of revenues (green) from 1990 to 2000 but has been flat up to 2005.[6]

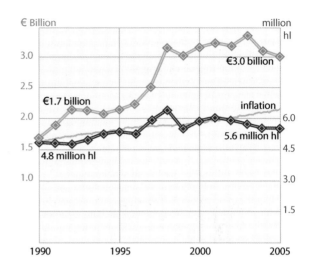

while Hyde represents the so-called petit châteaux (small producers) that cannot sell at any price. The gap has widened enormously in recent years.

Superficially Bordeaux has not done too badly in the past couple of decades. With 3 billion euros worth of sales each year, it is the most important wine-producing region in France except for Champagne. Allowing for the ups and downs of normal vintage fluctuation, since 1990 production has increased about 1% per year, but the total value of sales has increased by 4.5% per year (Figure 59). This is nicely ahead of inflation.

But the overall growth hides some serious underlying structural problems. Generic red Bordeaux, selling on average for under €3 per bottle, accounts for half of the market. The various Côtes appellations, accounting for another 15%, have seen no increase in average price since 1999. Dry white Bordeaux is in the doldrums, with production declining 40% in the past decade,[7] and an average price only just over €1 per bottle.[8] There is growth only at higher levels in the more quality-driven regions.

Bordeaux has problems in both its home and export markets. Within France, consumption continues to fall steadily, so there is no relief on the home market. After some years of decline, worldwide consumption overall has stabilized, but France has been steadily losing share in its export markets. Competition from the New World has been fierce.[9] France was the leading provider of wine to Britain for more than a century, but in year 2000 was bumped into second place by Australia.

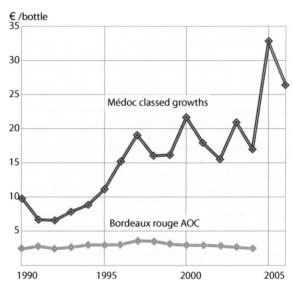

Figure 60

The average price of Bordeaux rouge AOC has been stuck under €3 per bottle, while the average release prices of classed growths (excluding first growths) have increased 3 fold since 1990.[10]

There has been a wine lake in Europe for decades, and Bordeaux is a major part of it. About 20% of the production of Bordeaux simply cannot be sold (this is about 10% of the total wine lake). For decades, the European Community has had a bizarre policy of paying producers for huge amounts of wine that is distilled because there is no market for it. Most of this wine is at the lowest level of Vin de Table, but for the first time in 2004, funds were requested to distill Appellation Contrôlée wine; by 2006, more than 6% of the crop was being distilled.[11] If you drive an ethanol-powered car in France, it may be running on the products of the Bordeaux vineyards!

The CIVB believes that 20% of the vineyards in Bordeaux need to be pulled up in order to bring supply back into proportion with demand. But offering compensation to growers to abandon their vineyards has been almost completely ineffective.[12, 13]

The top châteaux have been immune to these difficulties. Since 1990 the classed growths of the Médoc, and the equivalent châteaux on the right bank, have been on a roll. A series of good vintages, coupled with an increasing perception of fine wine as a collectible luxury item, have pushed prices to unprecedented levels. But the tipping point is well above the level of generic Bordeaux.

There's always been a difference between the top wines and the petit châteaux, but the past three decades have seen a major shift in their relationship. Previously, the top châteaux behaved as a locomotive pulling along the generic wines in its train. When speculative fever gripped Bordeaux in 1970-1973 (see later), the Deuxième Grand Cru Classés increased 4-fold in price; but generic Bordeaux shared the good fortune and also increased 3-fold.[14] Compare this with the past 15 years when classed growths increased 3-fold but generic Bordeaux remained stuck, creating an ever widening gap (Figure 60). A major difference, of course, is that now there is competition from the New World at the lower level, whereas the classed growths have maintained their unique mythic aura at the top end.

The bottom end of Bordeaux is often occupied by the cooperatives, which buy the bulk of their grapes from growers who cannot economically make their own wine. They are highly significant in terms of numbers, however, since 40% of the growers in Bordeaux use a cooperative.[15] Despair about the situation is typified by the story about the Director of a co-op, who was asked about the cost of production during a discussion about setting the price for the cooperative's wine. "Monsieur," he replied, "if I had to calculate our cost price I would have abandoned production long ago."[16]

The Players on the Place de Bordeaux

Most of the wine produced in Bordeaux is sold on the *Place*. The roles and relative importance of the players have changed over the years, but the basic system has remained unchanged; negociants make deals to purchase wine from châteaux only via the mediation of courtiers (Figure 61). Remember that until the railway extended through the Médoc and the Libournais in the late 19th and early 20th centuries, travel to the far reaches of the wine country was by no means easy; this made the courtiers an essential intermediary for the negociants, who remained in Bordeaux.

The courtier's role is much like that of a real estate agent in bringing together the buyer and seller. He takes a fee of 2% for his services, when the negociant buys the wine. Courtiers are best known in the Bordeaux market, where there are about 100 members of the Bordeaux syndicat. But 20 of them account for 80% of the transactions.[17] Courtiers also play a role in other regions in France; altogether about 450 courtiers in wine are registered outside of Bordeaux.[18]

Limited to their 2% commission, the courtiers are the least influential players in the system. Their role has diminished over the years. Originally, they would be essential for finding suitable sources of wine to match the specific needs of a negociant, for example, to make up a

Figure 61

The Place de Bordeaux connects châteaux, courtiers, and negociants.

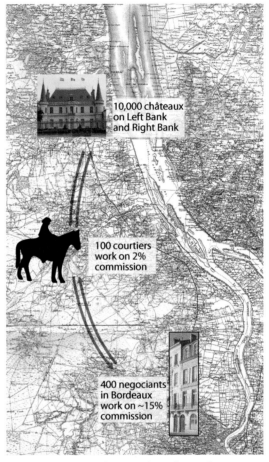

certain blend. This is still true to some degree for those known as courtiers de campagne (country courtiers). Usually based outside of Bordeaux, they maintain an intimate knowledge of the wine produced by the châteaux of the less well-known appellations. Courtiers based in Bordeaux are concerned more with facilitating transactions that would have taken place anyway between châteaux and negociants, ensuring that the formalities are completed properly. The courtiers do, however, guarantee the transaction, that is to say against failure to deliver or that the wine ultimately delivered will not be the same as provided in the samples. But it is rare these days for a courtier to need to meet the guarantee.

The negociants are a class apart. Until very recently, almost all were descended from foreign merchants who arrived in Bordeaux in the 18th and 19th centuries. In contrast with the local Catholic population, the merchants from England, Ireland, Holland, Germany, Switzerland were mostly Protestant. Forming companies such as Barton & Guestier, Nathaniel Johnston, Schröder & Schÿler, Mähler-Besse, and Louis Eschenauer, they lived in their own tightly knit society, largely intermarrying among themselves. (As recently as 1947, it created a scandal when a Johnston married a Catholic).

Establishing their companies on the Quai des Chartrons (Figure 62), close to the port, and outside the old city walls, the negociants became known as the Chartronnais. (Foreigners were forbidden to settle within the city walls.) At first, some dealt in other goods as well as wine, but by the mid 19th century, most had become negociants committed exclusively to wine. In their role as éleveurs of wine, they would physically take possession of the wine at some point after fermentation in order to mature it in their large caves.

Many negociants had extensive cellars running back from the Quai des Chartrons (in fact, this was one reason for their ability to store the wine; in the Médoc itself, the high water table makes it difficult for cellars to be built fully under ground, but the city of Bordeaux sits on rockier ground). Today there are about 400 negociants, of whom ~40 account for 85% of the market. Their combined turnover is about €2.1 billion, so this is pretty big business. Some are still located in Bordeaux, although those still engaged in production have often moved to new facilities outside the city.[19]

Figure 62 *A view of the Quai des Chartrons on the left shows a busy scene around 1900. Some courtiers and negociants still have their headquarters on the Quai, recently renovated as part of the gentrification of the waterfront in Bordeaux, as seen on the right.*

There is not much love lost between the players. The negociants' control over pricing was at the roots of continual conflict, not to say mutual loathing, between them and the château proprietors. Lamothe, the régisseur at Château Latour, said of the courtier Guillaume Lawton in 1812 that "the vulture hovers from time to time over the Médoc and especially over the heads of the needy whom he menaces with his cruel claws"[20]. A century and a half later, Comte Lur Saluces, proprietor of Château d'Yquem, was accustomed to saying more dryly "the interests of the proprietors and the negociants rarely coincide."[21] Not exactly a friendly relationship.

The courtiers tended to be regarded with scorn by the others as mere carriers of samples. Florence Mothe, a proprietor in the Graves, in her book on Bordeaux quotes an old ditty: "When one has lost all, honor and probity, one buys a *sonde* and becomes a courtier" (a sonde is the long pipette that is the symbol of the profession).[22] Philippe Courrian, proprietor of a Cru Bourgeois in the Médoc, recounts his interactions with courtiers: "The policy of the courtier was simple. He would say to the proprietor 'Your wine is not brilliant', then go to the negociant to confide 'I have found a remarkable wine, taste this'."[23]

The system continues, but the role of the negociants has been diminished, and that of the courtiers is often merely a formality, although some of the old trade lingers on. The courtiers are still important for oiling the trade in older vintages. I was sitting in the office of one courtier recently when there was a series of phone calls from negociants wishing to obtain often quite small parcels of specific wines from various vintages. The courtier was usually able to find a supply from another negociant.

The Place de Bordeaux Today

The balance of power changed on the *Place* following the market crisis of 1974 (see later). When the system was established, the negociants had a key role, but today it is the châteaux who largely have the upper hand in setting prices and making allocations to negociants. After 1974, many of the old negociant firms were taken over, and although some new and more dynamic ones appeared, an increased proportion of sales were made outside of the *Place*. Even so, 70% of the wine produced in Bordeaux today is still sold via the *Place*.[24]

Until château bottling became common in the mid-20th century, the vast majority of wine was matured and bottled by the negociants. Their role has diminished steadily since then. In the 1950s, virtually only the top châteaux bottled the wine themselves. As recently as 1982, only a third of wine in the Gironde was bottled at the château. Today most is château bottled.[25] The movement from sales in bulk to château bottling has effectively reduced the original, more complex role of the negociant to that of a distributor, especially remembering that all wines of high repute are now château-bottled. As May-Eliane de Lencquesaing, the proprietor of Pichon Lalande, said, "In the old days, the negociants often bought the wines in barrel, aged and bottled them, and retained stocks. Today, they buy and sell wines the same day. The telex has replaced the cellars."[26]

Negociants who function only as traders operate on a margin of about 15%. By undertaking to buy poor vintages as well as good vintages, they smooth out the market. It used to be the case that the negociants really made the market, sending out faxes when the vintage became available, and dealing with the responses, but now each negociant has his niche, often assisted (or appointed) by the château; the top châteaux choose who distributes their wines.

Some negociants still play more significant roles in production. Those closest to the old style are the generalists, who produce their own brands. With the consolidation in the industry over the past few years, the general negociants tend to be large firms, such as CVBG, who own a series of châteaux and vineyards and produce the well-known Dourthe #1 brand. But brands are handled in a completely different way from châteaux. Negociants do not hold substantial vineyard areas in order to produce brands; in fact, they directly own less than 5% of the vineyards.[27] Most of the wine for the brands comes from independent vignerons, often under long-term contract. The proportion handled by the traditional market has been reduced; in 1990 all the wine for Mouton Cadet was purchased on the market, but by 2004, the proportion was down to a quarter.[28] There's an increasing tendency for the negociant to exercise control over viticultural practices.[29] Production of brands is the most concentrated part of the industry: 90% of branded wine is produced by 10% of the negociants.[30] The wine is often made in modern plants located in outlying regions; the largest is that of Dulong, at St.-Savin de Blaye, with an annual capacity to handle 5% of the total Bordeaux harvest.[31] Mouton Cadet's white wine is produced at a plant at St. Laurent du Médoc, nowhere near the source of the grapes.[32]

Some negociants (these days really only the largest) are also château proprietors. But their role as proprietor is usually distinct from their function as a negociant; the château is managed as a separate entity, selling its wine under its own label.

Even with changes in the players, the basic operation of the Place de Bordeaux remains fairly static. The negociants do not have much freedom of action in pricing. The châteaux often set a "prix de revente," basically a minimum price for resale. The intention is to avoid price wars among the negociants, and possible damage to the reputation of the châteaux by price-cutting. (Under the pressure of trying to sell the indifferent 2007 vintage some châteaux abandoned the prix de revente.) Some new negociants have tried to buck the system, including the recently established firm of Millesima, which buys on the Place de Bordeaux but sells direct to consumers in many countries. This elicits mixed views in Bordeaux. On the one hand, it bypasses the usual players; on the other, it provides a ready means for disposing of excess inventory.

The importance of the *Place* has diminished, but still it remains a forceful presence with its own strictures on behavior. One château owner explained to me that he could only gain indirect access to consumers "to avoid violating the [unwritten] rules of the *Place*." Some proprietors who wish to sell direct but do not want to come into conflict with the *Place* set up their own negociant business as a fig leaf. One negociant in St. Emilion handles only 6 châteaux—all coincidentally owned by the same gentleman who owns the negociant business. Those who openly sell direct may suffer collateral damage, such as the difficulty of having their châteaux classified in St. Emilion (Chapter 9).

Negociants remain the key players in controlling distribution. The Place de Bordeaux insulates the château proprietors from their ultimate customers. The proprietor completely loses control of the distribution of his wine; once it has passed to a negociant, he can no longer determine its sales channel. Negociants may be quite secretive about revealing to whom they sell the wine. This is a source of continual frustration for proprietors who wish to track which distributors or retailers are selling their wine, let alone control where it is sold. "We want to know where our wines are sold and at what price," Michel Teysseron of Château Lafon-Rochet, said somewhat plaintively.[33] Sometimes the proprietors are reduced to generalized threats. "Shippers who sell to supermarkets will lose their allocations in 2006," said Jean-Claude Rouzaud of Roederer, owners of Château Pichon Lalande.[34]

Promotion is made difficult by the fact that the producers do not know who is selling the wine, and the distributors do not have enough to gain by promoting any individual wine. The proprietor cannot easily target retailers or consumers. A château may distribute its wines through a number of negociants, so that no single negociant along the extended supply chain has a big enough incentive or long enough term commitment to promote the wine. Together with the longstanding antagonism between the château proprietors and negociants, this may explain some of the strange gyrations of the market.

Promotion is a weak point in Bordeaux. Representation of Bordeaux as a whole is the responsibility of the CIVB (Conseil Interprofessionnel du Vin de Bordeaux). This is a private association with a public interest, subject to control by the Ministry of Agriculture. Its mandate is to promote the interests of its members, which essentially means anyone producing wine under the Bordeaux AOC. Its funds come from dues imposed on producers and negociants. The charge amounts to about 25¢ per case or roughly €15 million for all Bordeaux. This is a pretty pitiful amount compared with the €3 billion value of annual sales. All the major brands of Bordeaux together spend about another €10 million on promotion (most of it actually by the largest brand, Mouton Cadet).[35] It's roughly the same as the advertising budget for a single leading brand in the United States.[36]

The En Primeur Game

What sensible person would buy a product where full payment is required two years before delivery, the quality varies dramatically from year to year, significant changes occur in the period between production and delivery, the exact makeup may not be decided until shortly before delivery, and even the assignment of the product to lines of first and second quality may not have been completely decided? Well that is the en primeur system for buying wine. And aside from the need to pay well in advance, a subsidiary risk for the consumer is that the supply chain from the château can have several intermediaries; there is always a possibility one may fail before delivery.

The top wines are sold to negociants, and the château receives payment, in the spring after the harvest. The wine stays at the château where it is matured until it is bottled some one to two years later. The bottles are then shipped, via the mediation of the negociant, to distributors and retailers. The negociants have done no more than pay the château, while simultaneously selling the wine on to retailers.

Consumers have to purchase en primeur on the basis of reputation, or market hype, rather than on tasting. In a good vintage, the wine will sell all the way through to the ultimate purchaser, the consumer, who pays up front, although he will not receive the wine for another two years. In a poor vintage, commitments to buy the wine may stick with negociants and distributors, who therefore assume some risk. The Bordelais refer to the annual en primeur "campaign," somewhat suggestive of a war with the consumer.

The major advantage for the château owner is to smooth out the ups and downs that are inevitable in the pricing of an agricultural product whose quantity and quality fluctuate, sometimes dramatically, with annual vintage variations. Proprietors get a more even cash flow by selling their wine to the negociants soon after the vintage in both good years and bad.[37] The disadvantage, however, is that in a good year, prices can rise sharply after the wine has been sold to the negociants, so it is they, or people later in the chain, who reap more benefit than the château owner. Of course, once a château starts selling its wine en primeur, it is more or less locked into the system; a transition to selling after bottling would deprive it of cash flow for two years.

The advantage to the consumer is that in a good vintage, prices can increase sharply between the en primeur offering and arrival in the shops, so there is a reward for early purchase; also buying en primeur ensures availability. The days are long since gone when you could go to your local wine shop, buy a bottle, take it home to drink, and then decide at leisure whether you wanted to buy a case. Many high-end wines are on allocation, and demand is high enough that it may be impossible to purchase bottles on the shelf: the entire supply may be sold en primeur. (By contrast, in a poor vintage, or more pertinently a vintage that turns out not to be as good as expected, consumers who buy en primeur can get burned by price reductions when the wine is actually released.)

Buying en primeur is a relatively new situation for consumers. Wine from the leading châteaux has been sold to negociants en primeur through most of the second half of the 20th century; indeed at least for the first growths, there are price records going back to the previous century. Originally the wine was mostly sold in barrels to negociants who matured and bottled it. But the arrangement stayed largely within the trade until 1967, when château bottling became mandatory for the Grand Cru Classés of the Médoc. Negociants were then forced to trade in contracts for subsequent delivery of bottled wine; possibly to assist with their cash flow, it was around this time that the wine began to be offered at that stage to retailers and hence to consumers.[38] This was a significant part of the move to a consumer-driven wine market.[39] From relatively small beginnings with a few châteaux offered by a handful of merchants to cognoscenti, the en primeur offerings have now become a major annual event of full-scale consumerism.[40]

Roughly 700 châteaux offer their wines en primeur today (including most although not all of the top châteaux) and the majority of them become immediately available to the consumer. Wines are offered to the consumer *en primeur* basically during the spring or summer after the harvest, while they are still maturing in barrel. They will not be bottled for another 18 to 24 months.

Different châteaux make their *assemblage*, when the different grape varieties are blended into the final wine, at different points during maturation.[41] The need to show the wines en primeur creates some pressure to perform assemblage, or at least to take decisions in principle, fairly early, although most châteaux say it is usually pretty obvious soon after fermentation which barrels will be used for the grand vin and what the final blend will be. However, the final blend may not necessarily have been decided at the time of the en primeur showing.[42] This leaves the way open to accusations of manipulation,[43] such as selecting only the best barrels, or sweetening the blend by exposing the wine to a little American oak.[44]

En primeur wines are first shown to the world during the last week of March. During en primeur week, Bordeaux fills with thousands of buyers and critics from all over the world. They are put up at the châteaux: the most important stay at first or second-growths, while others are offered less impressive accommodation. There are fancy candlelight dinners each night at the châteaux. With several centuries of marketing experience, the Bordelais are masters at putting on a show to flatter and impress the visitors. The various professional bodies organize monster tastings: you can choose whether to taste blind or whether to know the identity of the wines. By the end of the week, faxes and emails are flying around the world with reports of the vintage.

Soon after, the first wines are actually offered for sale via the Place de Bordeaux, and slowly more are released, culminating with the release of the first growths. Whether they are snapped up or disdained depends on the success of the en primeur circus.

Because the wines are immediately sold all the way through the chain to the consumer, the success of the campaign depends on persuading people to buy on reputation and on recommendations based on barrel samples—consumers have no chance to taste. This increases the importance of the critic, but it is not an easy job to assess wines at such a young stage. The increasing number of people engaged in tasting en primeur (and their lack of traditional expertise) is partly responsible for a recent trend to make changes in vinification ensuring that the wines seem flattering at this stage (Chapter 10).

Gambling on the Vintage

The infection of speculative fever, giving rise to cycles of boom and bust, simply cannot be eradicated from Bordeaux. Perhaps it is an inevitable consequence of trading in a product long before it is actually ready for sale by obligatory middlemen who insulate the producer from the consumer. Everyone in the system plays games.

The major risk factor in buying en primeur is that it is not always easy to be completely certain of the quality and of the ultimate demand. It is not uncommon that down the road the vintage turns out not be quite as good as hyped at the time of the en primeur campaign. But the very existence of the system encourages the players to make other sorts of arrangements, among which the more speculative have been buying *sur souche* and by *abonnement*.

In order to achieve cash flow in periods of extreme difficulty, châteaux were sometimes compelled to sell the wine in advance of the vintage. The practice of purchase before the harvest is called buying *sur souche* (as opposed to en primeur which is after the harvest but before bottling).

Buying sur souche remained quite common in the 1930s and even into the post war years. It is a difficult judgment to make for the château. In 1961, panicked by the occurrence of coulure (a condition in which problems with fertilization reduce the size of the crop), some châteaux sold sur souche; this was a big mistake, since the vintage later turned out to be one of the best of the century, with a rather small, but very concentrated, crop. (The consequences were extreme at Château La Lagune, where the proprietor, Georges Brunet, ran out of money after selling en souche, and had to sell the château.[45]) At all events, there are no longer any sales en souche; the last examples in the records of the courtier Tastet & Lawton are for the 1964 vintage.[46]

In really hard times, such arrangements have been extended to cover longer periods. Indeed, in the period immediately preceding the 1855 classification, several châteaux, including some first growths, sold their crop for several years in advance at a fixed price. This practice, called an *abonnement* (subscription), often covered a period as long as 5 or 10 years. Then at the end of the century, the Médoc entered a long period of crisis when prices fell drastically. Between 1898 and 1910, strained financial circumstances forced 24 classified growths to sell their wine by abonnement.[47] Some châteaux did not come out of these difficulties until just before the First World War.

Much can change in the period between the sale of wines by the châteaux, soon after the vintage, and their appearance on the market two years later. The system encourages attempts to manipulate supply and demand. Sometimes these attempts have been successful; other times the producers or negociants have been victims. In a long series of speculative fevers followed by slumps, until very recently it has been the negociants who had the upper hand and who mostly benefited from changes in the market. But the balance of the supply:demand equation has fluctuated wildly in Bordeaux.

Back at the start of the 18th century, the frosts of 1708-1709 essentially killed the 1709 vintage. Because it was apparent that the forthcoming vintage would be tiny, the growers held back from selling the 1708 vintage, knowing that scarcity would push up prices. The producers were the clear winners on this occasion.

When there were vintages that no one wanted to buy for extraneous reasons, negociants who were bold enough could establish near monopolies. When fear of revolution in Europe suppressed demand for the 1847 vintage, the negociant Hermann Cruse bought up much of the crop (possibly as much as 90%).[48] A year later, the crisis over, he was virtually the sole supplier in a monopoly situation. A similar, although not quite so extensive coup, was mounted by the negociant Edouard Kressmann for the 1871 vintage, when demand was suppressed by the defeat in the Franco-Prussian war of 1870.

Historically, the châteaux have usually got the short end of the stick for advance sales, with good vintages leading to price increases that were profitable for those further down the chain.[49] Indeed, quite striking price changes after release en primeur have often led to significant profits being taken by negociants and others between the producer and the consumer, but with little benefit for the châteaux. One early example occurred just before the end of the First World War. The 1917 vintage (now long forgotten, but at the time considered quite good) doubled in price by the end of 1918; then the 1919 vintage, where it had not been sold as an abonnement, sharply increased in price. Many of the châteaux were bound by prior contracts to sell at what were now unreasonably low prices, but complaints to the negociants were met with the famous response, "il y a un contrat, Monsieur."

Getting the Upper Hand

The Bordelais are often accused of greed in setting their prices. The situation is complicated by two centuries of mistrust between proprietors and negociants, and by the insulation of the proprietors from the ultimate consumer. The proprietors have been able to ignore warnings from retailers that the market will not bear price increases by using their power to compel negociants to purchase poor vintages under the implied or explicit threat of being cut out from the next good vintage.

A negociant who declines to purchase because he feels the price is too high is likely to find that he will not be allowed to purchase any wine the next time there is a good vintage and the wine is in high demand. The negociant in turn passes the threat along to the next in the chain. This creates a balance of terror in which each player can be compelled to take wine of poorer vintages at higher prices than they like; but in return they expect an assured access for vintages where demand may outstrip supply. This has sometimes maintained prices above realistic levels. Insulation from the marketplace can give a significant delay before reality begins to fight back.

On the other hand, there have been vintages where speculative fever has driven up prices sharply after the initial release. Seeing large profits being taken after the wine had left the châteaux, infuriated proprietors increased their prices in the next vintage irrespective of its quality. The defense of the proprietors to criticism is that high investments are required to make good wine, that profits are erratic given the interspersion of poor with good vintages, and that if the market is prepared to pay for good vintages, the profits should go to them rather than those further along the sales chain.

A run of good vintages, coupled with the view of wine as a luxury item, has changed the supply:demand equation in favor of the châteaux. Originally prices were set at some point in the spring by negotiation between the châteaux and the negociants, who tended to have the upper hand since they controlled the market. Now the châteaux can dictate not only prices but also allocations.

Caught in the middle between the châteaux who insist they take wine in every vintage, and distributors and retailers who prefer not to become committed to poor vintages at high prices, the negociants are not much liked by either side. The reputation of the Chartronnais for sheer arrogance goes back at least a century, and was pilloried in a famous novel by François Mauriac portraying the society of the 1920s.[50] Florence Mothe, a proprietor in the Graves, comments sardonically that, "something perversely resembling a Cosa Nostra in embryo has developed in Bordeaux."[51]

The negociants may no longer have the upper hand with regards to the châteaux, but the speculative fever of good vintages since 2000 has enabled them to call the shots when selling to the retail trade. Simon Farr, a British merchant, is quoted by Stephen Brook as saying that, "Negociants never think strategically—they only react. But that's Bordeaux for you. Nobody thinks ahead or even thinks it's important to do so. From their point of view it's cheaper to make a mistake and then adjust to the consequences. If they lose a market or an important customer from time to time, well that doesn't bother them too much as they think there'll be another around the corner. There's no point arguing with a negociant as they never listen. They are totally self-interested."[52]

Price Is the Classification

Discontent over profits being taken further along the chain has led over the past twenty years to the development of the system in which the first growths no longer simply release their wines en primeur, but divide them into tranches. In a good year, the first tranche (also known as the prix de sortie) may be quite small to test the waters; usually the price is relatively attractive, but quantities are restricted. Second and then third tranches are released later at steadily increasing prices if the campaign is going well. It's a measure of the marketplace in recent years that the price almost always goes up in successive tranches. (But in older, poor, vintages, the first tranche was sometimes quite large.)

There are signs that even this strategy no longer satisfies the châteaux. Starting in 2005, with a vintage that promised to be spectacular, Château Latour reduced en primeur allocations to all negociants in order to hold back a proportion of the vintage for later sale. This is potentially a serious threat to the Place de Bordeaux. Will it succeed in reserving the profits for the château instead of those further along the chain? Stung by the strategy, one negociant commented that Château Latour "wants to sell like a grand cru of Burgundy using a distribution network like Champagne. But they are fooling themselves: Latour is too large to have the scarcity of a great Burgundy and too small to support a distribution network like Champagne."[53]

The châteaux may not have as much freedom as they would like. Following its new strategy, in 2006 Château Latour refused to supply the negociant Bordeaux Magnum with the 15 cases that it had provided annually for the past 20 years. Maxime Hamma of Bordeaux Magnum went to court. In 2007, he won his case, and obtained damages of €39,620 on the grounds that the continued supply for so many years amounted to a tacit contract.[54] Although still subject to appeal, this decision could considerably constrain the châteaux' ability to adopt a new strategy.

At the consumer level, you see tranches at all levels of classified growths, not just the first growths. Usually this is due to shortage of supplies on the after market. Below the first growths, the châteaux usually have a single release price. However, negociants who sell out their initial allocation from the château (at what amounts to a first tranche price) may then go back into the market to re-purchase from the *Place* (the château having now sold out), and the higher cost means that they sell the wine on at a higher price, effectively amounting to a subsequent tranche.[55]

One important aspect of Bordeaux is the explicit connection between price and classification, most notably in the Grand Cru Classés of the Médoc. Because the 1855 classification relied exclusively on price as the marker of quality, ever since then proprietors have felt that there is far more at stake than mere profits in setting the price: there is the reputation that will be inherited by future generations. Allowing your price to slip below your neighbor's has the possible implication that your wine should really be at a lower classification. There are endless stories of châteaux waiting for their close rivals to set prices in order that they will not be beaten.

Part of the reason for the crisis that developed in 1974 (see later) was that even those proprietors who were prepared to set "reasonable" prices abandoned any such intention as soon as they heard that other châteaux at the same level of classification were not showing such restraint. As Harry Waugh, a British wine merchant and writer (and at one time a member of the board of Château Latour) commented: "I arrived in Bordeaux at the end of March 1973 and was able for the first time to taste, but not enthuse over the young wine. Upon remonstration, grower after grower admitted the price was very high, but explained if he did not stick to it, his neighbor would succeed and he would lose face."[56] Even though there is no prospect of the classification being revised, the mindset that price determines status has been well and truly established.

It's the Vintage of the Century (Again)

The Bordelais are so quick to proclaim any vintage above the mediocre as the vintage of the century that it's become a joke even in Bordeaux.

The year when the phrase first appeared widely in the press was 1959, but vintages including 1929, 1945, 1959, 1961, 1970, 1982, 1990 all have been touted as the best of the century. Usually an appeal is made to records not broken since 1929. "The berries [for the 1990 vintage] have a richness never seen since 1928 and 1929, and it will probably be the vintage of the half century," was a fairly typical expression of enthusiasm from Le Monde in October 1990.[57]

Claims can certainly be made for some of the touted vintages, notably 1945 and 1961, but it's typically the vintage that needs to be sold that is the best of the century. And sometimes even when it turns out to be not such a good vintage, or actually a terrible vintage. Speaking of a vintage that is most kindly forgotten, Le Monde declared with eager anticipation in August 1997: "The châteaux of Bordeaux are waiting for the vintage of the century."[58] With a little more basis, although equally failing to withstand the test of time, was the report in 1970 that "Bernard Ginestet of the firm that owns Château Margaux said the 1970 vintage was the most successful he had ever seen. The Médoc was 'sensational'. He was still more enthusiastic about the Sauternes, which he called 'the best since 1947 or maybe 1929'."[59]

There are more vintages of the century in Bordeaux than in other wine regions, but the declaration is not unique to Bordeaux. The news usually goes hand in hand with warnings that there will need to be steep price increases. "The 1961 Burgundy vintage will be the most expensive ever. In the opinion of the experts here, the 1961 vintage is possibly the best of this century. Only 1929 is put in its class," the New York Times warned late in 1961.[60] There were fewer vintages of the century in Burgundy than in Bordeaux in the 20th century, but even so, 1961 is now all but forgotten.

Defying the Law of Gravity

What goes up must come down. Well, not necessarily in Bordeaux. Or at least, not straight away. The frequent proclamation of great vintages goes hand in hand with refusal to recognize the truly terrible, sometimes with disastrous consequences. Price almost always goes up in vintages that appear to be good (a judgment that is not always subsequently borne out). Prices do not necessarily go down in poor vintages.

A steep rise in price is common for great vintages or those that can be presented as such, but the extent has become magnified in recent years (Figure 63). Whereas 1982 and 1996 saw increases of about a third over the preceding vintage (in 1982 relative to an average vintage, although in

Figure 63

*Vintage ratings (top)
are compared with the
average release price
for classified growths
of the Médoc (bottom).*

*Great vintages (red)
usually have
significant price
increases. Poor
vintages (green) may
have price decreases or
increases.*[61]

price change from previous vintage in peak vintages							
+47%	+36%	-12%	-12%	+34%	+55%	+67%	+188%
1975	1982	1986	1990	1996	2000	2003	2005

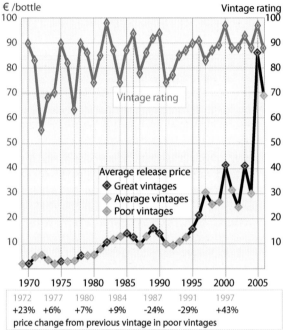

1972	1977	1980	1984	1987	1991	1997	
+23%	+6%	+7%	+9%	-24%	-29%	+43%	

price change from previous vintage in poor vintages

1996 the previous vintage had been good), increases became progressively steeper in subsequent good vintages, from 55% in year 2000 to more than doubling previous price levels in 2005. The only recent vintages to escape the pattern were 1986 and 1990, both vintages that followed quite good previous vintages. An earlier good vintage where prices had not been increased was 1970, although then subsequent attempts to compensate led to disaster (see later).

Poor vintages show little correlation between price and quality. Prices actually fell in 1987 and 1991, but they managed to remain more or less stable in 1977, 1980, and 1984. And what rationale can explain the sharp rises of 23% and 43% in the poor vintages of 1972 and 1997?

A high price ultimately was paid for the misjudgment of the 1972 vintage. The good vintage of 1970 had not been sold at any great increase in price over the poor vintage of 1969. The winners were the negociants, who were able to benefit from the rising perception of the quality of the vintage. Determined not to repeat this misjudgment in under pricing, the proprietors more than compensated by doubling prices for the 1971 vintage, actually quite a good vintage in its time, but with one or two exceptions not nearly the quality or longevity of 1970. And then 1972 came along: possibly one of the worst vintages of the century.

Boom and Bust

In the summer of 1972, the prospect of a poor vintage increased even further the speculative fever on current vintages. This was perhaps a normal enough response, but then release prices for the 1972 vintage (after harvest conditions fulfilled all the worst fears) increased roughly a quarter over 1971. Even for the Place de Bordeaux, known for its ability to support irrational behavior, at least in the short term, this was a striking demonstration of insulation from reality. In the longer term, players find themselves in a game of musical chairs, and the buck stops with the unlucky person holding the stock.

Caught in a frantic speculative fever, prices increased sharply to peak at the end of 1972. This was not confined to the Grand Cru Classés. The price per tonneau of the current vintage of AOC Médoc wine almost doubled during 1970, tripled during 1972, and then began to fall back in 1973.[63] By the end of 1974, prices were basically back where they had been at the start of 1971 (Figure 64).

There were plenty of warning signs of the crisis to come. As early as September 1972, le Monde noted that "counsels for restraint are increasing in Bordeaux, but apparently without any result. According to the President of the Syndicate of Courtiers, the market has become 'powerless watchers, tossed around by external events.' Many well

Figure 64

Price of Médoc wine during 1971-1974.[62]

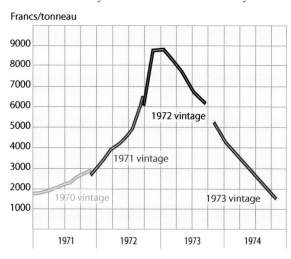

founded doubts are becoming more and more troubling in the stampede towards the red gold."[64] Actually the buck did not stop until 1974, when prices finally proved unsustainable. A huge vintage in 1973, somewhat variable in quality, basically flooded the market. Release prices dropped by comparison with the previous year. But it was too late by then. Prices fell back to earth during the en primeur campaign;[65] anyone who was committed to the wine had a rapidly depreciating asset.[66]

The biggest losers were the negociants. Intermediates in the chain were still holding large stocks of the 1972 vintage, with a magnifying effect on the price fall when it happened. This coincided with the general economic problems caused by the oil crisis, which saw large declines in exports—sales to the United States, an important market, fell by 42% in 1974.

The crisis was widespread: few of those dominating the market in the early 1970s now remain in business. Châteaux still holding unsold 1972 also were losers, all the more so when they had been reluctant to sell their remaining stocks of 1970 and 1971 in the face of rising prices, but now were caught by the rapidity of the fall. There were no winners.

This was the most dramatic of a series of boom and bust cycles. Next in line, 1997 was a distinctly poor vintage, but offered at a significant price increase over the classic 1996 vintage; this pushed its price to more than twice that of the equally poor 1994 vintage three years earlier. Once again, one driving force was the feeling of the proprietors that with the prior vintage their price increase had been reasonable, but that subsequent speculative increases had vastly enriched the negociants. There were warnings that these price increases might rebound in the future: "Seeing [the negociants] enrich themselves by the grace of a fax machine…left [the owners] with a taste of unripe tannins. As a result, the proprietors announced Himalayan increases for the 1997 vintage. The weak point in this agreeable plan is that 1997 is a minor year and it is necessary to avoid regarding new purchasers, essentially Asian, as chickens to be plucked," commented Le Point magazine.[67]

Since 2000, the en primeur campaigns have generally gone well for the producers and negociants, although with some sticky points in the lesser vintages of 2001, 2002, 2004, and 2007. One measure of success is the number of châteaux that sell out their production completely en primeur. In the highly successful 2000 vintage, more than 300 châteaux did so, but only 100 did so in 2001, and only 50 in 2002.[68] It's in vintages like this that the negociants justify their usefulness to the proprietors by absorbing the production. And by 2005 things were in full swing again, with demand for a great vintage far outstripping supply.

Which brings us to 2006. At first this was thought to be no more than an average vintage. But it was sold on the success of the previous vintage, like so many before it. As Jancis Robinson commented "I would say that, with a handful of exceptions, this is a vintage to be bought by wine lovers only if they have an empty cellar that they are dying to fill... Most years there is a common theme to the primeurs sales pitch. This year it has been that many vintages have in the past been erroneously overshadowed by the one that preceded it: 2004 by 2003, 1996 by 1995, 1990 by 1989, 1986 by 1985, for example. We are meant to believe that by association 2006 is in danger of being overlooked because we are dazzled by the greatness of 2005. Do not fall for this."[69] Other assessments were more optimistic, and en primeur prices fell only 20% (remember that they had more than doubled for the 2005 vintage), making 2006 merely 50% more expensive than 2004. The vintage seems to have sold fully through to the consumer, so if there is a loser, it will be the consumer rather than anyone in the supply chain.

And the 2007 vintage looks like a repeat of earlier excesses. A decent enough vintage of soft pleasant wines (what the trade calls a restaurant vintage), the wines will drink well enough in the next few years, but few will justify long-term maturation or achieve greatness. Yet prices have come down only slightly from 2005 and 2006. Past cycles would predict that the next poor vintage will magnify a fall in prices; with 2008 impacted by rain, and a worldwide financial crisis looming, will this be the vintage of reckoning?

As always with the en primeur system, it's impossible fully to judge the quality of the vintage before the bottles hit the shelves. It's certainly far more common for a vintage to be sold as much better than it ultimately turns out to be, although occasionally a vintage is under-rated en primeur. But with two mediocre vintages selling at prices scarcely below the record level of 2005, is it dèja vu all over again? Consumers purchasing en primeur may find it difficult to avoid being the losers.

The Fall of the Old Guard

Few of the negociants that were so dominant in the 18th and 19th centuries remain in existence in more than name. Of the top 10 at the start of the 20th century (Table 10), only Schröder & Schÿler and Nathaniel Johnston are still independent. In terms of economic importance, they are the only two of the old Chartronnais to be in the top 50 negociant firms of today (at positions 28 and 50).[70] All the others of

Table 10	Schröder & Schÿler	15%
Leading negociants 1890-1910.[71]	Rosenheim	13%
	Calvet	11%
	Cruse et Fils	11%
	Eschenauer	11%
	Journu-Kappelhoff	9%
	Armande Lalande	8%
	Barton and Guestier	8%
	De Luze	8%
	Nathaniel Johnston	5%

the old negociants still nominally in existence are parts of the large conglomerates that dominate the scene today. One of the oldest, Barton and Guestier, remained independent until the 1940s, when it was taken over by Seagrams. The châteaux owned by the Bartons, Léoville Barton and Langoa Barton, remained in the family, however.

Many of the old-line negociants fell by the wayside in the crash of 1974. Most of them were absorbed by larger companies, accelerating a

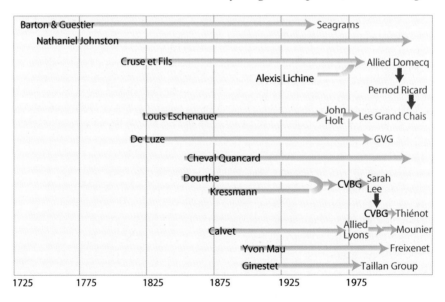

Figure 65 *Some negociants survived from the 18th or 19th centuries until relatively recently (green lines), but most now have been taken over by larger companies in the alcohol business (red).*

process of consolidation that has continued ever since (Figure 65). The top 10 groups now account for a major proportion of the market (Table 11).

Cruse fell after its involvement in the Winegate scandal (Chapter 12), although more as a result of imprudent purchases in the inflated market of 1973-1974. It is now part of the Grand Chais de France, which also own Calvet, Louis Eschenauer, JP Chenet, and Dulong, quite an amalgamation of the old negociants. Dourthe and Kressmann merged into CVBG, were purchased by the American food giant Sarah Lee, taken private in a leveraged buyout, and recently sold to Champagne Thiénot, all in a relatively few years. Many of the managers of the old negociants started up new companies, which today form quite a solid pack in the middle of the negociant hierarchy.

Along the way, not a few of the Grand Cru Classés have passed through the hands of the negociants, although they have usually been the one asset that was relatively easy to sell when times were hard. As Nicholas Faith comments, "the Chartronnais were always prepared to sacrifice their châteaux—however long they had been in the family—to preserve their businesses."[72] Of course, it was often the case that the business was in such trouble it was worth little, whereas there was usually a buyer for a château.

The house of Ginestet is a cautionary example of rise and fall. Founded in 1897, it became one of the most important of the old-line negociants. By 1949, Fernand Ginestet and his son Pierre were in a position to purchase the first growth, Château Margaux. But, like so many others, they acquired large stocks of the 1972 vintage at highly elevated prices; the rapid decline in prices left them unable to meet their debts, which at 55 million Francs were more than the annual cash flow of 34 million.[73]

Their only option was to sell Château Margaux, but this proved to be a difficult task, in part because the French government banned the sale to National Distillers (an American company) on the grounds that a first growth should remain in French ownership. Eventually it was sold for 75 million Francs in 1977 to the Greek entrepreneur, André Mentzelopoulos via his ownership of the French Potin supermarket chain. This was not enough ultimately to save the Ginestet firm, which was sold to Jacques Merlaut (for a symbolic Franc!) and absorbed in 1978 into the Taillan group. (By way of a sidelight into attitudes in Bordeaux, one Bordelais told me "The problem was that Ginestet tried to meet his obligations. He was a fool.")

Table 11 *The major negociants in Bordeaux*

Negociant	Owner	Subsidiaries	Brands	Turnover (millions)
Castel	Pierre Castel	Oenoalliance (2008)	Baron-de-Lestac, Blaissac, Malesan	€1100
Les Caves de Landiras	Grands chais de France	Eschenauer, Domaines de France (Alexis Lichine & Cruse (2004), Dulong (2006), Calvet (2007)	JP Chenet, Calvet	€600
CVBG	Champagne Thiénot	Dourthe, Kressmann	Dourthe	€275
Baron Philippe de Rothschild	Philippine de Rothschild		Mouton Cadet	€170
William Pitters	Marie Brizard group			€105
Grands Vins de Gironde	J.J. Mortier & cie	De Luze		€90
Ginestet	Taillan group		40% brands including Ginestet, Villa Burdigala, Mascaron	€80
Yvon Mau	Freixenet		Yvecourt, Premius	€80
Sovex-Woltner	Ballande group		35% are brands	€76
Cordier-Mestrezat	Val d'Orbieu (TAG)		Cordier Prestige, L'exception Cordier	€50

The leading firms are relatively recent creations. Castel (the largest supplier of table wines in France) was created in 1949. A drinks group with interests extending from mineral water to alcohol, in 2008 it swallowed up Oenoalliance, which had been number 9 on the list of negociants. William Pitters dates from 1964; created by Bernard Magrez, who is also an important château proprietor, it was sold to the Marie Brizard drinks group in 2005. CVBG has been in and out of private hands; presently it is owned by a champagne house. The large firms also have broad interests elsewhere in France and often in other countries. The largest of the firms with local origins is Baron Philippe de Rothschild. The Taillan group owns the greatest number of important châteaux; Cordier does more than half its business in distributing top châteaux.[74]

The Future of the *Place*

Superficially, Bordeaux has changed greatly in the years since the crash of 1974. But the underlying forces remain the same. The old negociants have gone, and their replacements are large firms, often with widespread interests extending well beyond Bordeaux. But the market is really split. The new negociants attempt to compete on the international stage with brands to match those of the New World. Large size is essential for any chance of success, as is flexibility in responding to the marketplace. The losers here are the small producers, who can neither sell their wine competitively on their own nor make a profit on the price they obtain from the negociants. Given the economic clash of interests, the antagonism between them and the producers is perhaps inevitable, and perpetuates the tradition of centuries. Yet in the market for named châteaux, the Place de Bordeaux functions much as it always has, albeit with a shift in power from the negociants to the proprietors. Using the muscle that comes from the combination of a series of good vintages with increased demand, the proprietors of the top châteaux have become the big winners, but the negociants also are doing just fine.

How will the Place de Bordeaux survive in the global market of the future? Its proponents argue that it provides a uniquely effective system for moving hundreds of wines to market in short order and that it lets producers do what they do best: making the wine. Detractors hold that for quality wines it divorces the producer from control of distribution and from contact with the consumer. The biggest criticisms come from small producers. The régisseur (manager) of one Médoc classed growth said to me, a little bitterly, that he was forced to sell the wine directly from his family property (a small château on the other side of the river), because the negociants of the Place were not interested in small producers. Certainly there is nothing like the Place anywhere else: but does it represent survival of the fittest or the last throes of a dinosaur?

8

The Price of Reputation

"YES, IT WILL WORK IN PRACTICE, but will it work in theory?" was the famous response of a French diplomat to an Anglo-Saxon initiative.[1] There is certainly a puzzling gulf between practice and theory in the effect of wine critics. Critics are believed to have enormous clout; their influence is supposed to make wines so scarce they cannot be purchased or so undesirable they cannot be sold. They are accused of causing producers to abandon their traditional styles. But how can we explain this? The critics are rarely in close agreement, it's only a small proportion of consumers who pay any attention to critics anyway, and isn't the classification by the French authorities meant to determine the reputation of the châteaux?

Virtually no one earned a living writing about wine until quite recently. Producers made the wines they wanted to (or that they could), consumers had relatively little choice, and high-end wine was Bordeaux or Burgundy. Information and advice about wine came largely from specialist shops.

The revolution of the last quarter century has greatly expanded the wine industry, with the majority of wine now sold through supermarkets rather than specialist stores, the traditional European producers seeing their markets eroded by competition from the New World, large scale brands replacing small scale production, and varietal labeling becoming as important as place of origin. Consumers have vastly more choices; producers who do not respond to the market are in the doldrums.

The transition from a producer-driven to a consumer-driven industry has seen the growth of consumer magazines and newsletters focused on assessing and recommending individual wines.[2] The effect of assessment by the critics is magnified for the great wines of Bordeaux, sold *en primeur* two years before any consumer has a chance to taste them in bottle. In a great vintage, the wines may sell out en primeur; it becomes virtually impossible to obtain them at retail after their release. Critics taste the wines from barrel in March, and by April their recommendations are in print, in time to influence purchasing decisions as the wines are offered to consumers over the spring and summer.

The World's Most Influential Critic

The corruption of wine writers was legendary until relatively recently. Stories used to abound about critics who visited famous châteaux and left the trunks of their cars open, ready for a few complimentary cases of wine. There are even embellishments about writers who returned the wine for a better vintage when they thought it was not good enough. Few critics were truly independent; almost all had some sort of trade in wine as their main occupation, with writing only subsidiary. Critical comment was rare.

This background was part of the impetus that led Robert Parker to start The Wine Advocate in 1978. Now by far the most dominant newsletter on wine, The Wine Advocate established the paradigm for assessing wines with a quantitative score out of 100, much simplifying the process of selection for the consumer. Right from the start, Bordeaux was a major focal point, spurred by the fact virtually no critics had exposed the poor quality of some first growths during the preceding decade. The Wine Advocate was different, starting off by slamming the quality of the 1973 vintage. Château Margaux was described as "a terrible wine... very thin and acidic."

It was with the (then) atypical 1982 vintage that Parker made his reputation. Relatively warm and prolonged vintage conditions led to a harvest of unusually ripe grapes, giving wines with lower acidity, much riper tannins, and higher alcohol than had previously been common. The low acidity caused many critics to write off the year, at least in terms of a classic long-lived vintage. Among these was Robert Finigan, author of the Private Guide to Wines, then the leading wine newsletter in the United States. This mistake, together with some financial problems, led to the decline and ultimate failure of the Private Guide,[3] opening the way for the Wine Advocate to dominate the market in fine wine assessment.

Robert Parker was one of the first to recognize the quality of the vintage, and his argument that 1982 would be a long-lived great vintage elevated him to become the high priest of wine criticism. From its initial issue of a few hundred copies in the local Washington-Baltimore area, the Wine Advocate has grown to tens of thousands of copies distributed worldwide. In April each year, the Wine Advocate now offers a detailed assessment of the preceding vintage complete with scores out of 100 for most wines.

Its dominance, initially of the market in the United States, later in Europe and Asia, has led to the description of Parker as the world's most influential wine critic, and indeed, taking all things considered, as the world's most influential critic, since in no other area does one person's view dominate so completely. Indefatigable in his tasting, now supported by a team of writers with responsibilities for particular wine regions, he has built the Wine Advocate into a voice that cannot be ignored by wine producers. Nowhere is this more apparent than in Bordeaux, for which he still takes personal responsibility.

A score of 90 from the Wine Advocate is the tipping point. The saying goes that a wine with a score above 90 cannot be kept on the shelf; but at a score below 90 it cannot be got off the shelf. The Bordelais both rely upon and deplore Parker's influence. They rely on his ability to give scores that sell wines worldwide. But they criticize the fact that one person should be so influential, and some worry that his taste is changing the nature of Bordeaux. One château owner recently said to me, without any perceptible sense of irony, "Nobody pays any attention to the Wine Spectator—it all depends on God's rating." (It goes without saying that God is Parker.) The proprietor went on to say that now the negociants just quote Parker, essentially replacing what used to be their own comments with his ratings.[4]

There's a strong element in Bordeaux's reaction to Parker of "can't live with him, can't live without him." Over the first decade or so of his growing influence, the attitude seems to have changed from resentment to dependence. When Parker reported in April 2002 that the 2001 vintage was overpriced, reaction was strong. "Except for the châteaux owners, everyone from Bordeaux... believes prices must drop back to 1999 levels for this vintage to move through the marketplace," he reported.[5] In response, May-Eliane de Lencquesaing, the proprietor of the super-second Château Pichon Lalande, said, "he's hurt and destroyed the market. That is a very big responsibility."[6] Parker had become so important that the success or failure of the vintage could be attributed to him, rather than to the decision of the Bordelais on pricing! The following year, Parker did not make his usual visit (this would have been in March 2003, but his wife did not want him to travel during the Gulf War) to taste the barrel samples (of the 2002 vintage). This was taken as a sign that the vintage was not worthy of interest (as indeed it was not), and as Jancis Robinson commented "the Bordelais are having to re-learn the art of selling a whole vintage without his help."[7]

The Wine Advocate shows a preference for wines that are dark colored, full bodied, showing forward fruits, and often high in alcohol. This is the modern style pioneered by the New World, and of which the 1982 vintage was a forerunner for Bordeaux. It is more typical of the Merlot-dominated wines of the right bank than of the more classically austere wines of the left bank driven by Cabernet Sauvignon. Without excusing or wishing to return to some of the "classic" vintages of Bordeaux that were thin, acid, and tannic, requiring years to come around and be drinkable (if they ever were), Parker's detractors believe that it destroys the typicité of Bordeaux to go to the far extreme of highly extracted wines made from super-ripe grapes in an international style.

Given this perception, it is ironic that early issues of the Wine Advocate (in common with other commentators of the period) took the view that Californian wines had alcohol levels that were too high, too much oak, and were altogether too massive. An early issue commented that "the better Bordeaux are elegant, delicate wines that possess incredible subtlety and complexity, whereas the best California Cabernets are massive, powerful, assertive wines often bordering on coarseness." Parker went on to comment that the California Cabernets did not age well beyond a few years, compared with the much greater longevity of Bordeaux. It is not easy to relate these early views to the wine reviews of the past decade.

It's beyond question that the style of Bordeaux has changed since 1982 (Chapter 10). Advances in viticulture coupled with a warming climate trend have seen increasing ripeness in the grapes at harvest. Instead of picking by the balance of sugar to acid, growers look for "phenolic ripeness." (Phenols are aromatic molecules involved in development of color and tannins.) Harsher or vegetal flavors have been much reduced by better sorting and selection to ensure use of only ripe grapes. Advances in vinification have created additional ways to extract color and tannins from the grapes or to concentrate the wine. Altogether, wines are now darker, fruitier, and more alcoholic. Of course, none of these developments are confined to Bordeaux: they are a worldwide trend. But how far is Robert Parker responsible for the progression down this path in Bordeaux?

The Uncorrelated Critics

Everyone agrees that Parker's scores have a major effect on the price of Bordeaux. Biographies are full of quotes from Bordeaux proprietors stating that the stakes may run to millions of Euros.[8, 9] Academic papers have purported to quantitate the effect. One claimed that Parker can change the price by €2.80 per bottle.[10] Another claimed that every Parker point above 90 adds £10 per bottle.[11] But it's not that simple. Many factors affect the price of wine; it requires an attack of terminal gullibility to believe it is possible to break out the exact effect of Parker scores with analytical precision.

If Robert Parker, or any other critic, has a direct effect on the market, there should be a correlation between the ratings and wine prices, especially in those cases where critics are in agreement. But there is no good correlation between the ratings of the leading critics (Table 12). There is rarely as much as 70% agreement between any pair of critics, and there is no particular pattern to the correlations, such as better levels of agreements between critics from the same country.

Table 12 *Correlations between critics' ratings and release prices for Bordeaux 2005 en primeur.*

	WS	JR	DE	BD	RVF	LEP	Euro
RP	67%	43%	60%	68%	53%	52%	56%
WS		49%	60%	68%	52%	55%	53%
JR			55%	50%	33%	48%	51%
DE				77%	59%	58%	61%
BD					62%	59%	57%
RVF						51%	43%
LEP							52%

The critics are: RP = Robert Parker (the Wine Advocate), WS = Wine Spectator, JR = Jancis Robinson (web site), DE = Decanter Magazine, BD = Bettane-Deseuve, RVF = Revue de Vin de la France, LEP = Le Pointe, Euro = release price in euros.[12] The results are very similar for other vintages.

Table 13 *Pair wise vintage correlations between en primeur château release prices.*[13]

	1995	1996	1997	1998	1999	2000	2001	2002	2003	2004	2005
1994	97%	91%	94%	89%	89%	86%	87%	88%	88%	77%	86%
1995		95%	78%	89%	86%	81%	83%	84%	84%	72%	79%
1996			96%	88%	89%	84%	62%	65%	81%	59%	64%
1997				95%	94%	65%	59%	61%	71%	55%	60%
1998					98%	94%	95%	93%	90%	85%	85%
1999						95%	97%	95%	91%	79%	83%
2000							98%	93%	92%	84%	90%
2001								97%	91%	88%	86%
2002									91%	86%	87%
2003										88%	94%
2004											85%

Table 14 *Pair wise vintage correlations for châteaux ratings in the Wine Advocate.*[14]

	1995	1996	1997	1998	1999	2000	2001	2002	2003	2004	2005	2006
1994	67%	61%	52%	37%	26%	41%	13%	27%	28%	13%	41%	32%
1995		69%	62%	58%	47%	58%	45%	48%	40%	32%	47%	46%
1996			65%	44%	45%	58%	45%	45%	55%	31%	50%	45%
1997				53%	51%	49%	39%	41%	36%	33%	40%	34%
1998					58%	52%	55%	27%	27%	37%	46%	47%
1999						70%	56%	48%	45%	40%	59%	44%
2000							61%	55%	56%	51%	68%	51%
2001								58%	51%	53%	64%	56%
2002									61%	45%	61%	42%
2003										57%	63%	40%
2004											63%	42%
2005												62%

None of the critics' ratings show close relationships with the release prices of the wines; correlations run between 40% and 60%. Some investigations of these relationships have suggested that critics have more effect on the right bank, where classification systems are simpler (and do not even exist in Pomerol), than on the left bank, where the hierarchies of classed growths and cru bourgeois may influence prices.

This seems eminently reasonable, except that it happens to be untrue! In fact there is better correlation with prices on the left bank than on the right bank.[15]

The single most important factor determining the price of a wine in one vintage actually is its price in the previous vintage (Table 13). The rank order of châteaux by price typically is about 95% the same from one vintage to the next. As years pass, the correlation drops; by six years later, the correlation is typically down to 85-80%.

The most important implication is that it takes several years for significant change to occur in the relative ranking of the châteaux. Christian Seely, in charge of AXA Millésimes, which owns several important châteaux in Bordeaux, believes that it takes about ten years for improvements in quality resulting from investment to be reflected in the price of the wine.[16]

By contrast, critics can react in each vintage as they perceive change. Correlations between the relative ratings of châteaux for successive vintages in the Wine Advocate are relatively poor, rarely rising above 65% (Table 14). This implies that Robert Parker is calling each wine as he sees it in that vintage, and is not so much influenced by its performance in prior vintages. The critic reacts much faster than the market.

This is not to say that the critic lacks influence on the market, but that other factors slow the recognition of changes at the level of price. There are certainly exceptions where an extraordinary result by a château may cause a dramatic (but usually transient) spike in its price (corrections in the other direction are much less common), but there is considerable inertia with regards to changing the relative prices of châteaux.

The wide range of prices for wines that get the same rating shows the

Table 15 En primeur retail prices for wines rated 95 points by the Wine Advocate in 2005.

Château Margaux	Médoc First Growth	$600
Château Lafite Rothschild	Médoc First Growth	$490
Château Léoville Las Cases	Médoc Super-second	$240
Château Magrez Fombrauge	Saint Emilion Grand Cru	$168
Château l'Évangile	Pomerol	$166
Château Pichon Longueville Baron	Médoc Super-second	$105
Château Canon La Gaffelière	Saint Emilion Grand Cru Classé	$77
Château Lynch Bages	Médoc Super-second	$70
Château Monbousquet	Saint Emilion Grand Cru	$44

strength of other influences besides the critics. Wines rated at 95 points for the 2005 vintage in the Wine Advocate have prices ranging from $44 to $600 (Table 15)! The first growths are at the top of the list, three super-seconds are widely separated in price, and there is a mix of Grand Crus and Grand Cru Classés from St. Emilion. It might well be that had any of these wines received a higher or lower rating its price would have been affected accordingly, certainly it might be that some of these wines owe much of their success to Robert Parker's advocacy (particularly those from St. Emilion), but, given the wide range, clearly the Wine Advocate's ratings are not the only factor influencing prices.

The Perfect Score

Even in an atmosphere given to exuberance and exaggeration, perfect scores are rare, but when the Wine Advocate gives a wine a score of 100 points, the effects are a powerful testament to its influence. (This has happened roughly a hundred times since its inception, representing a tiny proportion of the 10,000 wines tasted every year.) The effects are most visible when the wine is not a first growth or equivalent, but is raised above its usual position into another class by the score. This happened with Château Climens in 2001 (a great vintage for Sauternes) and with Château Montrose in 1990 (a top vintage for the Médoc).

The Sauternes classed growths have had a steady price relationship for a very long time. Château d'Yquem is always way at the top, typically 4-5 times more than any other Sauternes, but then there is a

Figure 66

Release prices for Sauternes premier crus show a steady relationship during the past decade.[17]

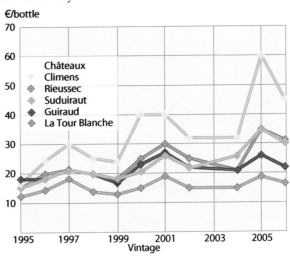

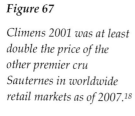

Figure 67

Climens 2001 was at least double the price of the other premier cru Sauternes in worldwide retail markets as of 2007.[18]

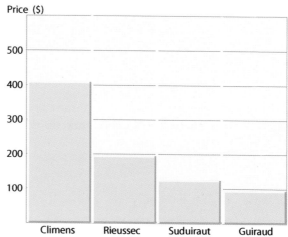

group of premier crus in a fairly tight price band. The top four of this group always contain Châteaux Climens, Rieussec, Suduiraut, and Guiraud, with Climens at the top, but the others switch position from year to year (Figure 66). (Château de Fargues, owned by Comte Lur Saluces, the former proprietor of Château d'Yquem before he was forced out, is also now right up there at the top.)

In the 2001 vintage, when prices were first released Climens was its usual one third above the price of Suduiraut and Rieussec. It was not mentioned in the Wine Advocate's brief review of the sweet white wines in April 2002, but was given a rating of 96-99 when the wines were reviewed in detail in April 2003, and then was promoted to a perfect score of 100 in the final review in June 2004. Rieussec was given 99, Suduiraut was given 98, and Guiraud 94, but there is no matching the effects of a perfect score.

The effect on the market was instantaneous and dramatic. Climens 2001 immediately became a scarcity item, and its price differential over the others increased to 200-300% worldwide (Figure 67). (Climens reached about 50% of the price of Yquem, which the Wine Advocate did not rate in this vintage.) But the effect did not carry over to subsequent vintages. After a spike in the price of the 2005 vintage, Climens returned to its usual position in the marketplace, ahead of Rieussec and Suduiraut, but not dramatically so.

Château Montrose has run neck and neck with Cos d'Estournel, the other second growth in St. Estèphe, for the best part of a century. During the 1980s, Cos d'Estournel, which adopted a more modern style in contrast to Montrose's more traditional style, began to pull somewhat ahead, becoming a clear member of the super-seconds in the 1990s. (The

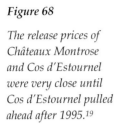

Figure 68

*The release prices of
Châteaux Montrose
and Cos d'Estournel
were very close until
Cos d'Estournel pulled
ahead after 1995.*[19]

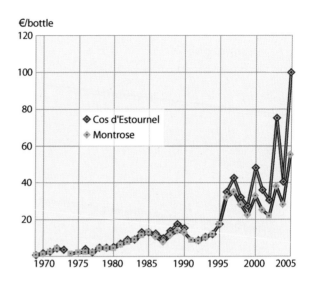

super-seconds are group of châteaux that price just below the first
growths.) Since 1995, Cos has led Montrose in release price (Figure 68).
In these vintages, Parker has usually rated Cos d'Estournel ahead of
Montrose; although this was reversed in the vintages of 2000 and 2003, in
neither case did it alter the lead of Cos d'Estournel in the release prices.

But as the eighties turned to the nineties, Montrose put in two
superlative efforts with its 1989 and 1990. Its release price was just
slightly below Cos d'Estournel. In its initial review in June 1992, the
Wine Advocate gave 1990 Château Montrose 94-98 points, but in a
subsequent review of the vintage in February 1993, pulled it up to the
perfect score of 100 points. Château Montrose 1990 then all but
disappeared from the retail market; and when it returned, the price was
greatly elevated. The effect has persisted: at wine auctions over the past
decade, Montrose 1990 has regularly fetched twice the price of Cos
d'Estournel (Figure 69); indeed sometimes it stretched into the price
band of the first growths. This is a dramatic demonstration of Robert
Parker's power to transform an individual wine into a collectible item.
The law of supply and demand does the rest.

This type of effect is not unprecedented; it has occurred previously
when a perception has arisen that a wine has performed *hors de classe*.
The great 1961 vintage well illustrates the ability of the market to adjust
as reality sets in when the wines are available to drink. When the prices
were first released, Lafite Rothschild was well at the top of the first
growths, with a prix de sortie of 27,500 francs/tonneau. The rest of the

Figure 69

*Château Montrose 1990
has sold for twice the price
of Cos d'Estournel 1990 at
auctions from 1999 to
2007.[20]*

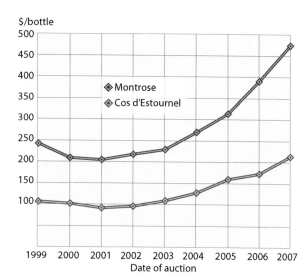

first growths were bunched in a range between 17,000 and 22,500 francs/tonneau. Well below them came Château Palmer in its usual position at between half and a third of the first growth release prices (at 8500 francs/tonneau), together with the rest of the second growths, including Château Léoville Las Cases.

Later it became apparent that the Palmer 1961 was exceptional. By 1978, it placed at the top at a blind tasting of the vintage.[21] It also became clear that 1961 was not a particularly good vintage for Lafite and its relative price declined. Palmer's price slowly rose to the top of the first growths.

But price adjustments took more than twenty years to occur. When wine auctions started at Christies in London in the 1970s, ten years after the vintage, the initial order of prices had not changed very much (Figure 70). Lafite Rothschild remained at the top of the first growths; Palmer remained below them. At the start of the 1980s, Palmer started to penetrate into first growth territory, with its price exceeding that of its neighboring first growth, Château Margaux. By 1986, Palmer had risen above the first growth prices.

Palmer has not quite had the staying power to remain at the top, although it continues to be well up in the first growths (Figure 71). Château Latour is now generally recognized as the best of the first growths in 1961, but in a dramatic indication of market reality, Palmer plays tag with Mouton Rothschild and Haut Brion for second place. Two first growths are now recognized to have significantly under-performed:

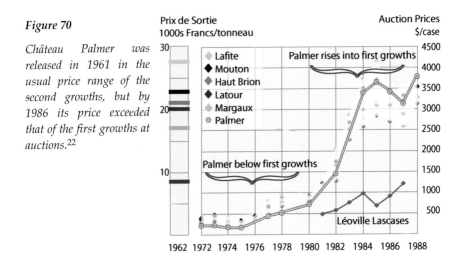

Figure 70

Château Palmer was released in 1961 in the usual price range of the second growths, but by 1986 its price exceeded that of the first growths at auctions.[22]

Lafite Rothschild and Château Margaux sit well at the bottom of the group. It's especially significant that Palmer 1961 prices well above its first growth neighbor (Château Margaux) in the same commune. No other classed growth reached even half of Palmer's level; Léoville Las Cases is a typical example.

Palmer has never achieved this result again (and even the people at the château say they have no idea what brought everything together in such a remarkable way in 1961), but it remains firmly established in the group of super-seconds. However, it is not the leader of that group, a position that usually goes to Léoville Las Cases, so its success in 1961 does not seem to have had any permanent effect.

Palmer made its lurch into first growth territory well before Robert Parker started the Wine Advocate. Indeed, its success cannot be laid at any one individual's door, but resulted from a general realization that the château had reached unprecedented heights in this vintage. The phenomenon of a château dramatically but temporarily changing its place in the hierarchy is therefore not at all new: what is novel about the present day is that one man, and only one man, has the power to create the perception that drives this effect; and thanks to modern communications, it can take place in days instead of decades.

Figure 71

Since the 1990s Château Latour has emerged as the top 1961, with Palmer, Mouton Rothschild, and Haut Brion in a group close behind. Lafite Rothschild and Margaux have dropped down towards the second growths.[23]

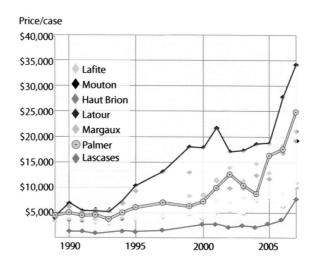

Wine as a Luxury Item

Is wine becoming a luxury item, out of reach of the ordinary consumer who used to enjoy high quality wine? The relationship between the price of wine at the top level and the cost of more mundane items has certainly changed. The average release price of the first growths more or less kept pace with inflation from 1969 to 1995 (Figure 72). In good vintages the price might pop up above inflation, and in poor vintages it might drop below. But the bank broke after 1996, and in spite of the ups and downs of subsequent vintages, the first growths maintained a new position in the economy. In 2005 they soared to unprecedented heights, and since then apparently have been immune to the relatively indifferent vintages that followed.

The stratospheric increase of the first growths has pushed prices to a point at which traditional purchasers are being excluded from the market by "new money." The prices of first growth claret have followed a very similar pattern to that of a more obvious luxury market, that of post-impressionist art (Figure 73). The parallel is striking: both started to increase sharply in 2005; art prices have more than doubled since the relatively stable period from 2000 to 2003, and wine prices have actually increased close to 3×. Wine may even have been a better investment than impressionist art! And it is more liquid.

Figure 72

*The average release price
of the first growths has
outstripped inflation only
in the past decade.[24]*

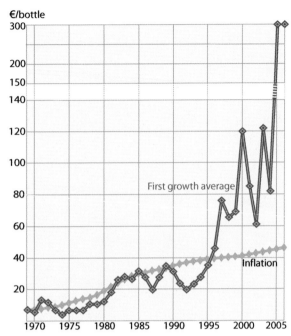

But what goes up must come down. As luxury items, both art and wine were hit by the financial crisis at the end of 2008. Wine reacted as extremely as art, with prices dropping sharply, and auctions in New York showing up to 70% of the lots unsold.[25] The sharp increase in prices immediately preceding an even sharper fall is characteristic of crashes, such as 1973 (Figure 64), with long-lasting effects. It remains to be seen whether the current drop foreshadows a permanent change in the market or is a temporary blip.

Another mark of growing interest in wine as a luxury item that appreciates in value is the creation of several wine investment funds. Of course, just as in the art market previously, this means that the consumer must compete with purchasers whose only interest is capital appreciation. This distorts the market by increasing the cost of "investment grade" wine relative to other wines, and no doubt has contributed to the enormous rise in the price of first growth clarets, which at more than $1000 per bottle en primeur for some châteaux of the 2005 vintage are now well out of the reach of the traditional consumer. Actually, it's not clear that any of the investment funds have done especially well, and the threat is that the short attention span of the "new money" will turn to other items for investment, allowing wine to return to more proportionate values (and possibly leading to a sudden decline

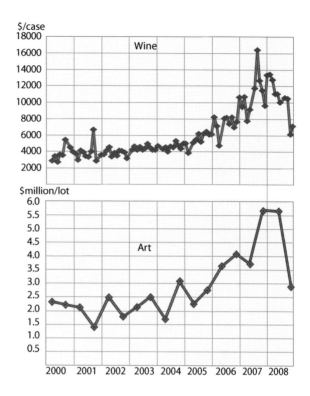

Figure 73

First growth claret increased from an average of $5,000 per case to $12,000 per case (for vintages 1982-1990) while the average post-impressionist painting increased from $2.0 to $5.0 million between 2004 and 2008.[26]

and loss for the investors). Will the financial crisis of 2008 spark a long-term collapse?

Until the end of 2008, however, the wine auction scene showed the same frantic quality as the art market. When auctions were held only in London in the 1970s and 1980s, they were a fairly sober scene—I remember a few personal buyers looking for wines of interest, but most of the clients were merchants buying stock. The situation changed following the opening of auctions in New York in the mid 1990s, when a new class of buyers—less experienced and wealthier—came into the market. I well remember the scene at the first Christie's wine auction, somewhat of a celebrity event presided over by auctioneer Michael Broadbent who came from London, when several lots of young vintages were purchased for prices significantly above what was being asked at the Sherry-Lehmann wine store just a couple of blocks away![27] The room was thronged with individual buyers, some of whom waved their hands in the air to bid and just kept them up there until the lot fell, irrespective of price. This sort of erratic, not to say irrational behavior, continues to mark the treatment of wine as a luxury item.

The Green Glass Ceiling

What effect does the classification have on price? Does the market set prices depending on the current success or failure of each château irrespective of the classification? Or does a higher classification allow a château to gain higher prices, even when growths with lower classification actually achieve better results?

Below the first growths, the contrast between the present order of the châteaux according to price and their order in the classification of 1855 shows the ability of the market to adjust to reality (Figure 34). Some châteaux have risen; others have fallen. One tier below the top, two of the super-seconds, with prices between the first growths and the rest of the seconds, are clear promotions: Lynch Bages was classified as a fifth growth in 1855 and Palmer was classified as a third growth. Some of the seconds have sunk down to lower levels: Rauzan-Gassies and Durfort-Vivens have sold at the levels of fourth and fifth growths over the past twenty years.

Yet there is one instance in which the classification seems to dominate all other considerations. The first growths always have a significant price differential over the second growths (Figure 74). In exceptional circumstances, an unusually good vintage of a super-second may reach first growth prices at auctions well after the vintage, but there has been no case since 1855 in which any second growth achieved a price en primeur penetrating the level of the first growths (although Léoville Las Cases came within a whisker one year).[29]

Critical opinion sees less distinction between the firsts and the

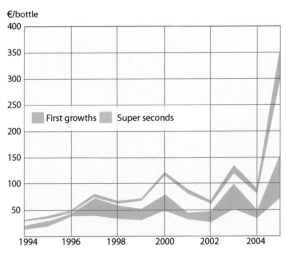

Figure 74

En primeur prices for the first growths fall into a narrow range that is always above the somewhat broader range of prices for the super-seconds.[28]

Figure 75

*Parker's scores for the
first growths and super-
seconds show significant
overlap, reflecting the
view that some super-
seconds produce just as
good results as the first
growths in some years.[30]*

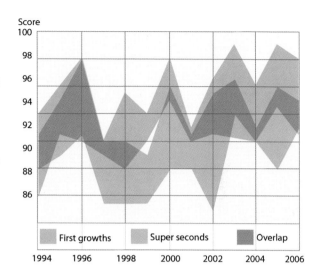

seconds, especially in recent years when some of the super-seconds have
been judged to produce results as good as the first growths. In most
years, Parker's scores for the first and second growths show some
overlap; and in some years several second growths are rated just as
highly as some first growths (Figure 75).

The reputation of the first growths supports their price even in
difficult circumstances. There have been periods where one or another
first growth has generally been acknowledged to perform below par:
Lafite Rothschild had a bad run in the 1960s, Margaux was poor in the
1970s; yet their prices, even if below those of the other first growths,
always remained above the second growths. For a brief period in recent
years, a narrowing gap between the first growths and the super-seconds
reflected the increase in quality of the super-seconds rather than any
problem with the first growths, but still the reputation of the first
growths prevented any of the second growths from achieving parity.

The price differential of the first growths is at least partly sustained
by the fact that the classification places them above the second growths.
They do not necessarily maintain a premium over wines of the right
bank, where the classification is different (in St. Emilion) or does not
exist (in Pomerol). In the past few years, Pétrus (in Pomerol), and
Ausone and Cheval Blanc (in St. Emilion) have usually been more
expensive than any of the Médoc first growths (Chapter 9).

Does the 1855 classification have a stultifying effect in the Médoc in
preventing châteaux below the top level from achieving true recognition
in the marketplace? What would happen if there was regular
reclassification, as occurs in St. Emilion?

9

The Rise of the Right Bank

CHÂTEAU PÉTRUS MAY BE THE WORLD'S MOST EXPENSIVE WINE. A tiny property of about 11.5 ha, producing a mere 3000 cases each year, it sits on a gravelly outcrop on the plateau of Pomerol close to the border with St. Emilion. Current vintages are released at more than $2000 a bottle. Yet until after the second world war, few people outside the region had heard of Pomerol. The right bank was the poor man of Bordeaux, a vast hinterland with difficult access, where wine was only part of the agricultural economy, and where most châteaux produced wine on a far smaller scale than the left bank. The châteaux themselves are correspondingly understated compared with the Médoc (Figure 76), although the style of the wines is contrastingly more flamboyant.

Wine production on the right bank is probably not as old as on the left bank, but goes back at least to the 4th century. The poet Ausonius, for whom Château Ausone is named, had a villa then in the vicinity of what

Figure 76

Château Pétrus used to be known for its shabby appearance; now somewhat smarter, it is still quite modest, in contrast with the style and price of its wine.

is now St. Emilion, and recorded 25 ha of vines out of a property of about 260 ha. By the 18th century, production in the region extended from the palus along the river to what had become the best areas of production in Canon-Fronsac and St. Emilion (Chapter 2).

But most of the wines of the Libournais were used only for distillation. Not included in the 1855 classification because there was much less market in the wines (remember that the mandate for the classification was actually to present all the best wines of the Gironde), its châteaux lagged far behind their counterparts in the Médoc in price and reputation. In the decade or so after the classification, the best wines of the right bank priced right at the bottom compared with those of the Médoc (Figure 20). St. Emilion may have missed a beat in 1855, but by 1867 the growers were aware of the effects of publicity, and their wines were entered in the Paris Exhibition, where they won several gold medals (and again in 1889).[1]

Although the wines of Pomerol and St. Emilion became steadily better known through the 20th century, even as recently as 1945 none reached even half the price of the Médoc first growths.[2] But the situation has changed dramatically; the top wines of St. Emilion and Pomerol now achieve prices well above any wine of the Médoc. Some of these wines are the long established leaders of the right bank, but others have been created only recently. St. Emilion in particular has become a source of innovation in Bordeaux. Methods in viticulture and vinification introduced in the past twenty years on the right bank, and initially scorned on the left bank, have now become commonplace in all Bordeaux.

The Lie of the Land

The right bank is a larger area than the left bank, and its terroir is correspondingly more diverse. It is here that the vast bulk of AOC Bordeaux is produced, from not very distinguished terroir. The best appellations are in the Libournais (named for the town of Libourne on the Dordogne river).

St. Emilion is by far the largest appellation in the Libournais, with roughly the same area of vineyards as the Haut-Médoc. Centered on the picturesque town of St. Emilion, it is at the heart of the Libournais vineyards. The other top appellation, Pomerol, adjacent to the northwest corner of St. Emilion, is much smaller, a little smaller than the individual communes of the Médoc.

The organization of viticulture is different here from the left bank. The estates are much smaller on the right bank; in Pomerol and St. Emilion the equivalents of the classed growths are typically estates of 12-14 ha (30 acres) with an annual production of 60,000 bottles (about 20% of the size of their left bank counterparts). The 5500 ha of St. Emilion are divided overall among close to 1000 châteaux; more than half are less than 5 ha in size.[3]

The right bank is Merlot territory. Contrasted with the gravel-based soils of the left bank, the right bank has more clay. This is the main factor driving the choice of Merlot as the principal grape on the right bank compared with Cabernet Sauvignon on the left bank. Air temperatures are closely similar—and if anything the right bank is slightly warmer than the left bank—but the clay-based soils do not retain heat as well as gravel, and their cooler nature requires grape varieties that ripen just a little sooner. Because Cabernet Sauvignon typically ripens a couple of weeks later than Merlot, it does not easily reach full ripeness on the right bank. So usually the more rapidly ripening Cabernet Franc is planted rather than Cabernet Sauvignon.

The right bank epitomizes a general trend in Bordeaux towards an increasing proportion of Merlot (Chapter 10). Merlot has increased steadily since the 1960s (Figure 77). The present mix of varieties was established when most of the vines had to be replanted after the great freeze of 1956. The Libournais were convinced at the time that they had too much Cabernet Sauvignon and should move more in the direction of Merlot, but were impeded by INAO, which recommended plantings of Cabernet Sauvignon.[5] Even worse, INAO recommended rootstocks and clones of Cabernet Sauvignon that were too productive and low in

Figure 77

The proportion of Merlot in the Libournais has increased steadily.[4]

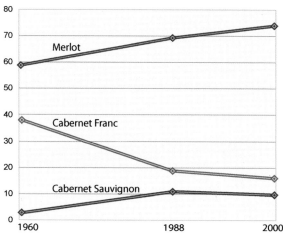

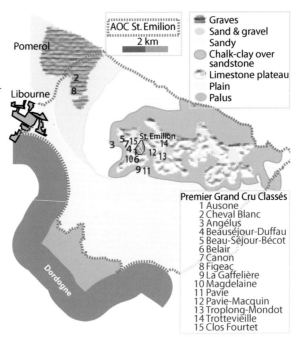

Figure 78

St. Emilion has several distinct terroirs.[6] The best vineyards are located either on the gravel soils of the Graves, in the northwest corner adjacent to Pomerol, or on the limestone plateau close to the town.

quality. After a battle with the local Syndicat Viticole, the present pattern emerged, with Cabernet Sauvignon around 10% of plantings in the appellations around Libourne. (It is somewhat higher in other right bank appellations.)

The best wines of St. Emilion come from the northern half of the appellation (Figure 78). The most general division of the terroir is into the Graves (no connection with the area of the same name to the south of Bordeaux) and the Côtes.

At the western edge, just adjacent to Pomerol, the Graves, as its name suggests, has gravel in the soil, more resembling the Haut-Médoc. Here there is a much higher proportion of Cabernet Franc, as much as 60% at Château Cheval Blanc, and there is even Cabernet Sauvignon at Château Figeac, which has one third of each of the major varieties planted.

The dominant feature of the Côtes, the slopes around the town itself, is a thick base of limestone, covered by loam and clay. The best terroir is in the immediate vicinity of the town. Falling away from the plateau surrounding the town of St. Emilion, the terroir has more sand; none of the better châteaux are located here. To the south is a large plain, the least favored terroir in the appellation.

Pomerol lies just to the west of St. Emilion, extending to the north of the town of Libourne. It is a plateau with gravel and clay lying on top of a base that is rich in iron (*casse de fer*). "You can taste the iron in the soil," they sometimes say of Pomerol. It is a very small area, roughly the same as St. Julien in the Médoc. This is real Merlot territory, even more so than St. Emilion, with many wines having 80% or even higher content of Merlot. Pétrus, the most famous, is 95% Merlot, the rest being a touch of Cabernet Franc.

Fifty years of Classification

The wines of St. Emilion were first classified in 1955. The driving force was the Syndicat Viticole, representing the châteaux. It had taken about twenty years for the plans to fructify, but in 1954 INAO agreed to undertake the classification, which became part of the Appellation Contrôlée. Basically the classified châteaux were divided into two categories. The top levels are the *Premier Grand Cru Classé* (further subdivided into groups A and B) and the *Grand Cru Classés*. Châteaux must apply in order to be included.

Following the initial release in 1955, the classification was revised twice at roughly 15-year intervals (in 1969 and 1986), but since then has been revised more systematically every decade (in 1996 and 2006). The criteria for classification are a mélange of terroir, quality of wine, and commercial considerations. This brings both strengths and weaknesses.

The list of Premier Grand Cru Classés has had several changes since 1955 (Table 16). Demotions have been rare, the only one being for technical reasons. Promotions have gained pace a little, from none in the first reclassification to two in the most recent. There has been more change in the numbers of the Grand Cru Classés, which started out with 63, increased to 72 in the first reclassification, but since then has been decreasing steadily to its current level of 46.

Including terroir as a criterion prevents the free trade in land that occurs in the Médoc. If a Premier Grand Cru Classé purchases a new plot of land that was not previously classified at the same level, the wine made from it must be vinified separately for ten years so that its quality can be assessed before it is approved for inclusion under the appellation. Château Beauséjour-Bécot ignored this rule and was demoted from Premier Grand Cru Classé in 1986 as a result (its status was restored in 1996 after it agreed not include the production in the grand vin). On the other hand, in 2000 Château Canon purchased the 4 hectares of Château Curé-Bon (a Grand Cru Classé), but INAO reclassified the terroir as

premier grand cru, allowing it to be incorporated into the grand vin of
Château Canon. It all depends on your relationship with the authorities.

The system is now in chaos because the 2006 classification was
successfully challenged in court on grounds of unfair practices. The
wines were not tasted completely blind (which would have ensured the
judges would have had no knowledge at all of which was which).
Apparently, the châteaux that had been classified in 1996 were tasted as
one group; then applicants for promotion were tasted as a separate
group. On top of this, the committee visited some châteaux, but not
others. The classification was suspended by court decision in November
2007, but the government used its emergency powers in July 2008 to rule
that the 1996 classification should be restored for the next three years
while things were sorted out. Requests from the châteaux that were
promoted to use their new status were denied.[7] The most recent court
ruling, in March 2009, confirmed the suspension. It is unclear what will
happen when the extension of the old classification runs out in 2010. The
château proprietor Jean-Luc Thunevin commented that "in my (perhaps
biased) opinion, [the situation] is getting worse and totally immoral."

Table 16 Classification of Saint Emilion Premier Grand Cru Classés since 1955

Château	Year classified
Ausone	1955
Cheval Blanc	1955
Angélus	1996 (promoted from Grand Cru)
Beauséjour Duffau-Lagarrosse	1955
Beauséjour-Bécot	1955 (demoted in 1986, restored in 1996)
Belair	1955
Canon	1955
Figeac	1955
La Gaffelière	1955
Magdelaine	1955
Pavie	1955
Pavie-Macquin	2006 (promoted from Grand Cru)
Troplong-Mondot	2006 (promoted from Grand Cru)
Trottevieille	1955
Clos Fourtet	1955

The first two are group A, the rest are group B.

When you see a label on a current vintage from St. Emilion, then, you have no idea of whether it really reflects the present status of the château. Needless to say, the proprietors that have been deprived of their promotion are up in arms. And just to add insult to injury, the United States government opened an investigation as to whether the eight châteaux that had been promoted, and then denied use of the higher classification, had committed a fraud in using the new descriptions on their labels for the 2006 and 2007 vintages.[8]

Commercial considerations used in the classification include its reputation, a somewhat nebulous concept, and the price. Including price runs the risk of having the same effect as in the Médoc of encouraging price increases in order to improve position in the classification. Château Figeac has long been pursuing promotion from group B to join Ausone and Cheval Blanc in group A, but was denied promotion on the grounds that "that Figeac does not sell at the same level of price as Cheval Blanc or Ausone." As Thierry Manoncourt, the proprietor, fumed "It's a circle — you can't sell at the same price because you're not Premier Grand Cru Classé A!"[9]

The most pernicious of the commercial considerations is felt to be the role played by negociants on the jury. Until 2006, the jury consisted almost exclusively of people making their living through the Place de Bordeaux. Consequently, wines that are not distributed through the Place were not classified. By 2006, others were also included on the jury, but negociants still amounted to one third. Jonathan Maltus, who distributes the wines he makes at several properties himself, was considering applying for classification for Le Dôme (which regularly prices in the top twenty wines of the appellation), but "when I asked if Le Dôme would be considered, I was advised there would be no point because we don't release our wine to the Place de Bordeaux."[10] The medium is the message, said Marshall McLuhan in the 1960s, but it's a new concept that wines should be classified by their distribution mechanism.

Overtaking the First Growths

The top wines of the left bank clearly outpaced their counterparts on the right bank until the early 1970s. But since then the top wines of the right bank—Pétrus, Ausone, Cheval Blanc—have been regarded as essentially equivalent to the first growths of the Médoc. Pétrus, unclassified since there is no classification in Pomerol, is usually the most expensive of the traditional châteaux, its position reinforced by small production (less

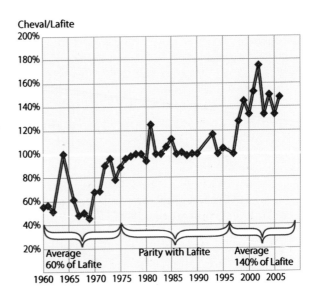

Figure 79

Until the mid 1970s, Cheval Blanc was well below the price of the Médoc first growths en primeur. It maintained a close parity until the mid 1990s, when it increased well above Médoc first growth prices.[11]

than 10% compared to Lafite Rothschild, for example) and lack of availability on the en primeur market. Leadership in St. Emilion has oscillated between Cheval Blank and Ausone, the two class A members of the Premier Grand Cru Classés.

All of the Médoc first growths and their right bank counterparts have increased sharply in price since the mid 1990s, but the right bank has now pulled well ahead of the Médoc. The change in fortunes of the right bank is evident when comparing Cheval Blanc with Lafite Rothschild (Figure 79). Cheval Blanc was about half the price of Lafite Rothschild during the 1960s, and then increased to parity during the 1970s. In the mid 1990s it showed a sharp increase, together with other top wines of the right bank, to exceed the prices of the first growths.

Garage Wines: Antithesis of Terroir

The estates of the right bank have always been much smaller than those of the left bank, but in recent years a new group of wines has been created, involving limited production from very small vineyards, typically less than 5 hectares. The wines are usually heavily dominated by Merlot (some are 100% Merlot), and generally associated with the new style of super concentration, reflecting very low yields, mature or over-mature grapes, increased extraction during vinification, and a strong emphasis on toasty new oak.

Because most of these operations were housed in rather modest accommodations, some literally in basements or garages, the French writer Nicolas Baby came up with the name *vins de garage* and called the vintners *garagistes*.[12] Production is usually very small; few garage wines produce more than 1000 cases per year.

The people who make garage wines tend to be foreigners, often newcomers to the scene rather than part of the traditional Bordeaux wine establishment. They share a disdain for the traditional system and a love of shaking things up.

Jacques Thienpont, who created Le Pin in Pomerol, the very first garage wine, is not entirely a foreigner since his family had long owned châteaux in Bordeaux, although he was working as a merchant in Belgium before he purchased a plot of land near Vieux Château Certan, a family property in Pomerol. The plot was only about 2 ha and was called the Clos du Pin; it produced a generic Pomerol that was sold off in bulk. The soil is clay and gravel, contrasting with the clay and limestone of Vieux Château Certan. The original intention was to extend the vineyards of Vieux Château Certan, but Thienpont realized he could make a special wine from this plot. Using low yields and modern production methods, he produced a tiny amount of wine that rapidly acquired a cult reputation. In 1985 the Thienponts acquired another hectare, adjacent to the original plot (from the local blacksmith), but production remains very small.

The craze for garage wines really took off in St. Emilion at the beginning of the 1990s, with Jean-Luc Thunevin's Château de Valandraud leading the way. Thunevin came to France from Algeria, worked as a bank teller, opened a wine bar, and eventually bought a tiny parcel of less than an hectare. Together with his wife Murielle he started producing wine, and created Valandraud (named by combining *val* for valley with Murielle's surname, *Andraud*). Their first harvest in 1991 produced only 1280 bottles. Valandraud was initially made from a relatively sandy plot of land. Now it has acquired better terroir, comprising various plots of land scattered around St. Emilion, producing 75,000 bottles of wine a year. (Is this still a garage wine?) The Thunevin's have a negociant business in St. Emilion, and now it's hard to get an appointment to meet Jean-Luc. Murielle Andraud is responsible for one of the first forays of garagistes into the left bank, with Château Marojallia in Margaux.

Jonathan Maltus is an Englishman who sold a successful engineering business, fell in love with a (then) fairly indifferent property called Château Teyssier, bought it in 1994, and slowly expanded his holdings

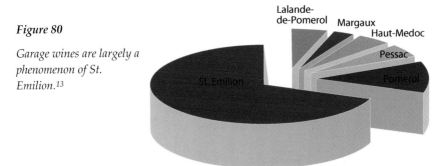

Figure 80

Garage wines are largely a phenomenon of St. Emilion.[13]

by buying small plots of high quality as and when they became available. Now with 55 hectares of vineyards, he has become a sizeable player in St. Emilion and makes several garage wines that have cult status, including Le Dôme and Les Astéries. He also produces a rarity, a white wine from St. Emilion (although it can be sold only as generic Bordeaux), Clos Nardian, which sells at prices comparable to the top white wine of Bordeaux, Haut Brion Blanc.

When garage wines made their first widespread impact on the market in 1991, there were only about five of them. Since then, numbers have increased fairly steadily until reaching a plateau in the past five years at the present level of 30-40. The majority of garage wines still come from St. Emilion (Figure 80), but others on the right bank come from Lalande-de-Pomerol as well as Pomerol.

A handful of garage wines on the left bank follow the same general principles, although here more often dominated by Cabernet Sauvignon. With success, several of the garage wines have expanded from their original, very small production; some even have second wines.

"We Are All Garagistes Now"

Most garage wines do not come from great terroir. In most cases, their terroir is quite ordinary. Extreme viticultural and vinification techniques have been used to compensate for the lack of terroir, using very low yields and other means to achieve super concentration. Some proprietors of larger châteaux have been known to comment sourly that it is easy enough to produce high quality wine on a miniscule scale by using all the tricks of viticulture and vinification, but the real issue is to get quality wine when you have tens of hectares to cultivate.

In most cases, the land for the garage wines came from purchase of small plots that had been part of an existing château; sometimes it was split off by the same owner from an existing château; and in a few cases, established châteaux that had very small vineyards in effect converted their production to the style of a garage wine.

The market success of the true garage wines has led to various imitations. Garagistes have gone into terroir, purchasing small but special plots of land from which very concentrated wines can be made. Some established châteaux began to produce super-cuvées along the same principle, either using grapes from a small, superior terroir within the estate, or simply selecting the very best barrels, to produce a more concentrated wine than that of the château itself. This is the reverse of the phenomenon of second wines, where the grapes from inferior terroir that are not considered good enough for the Grand Vin are relegated to a second wine. Of course, whereas the production of a second wine is likely to improve the Grand Vin, taking the best lots for a super-cuvée is likely to have the opposite effect.

As wines made from more established châteaux, super-cuvées tend to have a different group of proprietors, but among them are several who are shaking up Bordeaux by introducing a more international style at the châteaux they purchase. Gérard Perse owns Châteaux Pavie and Pavie-Macquin, but on a smaller scale makes garage-type wines at Châteaux Monbousquet and Bellevue-Mondotte. Bernard Magrez (who recently sold the major negociant William Pitters) now owns a whole portfolio of châteaux on both left and right banks, and makes super-cuvées such as the Serenité Cuvée d'Exception in Pessac-Léognan.

Garage wines have had an effect out of all proportion to their number and size. There are probably less than 200 ha of vineyards devoted to production of garage wine, generating fewer than 40,000 cases each year in total. This is roughly equivalent to the size and annual production of a single Grand Cru Classé of the Médoc. But they have moved the whole market.

Garage wines remain intensely controversial, and are especially subject to derision on the left bank. "Vins de garage are finished," one proprietor said to me. "They are grotesque," said another. Steven Spurrier, who organized the famous "Judgement of Paris" tasting in 1976 that catapulted California wines to equality with top French wines, said: "The belief that ridiculously low yields make better wine has finally been exploded by the quality of 2004, as it should have been by 2000, 1996 and 1990. Goodbye to a fad."[14] Yet their influence has been widespread. It was the garagistes who introduced viticultural techniques for reducing yields that have become common all over Bordeaux and led the trend towards harvesting riper grapes. From the epicenter in St. Emilion, the trend towards richer wines spread across the right bank and left bank. "St Emilion in the nineties was the engine for change for fine winemaking," says Jonathan Maltus of Château Teyssier.[15]

There is some doubt about the staying power of the garage wines themselves, but there is not much doubt about the effect they have had on the style of Bordeaux generally. As Comte Steppan von Neipperg of Château Canon La Gaffelière in St. Emilion says, "Garagistes try to make outstanding wine without outstanding terroir, but it's not really possible in this way to make a wine that ages for 10 years, although it will drink well earlier. Garage wines have influenced the whole Médoc. In the early 1990s people in the Médoc were laughing at the garage movement in St Emilion, but now they have adopted many of the same methods."[16]

Undue Influence

Phenomenally expensive garage wines have provided a driving force for the auction market in Bordeaux wines. Le Pin is famous for the period when it became one of the most expensive wines on the London auction market, pushed up by highly competitive buying from collectors in the Far East. It set a record for the most expensive bottle of Bordeaux of any vintage since 1978 ($11,750 for one bottle of the 1982 vintage), beating out even Pétrus at a mere $8,500.[17]

Although some of the pressure has subsided, the price of available vintages on the auction market continues to hold up well enough. There has not been much attrition in its relative price since the level settled down at the end of the eighties (Figure 81). Depending on the vintage, Le Pin maintains a price at several times the average of the Médoc first growths.

Figure 81

Auction price of Le Pin relative to the average of the first growths of the Médoc (defined as 100%) for the same vintage.[18]

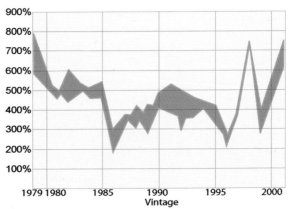

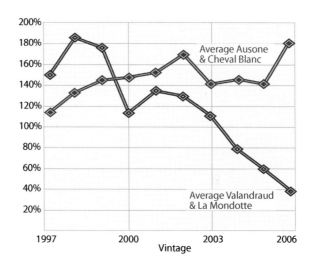

Figure 82

Comparison of the release price of Ausone and Cheval Blanc with two leading garage wines since 1997.

All prices are relative to the average of the Médoc Premier Grand Cru Classés.[19]

En primeur prices are a useful indication of opinion at the time of release. However, the small quantities and distinctive origins mean that garage wines often bypass the Place de Bordeaux, so only a few are available en primeur. They started out well in the late 1990s (Figure 82). The garage wines at first soared above the established wines, but then saw their relative position decline after the turn of the century. Is the fizz going out of the market?

Classification: a Moving Target

Has change in St. Emilion outstripped the classification? Is the present rate of revision every 10 years enough to keep up with changes at the classified growths, let alone the changes impelled by the introduction of garage wines, super-cuvées, and second wines?

The classified growths in St. Emilion occupy only half of the top twenty wines ranked by price. Châteaux Ausone and Cheval Blanc remain unchallenged as the most expensive wines of St. Emilion (Figure 83). After their brief success in the nineties, the garage wines now have slipped to a position just below the Premier Grand Cru Classés, but well above most of the other classified growths. A mix of Premier Grand Cru Classés and Grand Cru Classés, with one second wine, fill the rest of the top twenty positions. The classification offers little guidance to position in the hierarchy as ranked by price, with quite extensive overlap between wines in the Premier Grand Cru and Grand Cru groups.

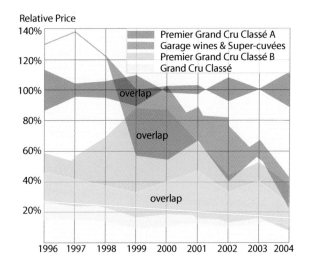

Figure 83

Release prices of the top wines in St. Emilion show Châteaux Ausone and Cheval Blanc followed by garage wines and then overlapping groups of Grand Cru Classés and Grand Crus.[20]

Prices are relative to the average of Ausone and Cheval Blanc.

Ranking the wines of St. Emilion by release price for recent vintages shows the importance of garage wines and super-cuvées (Table 17). Although produced in quite small amounts, and therefore of relatively small overall economic importance, they comprise the largest group (15 wines) in the top 40 wines. The second group of wines in the classification, the 13 Premier Grand Cru Classé B, extend over positions 4 to 39 in the list. But some Grand Cru Classés achieved higher prices in these vintages than some Premier Grand Cru Classés.

With changes occurring over short periods of time, such as the decline in the position of the garage wines from 1996 to 2001, the difficulty for a classification in keeping up with the marketplace is clear. Is the assumption that garage wines are a passing fad, and the classification will outlast them?

At the very top, Châteaux Ausone and Cheval Blanc have a large price lead over all other wines. It's notable that their second wines now rank ahead of the majority of Premier Grand Cru Classés. (A similar effect is seen with the second wines of the first growths in the Médoc.) Since 2001, the top two wines have been followed by the same group of four wines, perhaps a sort of counterpart to the super-seconds of the Médoc. Order within the group has changed between vintages. Château de Valandraud was the original garage wine; Bellevue Mondotte and La Mondotte are also garage wines; and the only classified growth in the group is Château Pavie, which has been controversial since its purchase in 1998 by Gérard Perse and the subsequent change to a much richer, more extracted style.

Château Ausone		147.0%
Château Cheval Blanc		100.0%
Château Bellevue Mondotte		35.1%
Château Pavie		34.2%
La Mondotte		34.2%
Château de Valandraud		30.6%
Château Angélus		26.4%
Château Pavie-Decesse		23.5%
Château Magrez Fombrauge		19.8%
Château Le Tertre Rôteboeuf		16.7%
Château Troplong Mondot		15.7%
Chapelle D'Ausone		15.7%
Le Dôme		15.2%
Château Gracia		14.9%
Petit Cheval		14.4%
Château Figeac		11.5%
Château Péby-Faugères		10.1%
Château Trottevieille		9.7%
Château Clos de Sarpe		9.7%
Château Canon La Gaffelière		9.6%
Château Canon		9.3%
Château Larcis Ducasse		9.3%
Château La Gomerie		8.8%
Château Pavie-Macquin		8.7%
Clos Fourtet		7.5%
Château Belair		7.5%
Château Beauséjour-Bécot		7.4%
Château La Gaffelière		7.1%
Clos Dubreuil		6.8%
Clos Saint Martin		6.6%
Château La Croix de Labrie		6.4%
Château Beausejour Duffau Lagarrosse		6.2%
Lynsolence		6.2%
Château Magdelaine		6.0%
Château Rol Valentin		5.7%
Château Monbousquet		5.5%
Lucia		5.4%
Virginie de Valandraud		5.3%
Château La Couspaude		5.2%
Château L'Arrosée		5.1%

Table 17

Wines of St. Emilion ranked in descending order of retail release prices in vintages 2005 and 2006.[21]

Prices are relative to Cheval Blanc = 100%.

 Premier Grand Cru Classé

 Grand cru classé

 Unclassified

 Garage wine

Super-cuvée

 Second wine

Figure 84

Release prices on the Place de Bordeaux show significant changes in order among some leading Premier Grand Cru Classé B group.[22]

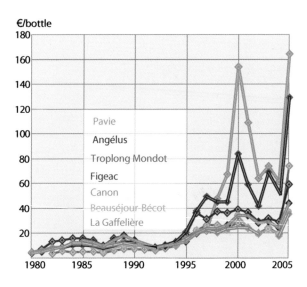

€/bottle

Pavie
Angélus
Troplong Mondot
Figeac
Canon
Beauséjour-Bécot
La Gaffelière

The Premier Grand Cru Classé B form quite a diverse group of wines, extending over a very wide price range for what is nominally a single class. Within a 10-fold price range, there have been significant changes in leadership over the past twenty years (Figure 84). Until 1990, Châteaux Figeac and Canon were the clear leaders of this group. Indeed, Figeac has been always considered the only likely candidate for promotion to group A. However, in the past ten years Château Pavie has moved to the head of this group, followed by Château l'Angélus. Château La Gaffelière has drifted from close to the top of the group to almost the bottom; indeed, it is sometimes considered a candidate for possible demotion.

The wines of St. Emilion show more change in leadership than has occurred in the order of wines in the Médoc over the same period; could this be because the ancient classification of the Médoc has a fossilizing effect? Or is this due to the impact of garage wines, whose introduction of a new style has caused others, including some of the classified growths, to follow? Whether you love or loath the garage wines, there is no denying the vibrancy they have brought to the wine scene first in St. Emilion and then elsewhere in Bordeaux. Have they pushed the style of production past a tipping point into a new Bordeaux?

10

The New Bordeaux

EVERYTHING CHANGED IN 1982. Before then, it was accepted that a great vintage of Bordeaux would be very tannic, quite acidic, and generally unpleasant to drink for many years, until it matured. The tannins and acidity were regarded as necessary to provide the structure for aging. The 1982 vintage broke the mold: ripe grapes had soft tannins and lower acidity than usual, making wines that could be drunk quite soon.[1] The great debate was whether the wines would age. Reputations were made and broken on the issue.

But let's just step back a bit and see where this concept came from that great vintages must be nasty when young. From medieval times until the 18th century, wine was an extremely short-lived product, drunk within the year (Chapter 2). After it became possible to preserve older vintages, the concept of improvement with age developed. Since then, the nature of "typical" Bordeaux has changed, but perhaps never as rapidly as in the years since 1982.

At the end of the 18th century, Thomas Jefferson commented that first growths could be drunk 3-4 years after the vintage, and that Bordeaux could age for as long again. "All red wines decline after a certain age, losing color, flavor, and body. Those of Bordeaux begin to decline after seven years."[2, 3]

By the end of the 19th century, a market in old wines had developed in England; Saintsbury, the celebrated author of "Notes on a Cellar-Book", purchased Lafite of the 1878 vintage when it was twenty years old (it had not been properly stored and he was not happy with it!), and mentions the fact that the 1870s were drinkable at 40 years of age.[4] (They still appear from time to time at current auctions, well over a century after the vintage!)

By the 20th century, wine could be enjoyed at all stages from youthful exuberance to maturity, but still references seem to be to the delicacy of Bordeaux rather than to strong tannins.[5, 6, 7] Distinctions were made between ordinary claret (to be drunk after two years) and top wines (to be drunk after a decade).[8] So far as I can determine, the association between youthful harshness and longevity seems to have taken hold in the mid-20th century, most likely as a means to sell second-rate vintages. ("It may be acid and tannic now, but just wait ten years…")

It's true that for the past half century or so, only the lightest, and relatively most short-lived, vintages of Bordeaux have been enjoyable in the first decade of life. Many great vintages have started out with strong tannins that took a decade to soften. But you can't reverse the effect; really acid, tannic vintages will not necessarily improve after a decade.[9] And as the famous oenologist Emile Peynaud pointed out, many of the greatest vintages of Bordeaux were actually relatively low in acidity.

Since 1982, grapes in Bordeaux (and elsewhere) have been harvested at increasing levels of ripeness, with higher alcohol, softer tannins, and lower acidity. The trend is due partly to improvements in viticulture allowing grapes to be harvested at a later point in the ripening cycle, and partly due to changes in vinification that allow better control of extraction. It has also been reinforced by a series of vintages that have been significantly warmer than those of previous years. The question is hotly debated as to how far this trend can go before wines in the new style of Bordeaux lose their character and their traditional age worthiness. (Cooler vintages that do not conform to the trend are now sometimes called "classic" to contrast with the new style.)

Yet the most significant effect of the new style is its impact on poor vintages. Great vintages require less intervention; and there have been more of them since 1982. But a vintage with problematic weather conditions that fifty years ago might have been lost altogether can today make quite respectable wine. "There are no bad vintages any more," they like to say in the trade. Fifty, perhaps even twenty, years ago the 2007 vintage would have been lost to mildew; but in fact it has turned out quite good, soft wines that will drink well in the short term—a restaurant vintage is the general euphemism used in the business.

Vintages both good and not-so-good now can be drunk sooner after their release than used to be the case. More recent vintages, such as 1990, 2000, 2005 pose the same question as 1982 but even more forcefully: can wines that are enjoyable so young be expected to mature and develop for fifty years like the greatest vintages of the past? The big question is whether the components needed to support long aging necessarily make the wine unpleasant when young.

The 1982 vintage, with which it all started, now offers a prospect that these modern vintages will in fact age well. Initially, the wines seemed to emphasize soft fruits, but I observed that some time around 2000, those of the left bank began to revert to type, with more savory aromas and flavors beginning to show, even a touch of the old herbaceousness of Cabernet Sauvignon that so typifies the Médoc. They show every sign of becoming classic Bordeaux in the tradition of the past in spite of their unusual beginning.

Things Aren't What they Used to Be

A fight among the wine critics about the 2003 vintage of Château Pavie from St. Emilion typifies reactions to the new Bordeaux. According to the eminent American critic Robert Parker, this "is a wine of sublime richness, minerality, delineation and nobleness."[10] But the British critic Jancis Robinson MW wrote "Ridiculous wine more reminiscent of a late-harvest Zinfandel than a red Bordeaux," in her 2003 Pavie note.[11] Clive Coates, another British Master of Wine, was even more severe: "Anyone who thinks this is good wine needs a brain and palate," he wrote.[12]

This well publicized dispute followed a change in style at the château following its purchase by Gérard Perse, a controversial newcomer in Bordeaux. The new style of Pavie followed the same path as many other châteaux in turning to much richer, more extracted flavors. The differing opinions of the results epitomize the continuing clash over styles. Robert Parker and his followers view the new style wine as richer, riper, more concentrated and exciting. More traditionally inclined critics view it as a New World-style wine, a super-ripe fruit bomb with blockbuster tastes clashing with food. Personally, it is not a wine I would enjoy with dinner.

Of course, change is nothing new. A Bordelais from the 18th or even 19th century would be astounded by today's wines (Chapter 4). And fashion can determine what constitutes typicity. A major change in vinification practices occurred in the early 19th century when Chaptal (one of the first oenologists, who went on to become Minister of the Interior under Napoleon) introduced the notion of strengthening a wine's alcoholic content by adding sugar before fermentation. (The extra sugar is converted into alcohol along with the sugar naturally present in the grapes.) Chaptalization (as it soon came to be called) was quickly taken up in Burgundy.

Reactions were mixed at the time. Dr. Morélot, a well known commentator of the time on the wines of Burgundy (he may have introduced the idea of terroir), commented in 1831 that "one makes better wine, with a good taste; but this wine, I do not know if I am fooling myself, is no longer a true wine of Burgundy. Stronger, more alcoholic, and darker in color, it has lost its bouquet, and become more southern in style."[13]

But chaptalization became the norm in Burgundy, occurring in more vintages than not. Indeed, we would hardly recognize Burgundy today (or for that matter Bordeaux) without chaptalization. Actually, chaptalization nominally was introduced into Bordeaux more recently, since it became legal only in 1938 (although it is hard to believe it was not practiced previously). It has been routine since the 1950s (although less common in the past decade).

The clash between tradition and modern trends is by no means confined to Bordeaux. The same issues occur everywhere: how much riper should the grapes get, how much should extraction be increased, how much exposure should the young wine have to new oak? The Italian regions of Barolo in Piedmont and Brunello di Montalcino in Tuscany, long known for savory wines produced from the Nebbiolo and Sangiovese grapes, respectively, have even fiercer clashes between the traditionalists and the modernists (who commit the heinous crime of maturing their wine in new oak barriques compared to the traditional [much larger] foudres of old oak; some father and son winemakers are no longer on speaking terms as a result of the split). It's not so violent in Bordeaux. Although each producer is generally committed to his style, it can be jarring when a new proprietor takes over and changes the style, as in the case of Château Pavie. But with the passage of time there are fewer holdouts for tradition.

The Simplification of Varieties

The concentration of grape varieties grown in Bordeaux today is relatively recent. Until the end of the 19th century, there was a much greater variety of types of vines, both black and white. Crisis in the vineyards subsequently led to a simplification of the encépagement (the mix of grape varieties) more than once, the driving force usually being the need to resume production as rapidly as possible with wines that would be available to drink as soon as possible. Extensive changes have resulted from at least two crises, phylloxera in the late 19th century, and the massive freeze of 1956.

The first lists of cépages grown in Bordeaux, dating from the early 18th century, identify about 18 black varieties and about 20 white varieties.[14] However, naming was erratic, the same varieties could be found in different locales under various names, and it is not possible to get any real sense of the dominant varieties. In fact, things were so confused that the first attempt to make a systematic account of varieties was abandoned in 1774.[15] But a list of a list of cépages grown in the Gironde published in 1785 included about 20 black varieties, with only Merlot of the modern varieties missing.[16]

It was not until 1841 that the major varieties of the Gironde were defined as Cabernet, Carmenère, Verdot (Gros and Petit), Merlot, Malbec, and Tarney-Coulant.[17] Two years later, a proprietor of the Graves listed the major varieties in order of merit as Carmenère, Carmenet-Sauvignon, Verdot, Merlot, and Malbec.[18] By 1874, opinion had changed and Féret placed the varieties in order of importance as Malbec, Cabernet, Merlot, Verdot, and Syrah.[19] Malbec was more important on the right bank, representing 30-60% of plantings depending on the commune, with most of the rest consisting of Merlot. Cabernet was more important on the left bank. The various communes of the Médoc varied from 40-75% Cabernet, with the rest in Merlot and Malbec.[20]

Following the devastation caused by phylloxera, the present varieties came to dominate the left and right bank. With replanting, Verdot disappeared from the Graves. Cabernet Sauvignon became the major Cabernet of the Médoc, at the expense of Cabernet Franc, and Carmenère largely disappeared. On the right bank, Merlot was replanted in place of Malbec, and by the turn of the century Merlot had become the major black grape.[21] The pattern of plantings established then did not change very significantly over the next half century.

The next big change was triggered by the winter freeze of 1956, which caused almost as much damage as phylloxera, but in a much shorter period. Unprecedented cold weather persisted throughout the whole of February; temperatures never rose above 0 °C, and went as low as –20 °C. Nothing like it had been seen since the Garonne froze in 1870. Vines were killed in vast quantities; major replanting was necessary. Overall, 45% of the vines were killed and another 40% were damaged. Almost 40% of the growers in Graves gave up that year.[22] Conditions were most severe in the Libournais, where Pomerol lost 50-80% of its vines, leading to a permanent change when replanting concentrated on Merlot, which accounted for more than half of the new plantings.[23] The Haut-Médoc, losing only 5-10% of its vines, was the least affected.

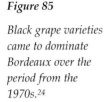

Figure 85

Black grape varieties came to dominate Bordeaux over the period from the 1970s.[24]

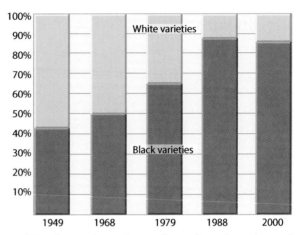

The great reputation of Bordeaux has always been based on its red wines, but in terms of overall production, its devotion principally to red varieties is relatively recent. Until the 1960s, plantings of white grape varieties were in the majority. As recently as 1968 they were still 50%, but fell dramatically to a small minority by 1988 (Figure 85). In one sense, this gives the lie to the notion that the French system strangles response to the market; this response to the preference for red wine is just as striking as a comparable transition in, for example, Australia (although the change in Australia was more rapid).[25]

Changes in the balance of red to white plantings were accompanied by major changes in the proportions of the different varieties. Plantings of quality varieties were encouraged by regulations introduced in 1953 (later strengthened in 1964), when varieties were divided into "recommended," "authorized," and "tolerated." Recommended varieties could be freely planted, authorized varieties could be planted only in smaller amounts, and tolerated varieties could not be replaced when vineyards required replanting. As a consequence, the good side of the disaster of 1956 was a general improvement in the quality of the cépages. Even so there was a tendency to concentrate on plantings that would rapidly give high yields; in 1964 almost 20% of plantings still consisted of old varieties rather than those being encouraged by the authorities.[26]

Since then, however, there has been a significant improvement in the quality of plantings in the Gironde. By 1988 varieties other than the major blacks and whites had largely been eliminated.[27] Regulations are much stricter today, and since 1998 in the communes of the Médoc, red wine can be produced *only* from Cabernet Sauvignon, Cabernet Franc, Merlot, Petit-Verdot, Malbec and Carmenère (although there is actually very little of the last two).[28]

The Inexorable Rise of Merlot

When you think of Bordeaux, you think of Cabernet Sauvignon. Yes, but this is really true only of the Médoc; actually by far the dominant grape variety in Bordeaux as a whole is Merlot. According to the latest figures from the CIVB (the Conseil Interprofessionnel du Vin de Bordeaux), Merlot is approaching two thirds of all plantings and Cabernet Sauvignon in fact is only a quarter (Figure 86).

Figure 86

Plantings of black grapes in Bordeaux are dominated by Merlot.

Black grapes are 89% of all plantings in Bordeaux.[29]

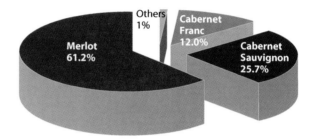

The growth of Merlot has scarcely slowed over the past half century (Figure 87). Cabernet Sauvignon increased sharply up to 1988, but has eased off since then. Cabernet Franc has seen a small decline and Malbec has gone from a significant variety to an insignificant one. The miscellaneous varieties have all but disappeared.

Figure 87

Concentration on the major varieties occurred in the 1970s and 1980s.[30]

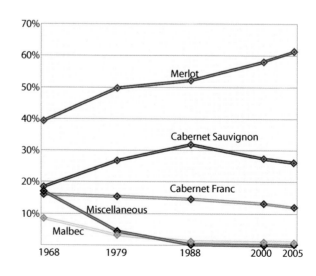

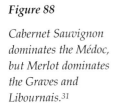

Figure 88

*Cabernet Sauvignon
dominates the Médoc,
but Merlot dominates
the Graves and
Libournais.*[31]

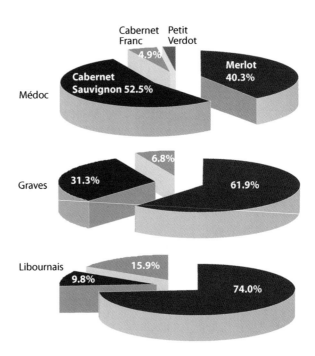

The Médoc, Graves, and Libournais are virtually different regions in terms of the dominant grape varieties (Figure 88). With three quarters of plantings, Merlot dominates the Libournais, it is the most widely planted grape in the Graves, and it falls to a minority only in the Médoc.

The supremacy of Cabernet Sauvignon in the Médoc isn't in fact entirely universal. It is certainly the dominant variety in the great communes of St. Estèphe, Pauillac, St. Julien, and Margaux, but actually occupies just under half of plantings elsewhere in the Haut-Médoc and Médoc (Table 18).

Table 18 *Cabernet Sauvignon is the most widely planted grape in the four communes of St. Estèphe, Pauillac, St. Julien, and Margaux, but is just under half of all plantings elsewhere in the Médoc at the classified growths and Cru Bourgeois.*[32]

	Cabernet Sauvignon	Merlot	Cabernet Franc	Petit Verdot
4 communes	57.0%	34.1%	7.7%	4.6%
rest of Médoc	49.9%	43.1%	7.3%	4.7%

The proportion of Cabernet Sauvignon more or less reflects the reputation of the château and the longevity of its wines. It is concentrated in the best appellations and châteaux of the Médoc. The classed growths have greater proportions of Cabernet Sauvignon and less Merlot than the other châteaux. Within the classed growths, the first growths have the most Cabernet Sauvignon (about 70%), and the seconds are just above the third to fifth growths (all around 60%). The Cru Bourgeois have notably less Cabernet Sauvignon (average 50%).[33]

Yet the trend towards producing wines that are ready to drink sooner has been accompanied by a decrease in the ratio of Cabernets to Merlot in all appellations. In fact, the largest percent increase in Merlot in the last decade of the twentieth century was in the Médoc. The trend extends even to the classed growths. Over the past 20 years, the total proportion of Cabernets planted at the classed growths has decreased steadily, while Merlot has increased (Figure 89). Petit Verdot has held its own around the 3% level.

The increase in total plantings contributes to the increase in proportion of Merlot. The very best areas, identified long ago, are planted with Cabernet Sauvignon. New areas naturally are not such good terroir, and therefore tend to be planted with Merlot. However, perhaps the recent warming climatic tendency may make it possible to reverse the trend and to plant more Cabernet Sauvignon (and also Petit Verdot, another variety that has some difficulty in ripening).

Figure 89

Changes in grape varieties planted at the classified growths show a trend for increasing Merlot and decreasing Cabernet.

The total plantings include grapes used for the second wine as well as for the grand vin.[34]

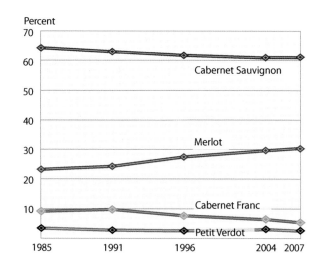

Vintage and Assemblage

Because the assemblage (the blend of different grape varieties) of each wine changes significantly from year to year, depending upon which varieties are successful in each vintage, it is not possible to predict the constitution of any particular wine from the vineyard plantings. Over a decade at Pichon Lalande, for example, the proportions of Cabernet and Merlot in the wine have varied widely, although the varieties planted in the vineyard have scarcely changed at all (Figure 90).

Compared with the proportion of 45% Cabernet Sauvignon in the vineyard (actually a relatively low proportion for the Médoc), the proportion of Cabernet Sauvignon in the wine varied from 75% in 1996 (a year generally dominated by Cabernet in the Médoc) to a low of 35% in 1999 (when Merlot was actually the major single variety in Pichon Lalande). Proportions of Cabernet Franc and Petit Verdot are quite variable, ranging from 15% to zero depending on the conditions of the year.

So even though there is a general trend in the Médoc at all levels of châteaux towards an increased proportion of Merlot, this has little predictive value for any particular year, given the wide variations in assemblage that result from individual vintage conditions. And in comparing different vintages in Bordeaux, it is not only the basic quality of the year that affects the nature of the wine, but also what assemblage was used that year.

Figure 90

Cabernet Sauvignon together with Cabernet Sauvignon forms a majority in Pichon Lalande, but actual proportions vary depending on vintage conditions.[35]

The bars on the left show the proportions of each variety planted in the vineyard.

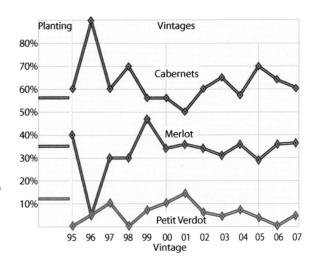

Ripe or Over-Ripe?

No one wants to make wine from under-ripe grapes any more. Vegetative flavors from vintages when the grapes failed to ripen are really something of the past. But has the reaction gone too far the other way, towards super-ripe grapes? Mention "herbaceous" when describing a wine in Bordeaux and the château proprietor will bristle visibly. Yet it's those faintly herbaceous notes of bell peppers coming from Cabernet Sauvignon that characteristically identify a wine of the Médoc. Personally, I believe that great wine requires that touch of herbaceousness coming from grapes before they go into super-maturity; when all the grapes are uniformly ripe or super-ripe, there's less variety, and you can get a fairly monotonic set of aromas and flavors. But only a touch, of course.

Changes in climate, viticulture, and vinification have combined in a trend to harvest riper grapes and to extract more matter from them. The warming trend resulting from climate change creates the basic circumstances in which grapes become riper during the growing season. Changes in viticulture have created more sophisticated control of exposure to the sun, allowing grapes to be better protected or exposed as appropriate, to achieve better ripeness. A vastly sophisticated array of vinification techniques allows much better control of fermentation, extraction from the skins, and extraction from oak. All of these factors have contributed to a significant change in the nature of the wine made in the past two decades.

Pruning adjustments to the grapevine during the growing season have made a significant difference to ripeness of the berries. "Canopy management" is the buzzword, meaning that the structure of the grapevine is arranged so as to control sun exposure. Vendange en vert, or green pruning, is used to reduce yield, by removing excess numbers of berries early in the season. (It is not completely successful because the grapevine adjusts by increasing the size of the remaining berries, and it remains somewhat controversial.) Later in the season, leaf pulling is used to remove leaves where they seem to be providing excess shade and preventing the berries from getting the exposure to sun that they need for ripening. Leaf pulling is sometimes done specifically on the shady side of the canopy; the leaves may literally be pulled off, or sometimes burned off. The intention of these treatments is to get the grapevine to have a limited load of berries that are equally exposed and therefore ripen evenly. It may well be that the effects are more pronounced in poor vintages than in really good ones, when conditions anyway would have given a good, ripe crop.

Before it became possible to control the temperature of fermentation (during the 1970s), growers tended to harvest grapes once they reached 11.5% potential alcohol, because otherwise the higher sugar levels would cause vigorous fermentation, pushing up the temperature, and running the risks of developing volatile acidity (by generating acetic acid) or getting stuck fermentation. (If fermentation stops when it gets too hot, it can be very difficult to restart.) Harvesting at this point went hand in hand with higher acidity and less mature tannins in the grapes. The ability to harvest riper grapes that can be fermented under temperature control has been one major cause in the change of wine style. The introduction of sorting tables to eliminate unripe berries also has had a large effect. And warmer vintages have provided the riper grapes more and more often recently.

Acidity has decreased, alcohol has increased, and tannins have increased. Acidity has been declining at roughly 10% per decade, so that it is now only about two thirds of the level in the 1970s. Potential alcohol levels (the amount that would be produced by complete fermentation of the sugar in the grapes) have increased by 15-20% since 1970 (Figure 91). True, levels in the grapes at harvest don't exactly predict levels in the wine, because during winemaking, acidity is decreased (as a result of malolactic fermentation) and alcohol can be increased (as a result of chaptalization). But the trend found in the grapes is more or less reflected in the wine.

Figure 91

Potential alcohol has increased and acidity has decreased steadily since 1970. [36]

These values were obtained with Cabernet Sauvignon; Merlot gives significantly higher alcohol levels.

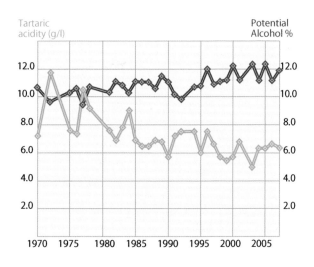

The average alcohol level in Bordeaux wines has increased steadily from a range of 12-12.5% thirty years ago to a range of 13-13.5% today. The trend to higher alcohol is a significant factor in a transition to the more powerful new international style at some châteaux, and has been especially marked in the past decade. Personally, I believe this represents a decline in elegance—if you go back to older Bordeaux at lower alcohol levels, you can see what we have lost. One oenologue of the old school said to me recently, "in a vrai [true] Bordeaux you have no alcohol perception—if you feel alcohol it is not a true Bordeaux."[37]

There is often a large difference between Cabernet Sauvignon, which may struggle to reach 12.5%, and Merlot, which may easily reach 14%; the final alcohol level reflects the proportions in the blend. My sympathies are with a Médoc château whose winemaker told me recently that in the 2005 vintage, with the Merlot at 14% alcohol, virtually none was included in the blend (which ended up as almost exclusively Cabernet Sauvignon) in order to retain elegance.

Chaptalization can be taken as a measure of whether satisfactory ripeness is achieved. Historically, the grapes have had insufficient sugar at harvest, so chaptalization has been used more often than not in both Bordeaux and Burgundy. Reflecting the warming trend of recent years, however, many producers in Bordeaux say that the last time they chaptalized was in 1997 or 1999. (It would be nice to confirm this factually, but the French authorities are strangely reluctant to disgorge information on the extent and frequency of chaptalization.) Of course, the need to chaptalize depends on the variety; at one great château, the winemaker told me that they have chaptalized Cabernet Sauvignon in every year except 2005, but the Merlot has usually been over the limit where it would be legal to chaptalize.[38]

Various criteria have passed in and out of favor for deciding when grapes are ripe. The most primitive is the ratio of sugar to acid. As grapes mature, they accumulate sugar and lose acid. The optimum time for picking used to be regarded as a matter of finding the moment when sugar was high enough to give good alcohol levels and acidity had declined below oppressive levels. Then the concept of tannin ripeness came to the fore, sometimes assessed by looking at the color of the seeds (they turn from green to brown at ripeness), sometimes simply by tasting the grapes. This idea broadened into the whole concept of "phenolic ripeness" that is popular now. (Phenols are molecules largely extracted from the skins of the grapes; they include the anthocyanins, responsible for color, and the tannins, needed for the structure to age.) Phenolic ripeness typically is achieved well after sugar levels have passed the point at which it used to be customary to harvest, which is one of the reasons why wine has become more alcoholic.

One measure of the change in wine is the IPT (index of total polyphenols), which was about 62 in 1982, 70 by year 2000, and 78 in year 2005.[39] The change in IPT means that total phenol levels have increased from 5 g/l to 6 g/l over 20 years, reflecting both increased ripeness of the grapes and better methods for extraction from the skins. Less obvious from the numbers is that the tannins have also changed in nature. Although there is no exact measure of it, it seems that tannins mature from more vegetative to rounder qualities as the grapes ripen.[40] Harvesting later in the cycle means that tannins are riper now than the green, stalky tannins of the past.[41]

Global Warming: Threat or Promise?

The French would argue that a thousand or more years of experience have gone into matching grape varieties with terroirs, so that each plot of land gives the very best wine possible. While Pinot Noir and Chardonnay are uniquely matched to Burgundy, Cabernet Sauvignon and Merlot have been perfected for the left and right banks of Bordeaux. Will all this be upset by global warming?

Climate is the most important factor in determining which grape varieties are appropriate for each region. Each variety does best in a characteristic temperature range; below the range it will fail to ripen properly, while above the range it is likely to give jammy wines lacking the usual typicité of the variety. Among common black varieties, Pinot Noir does best with an average growing season temperature (the average daily temperature between April and October) around 17 °C, Cabernet Sauvignon around 20 °C, and Syrah around 22 °C.[42] This explains why Pinot Noir was planted in Burgundy, Cabernet Sauvignon in Bordeaux, and Syrah in the Rhône.

Varieties have traditionally been planted in France more at less at the northern limits for achieving full ripeness, with the result that usually there would only be a few really good vintages each decade. In the 1950s, average growing season temperatures were 15.5 °C in Burgundy, 16.5 °C in Bordeaux, and 18.5 °C in the southern Rhône.[43] This is consistently a bit lower than the optimum for the predominant varieties. About three times every decade, a warmer year than average would bring really good ripening and create an excellent vintage.

Global warming has changed all this. Over the past 50 years, the warming trend has resulted in more vintages when full ripeness is achieved in the growing season, and the results have been especially striking in the past 20 years. A change like this is not unprecedented. Until the late 15th century, the Champagne region produced still red wines that were exported to Paris. However, the temperature plunge of the mini ice age was followed by sustained cooler temperatures, making it impossible to ripen the grapes fully. Burgundy then became the favored supplier. The annual temperature decline may have been only ~0.2 °C.

Over the past 10-20 years, the average growing temperatures in many regions reached or even exceeded the optimum value for its traditional grape varieties. One of the effects is that harvest dates have become progressively earlier. The average growing season temperature has increased by 0.4 °C per decade since 1950 in Bordeaux, and the average harvest date has moved earlier by 2.2 days per decade (Figure 92).

The typical temperature difference between Bordeaux and Burgundy over the past century was only 1.2 °C, so the increase in temperature over the past 50 years means that Burgundy now has an average temperature close to that of Bordeaux in the 1950s, while Bordeaux now has an average temperature approaching that of the southern Rhône in the 1950s.

Figure 92

Temperatures have become warmer in Bordeaux over the past 50 years and harvest dates have moved earlier.[44]

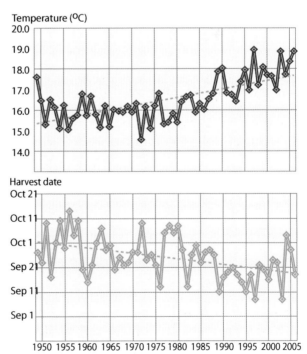

Figure 93

The warming trend of the past 50 years has brought the average growing season temperature in Bordeaux close to that of Napa Valley.[45]

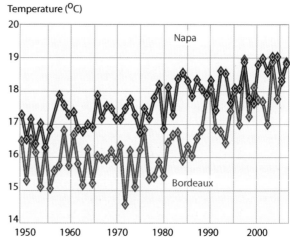

We may be fortunate in the present period that climate warming is producing an increased proportion of vintages in which Cabernet Sauvignon ripens perfectly in Bordeaux. But how much further can the trend continue before it becomes necessary to rethink whether the traditional varieties can continue be grown in each region?

The warming trend has been greater in Bordeaux than in California, so the gap in temperatures between Bordeaux and Napa Valley, one of the major New World competitors to Bordeaux, has narrowed considerably. In the past decade, Bordeaux has warmed up to reach almost the same average temperatures as those of Napa (Figure 93). This may be part of the reason for the increased convergence in style between the regions, with Bordeaux showing more of the riper, richer features associated with Napa valley.

The warming trend advances the entire cycle of grapevine maturation, from bud break (the start of the growing season), through flowering, véraison (when the berries start to develop color), to ripening and harvest. In fact, in France as a whole over the past 50 years, bud break has advanced by 5 days, and harvest has advanced by 17 days. This means that the overall growing season has become shorter, another point of convergence with the New World, especially between Bordeaux and Napa.

Rainfall has always been an issue in Bordeaux. The maritime climate is pretty wet and many vintages have been spoiled by rain. Drainage to get rid of surface water has always been a problem. Collateral problems are associated with high humidity, especially susceptibility to fungal infections (the 2007 vintage was almost ruined by mildew). More recently, however, the Bordelais have been worried by a decline in

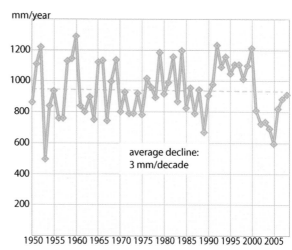

Figure 94

Bordeaux usually has 800-1000 mm of rainfall each year.[46]

rainfall, and some have even been heard muttering about drought. Historically rainfall has been between 800 and 1200 mm. annually. This was reduced to less than 700 mm during the period 2001-2005, the driest half-decade of recent times, and indeed in 2005 the level was only just above the minimum of 600 mm required by the grapevine (Figure 94). But the 2007 and 2008 vintages were back to only just below the historic average, so this may not necessarily be the beginning of a trend.

Changes in climate have the potential to alter significantly the effects of terroir. When vineyards are planted on a slope, for example, it is usually the middle of the slope that is the best terroir. Along the escarpment of Burgundy's Côte d'Or, the Grand Crus lie in the middle of the slope, because this is where the grapes reliably ripen best. This could be changed by global warming. And it's also true that terroirs higher up the slope do better in wet seasons, whereas terroirs at the bottom do better in dry seasons, because of drainage patterns, so a general change in rainfall could have a significant effect on relative qualities of terroirs. These issues are less pressing in Bordeaux, where the terrain is flatter, and where furthermore there is the potential to change which grape variety is planted in each spot. But it would be dangerous to assume that the traditional hierarchy will be immune to change by global warming.

The Rise of the Oenologue

Criticism of oenologues is almost as old as oenology. Emile Peynaud did more than anyone to bring vinification into a modern era based on rational analysis, but was criticized for making all wines taste the same.

"I am not sure of the appellation, I do not recognize the vintage, but I can tell this wine was made by Emile Peynaud" was one famous comment. (Similar comments have been made since, with perhaps more pertinence, about the oenologues of today.) Peynaud's retort was that "The wines of yesterday were more stereotyped than today's. They were all similar because they shared the same defect. They were oxidized."[47]

Peynaud revolutionized winemaking in Bordeaux in the 1950s by introducing methods based on understanding of the processes of vinification. Before Peynaud, malolactic fermentation was a mysterious event that might (or might not) happen in the spring. There were even winemakers who ascribed its occurrence to a mystical sympathy of the wine with the rising of the sap in the vines! Peynaud demonstrated that malolactic fermentation occurred in the spring because it is caused by bacteria that are sensitive to temperature; they become active as the cellars warm up.[48] (The bacteria convert the harsh-tasting malic acid to the softer lactic acid, reducing overall acidity, softening flavors, and introducing more buttery aromas. Malolactic fermentation is considered essential for almost all red wines and for many white wines.)

Peynaud caused winemakers to replace old barrels, often infected with spoilage bacteria, with clean, new barrels—leading to criticism that he had introduced the taste of oak into wine. The changes that he championed, from using the best grapes to maintaining cellar hygiene, made wine that was much easier to drink sooner. To those accustomed to the view that young wine was tart, tannic, unpleasant, and even undrinkable, this was heresy. Traditionalists distrusted him and claimed that his wines had been homogenized, "Peynaudized" as they put it.

Similar accusations reverberate, but with more force, in the present era. Many châteaux are advised by oenologues, of whom Michel Rolland, Stéphan Derenoncourt, Denis Dubourdieu, and Jacques Boissenot are the best known. Each advises a considerable number of château—Michel Rolland more than 50, Stéphan Derenoncourt around 40, Denis Dubourdieu and Jacques Boissenot some 20-30 each. Altogether some 200 of the leading wines of Bordeaux depend on advice from these four oenologues.[49] (And of course they also advise wineries in other regions and countries.)

Michel Rolland in particular is known for producing wines with intense fruit and new oak, very much the modern style of Bordeaux, in some ways more resembling wines of the New World than those of Bordeaux in the past. He is the owner of Château Bon Pasteur in Pomerol, and among the châteaux he advises on the right bank are the producers of many of the garage wines. He is often felt to be the arch apostle of the international style, and indeed was portrayed as a somewhat Mephistophelean figure in the film Mondovino, which took target at the globalization of wine.

The "international style" wines depend on changes in both viticulture and vinification. Not only are grapes are harvested at increased levels of ripeness, with greater sugar levels (giving higher alcohol levels) and more (and riper) tannins, but the wine is exposed to new oak at a much earlier stage.

After Emile Peynaud discovered the cause of malolactic fermentation, it became common to induce the process by adding the bacteria instead of waiting for chance. This allows the winemaker to decide exactly when malolactic fermentation should occur. Usually this remained in the spring following the harvest. After completion, the wine was transferred to oak barriques.

But wine is difficult to taste and assess when it is going, or has just gone, through the malo (as it is called in France). The original timing sometimes made it awkward to assess the wines when they first shown to critics at the start of the en primeur campaign in March. So now there is a trend to perform the malolactic fermentation immediately after the alcoholic fermentation, so that it is completed well before the spring. And often the wine is transferred to barriques immediately after alcoholic fermentation—sometimes it is even run off straight from the fermentation vats while it is still warm— so the malo can be performed in the barriques. Performing it in oak barriques gives a wine that is more pleasing and easier to taste, basically better rounded and showing its oak more distinctly, at this early stage.

No one knows whether there will be adverse effects on its development in the longer term. Bill Blatch of the negociant firm Vintex, who is widely respected for his annual authoritative newsletter about the vintage, comments that, "the trend towards malolactic fermentation in barrel continues. It is a laborious process, which, on the admission of most cellar masters, adds nothing to the wine in the long term, so the regrettable conclusion is that it is designed to make the young wines more pleasing for the journalists and customers to taste in the spring. Like reverse osmosis, microbullage and reductive élevage, investment in this process has gone all the way down the line to the petits châteaux, or at least to those estates having a distribution system that doesn't work unless the wines taste good en primeur."[50]

The new style wines tend to be powerful rather than elegant, bursting with fruit, sometimes with jammy rather than savory aromas and flavors. These wines tend to show well at comparative tastings because their intense flavors make it difficult to appreciate wines with more subtle constitutions; even experienced tasters can be fooled. Personally I would question whether these wines are really suitable to accompany food. However, they are much favored by some influential wine critics, including Robert Parker; reflecting the extent of his influence, in France, they sometimes say that a wine made to this prescription has been *parkerisé.*

The Heat Wave of the Future

Wine made in Bordeaux today is quite different from wine made in Bordeaux in the past. A wine of 1955 was more deeply colored, more alcoholic, more tannic, and longer lived than a wine made in 1855 (Chapter 4). Almost everyone would agree that wine got better over the century. This is a continuing trend. The wine of today is more deeply colored, more alcoholic, and more tannic than the wine of fifty years ago. But is it better?

It is more agreeable to drink sooner, and most people would take that as an indication that it may not be so long lived. Part of the reason for the increased softness of wines today is that the tannins are riper, but the verdict really is still out on the implications for longevity.

How far can the trend go before Bordeaux loses its typicité? In fact, what is the typicité of Bordeaux? Personally I view it (admittedly biased more toward the left bank) as wine that is elegant, possibly a little tannic when young; but when aged from a great vintage, becoming savory with layers of flavor all seamlessly integrated. I have my doubts that wines with more than 13% alcohol, and with heavy solid extract, will ever be able to achieve this quality.

This description, to be sure, applies to the top wines. Unable to achieve this type of quality, the lesser wines inevitably must be drunk younger, in which case "typicité" may mean something rather different. In fact, you might take the inability of the lesser wines to abandon their traditional "typicité," and to acquire softer, more forward, approachable fruits as part of the problem in competing with the New World.

If global warming continues, will the wine adjust or will we adjust? How far is it possible to further adjust viticulture and vinification to maintain freshness and elegance in the wines? Or will consumers have to become accustomed to the new style of wine, fruity and powerful, more southern as Dr. Morélot commented on the change in Burgundy almost two hundred years ago? Indeed, has the market already adjusted as seen in (sometimes hostile) criticisms of wines made to a more "classic" style?

11

Grand Vins and Second Wines

"THE VERTIGINOUS RISE IN PRICES has rendered the grand crus inaccessible to mere mortals," reported L'Express in 2005.[1] "Can't afford Château Margaux any more? Or Château Latour, or Château Any-Other-Famous-Bordeaux? Have you thought of trying your favorite château's second wine?" asked Frank Prial in the New York Times previously.[2]

Twenty years ago, most châteaux in Bordeaux produced a single wine. Today, almost all leading châteaux also produce a second wine, ostensibly offering a chance to experience their style and expertise at a much lower price. Initially, second wines were important for protecting the name of the château in poor vintages by finding a use for lots that did not quite meet the standard. But from these humble beginnings, second wines have become a phenomenon in their own right. In fact, some châteaux have quite reversed the roles of their grand vins and second wines in terms of relative production: more than 50% of production, they claim, goes into the second wine.

When you have 55 hectares of vineyards and are producing 25,000 cases of wine a year (the average for a Grand Cru Classé in the Médoc), there will inevitably be significant variation in the quality of wine made from different parts of your vineyards. Probably some plots will always give better wine than others; this is the essence of terroir. But the quality of the grapes in different parts of the vineyard will also vary with the particular vintage. It used to be that the vintage was the vintage and basically all of the production went into the wine, but the past couple of decades have seen an increasing trend towards setting aside the lots that do not meet the objectives of the Grand Vin, for whatever reason, and using them for a second wine. Only the best lots go into the grand vin.

The close relationship between grand vin and second wine is virtually unique to Bordeaux, made possible by the classification system that effectively treats châteaux as brand names. By contrast, while a Burgundy producer can offer wines at a range of levels (and prices), the emphasis on terroir creates an expectation of differences beyond simple quality levels: we expect any producer's grand cru and premier cru Burgundy to be in the same general style, but the grapes come from different plots of land, each with its own characteristic terroir. The titillation of second wine in Bordeaux is that, in another vintage, the grapes that went into the second wine might have been part of the grand vin.

The origins of second wines are not so simple as they appear. In reality, they encompass a range of sources: inferior plots of land, production from young vines (where the quality is not so good), cépages that were less successful in a given vintage, use of vin de presse (what's made by pressing the grapes at the end of fermentation, which is of lower quality than the wine made from the juice released earlier). At one extreme, they may come completely from lots that are declassified from the grand vin; at the other, they may come from vineyard plots that never contribute to the grand vin. And their production is somewhat simpler, with less extended maturation and exposure to new oak.

The lack of any precise definition for second wine leaves opportunity for confusion and misunderstanding. Almost 20% of the names that are reported for second wines in the standard books on Bordeaux are incorrect: they include other châteaux owned by the same proprietor, commercial marques (wine made from sources other than the vineyards of the château itself), or other types of wine altogether.[3] Yet second wines have become an important commercial part of the market, representing roughly 10% of the retail value of Bordeaux—more than sales of either dry or sweet white wines.

What does this do to the economics of production? Is the consumer who buys the second wine getting an opportunity to experience something he cannot afford at the level of the grand vin? Or is the second wine simply a brand extension that sells at a price inflated by the reputation of the château?

The Old Market in Second Wines

In 1982 there were only a handful of second wines; today there are about 700. Only the growth of garage wines has been more explosive, but garage wines are far fewer in number and far smaller in scale of production (Chapter 9). In a market where everything is tightly regulated by appellation rules, second wines stand out for bypassing the system. (True they must conform to the rules of the appellations in which they are located, but their relationship with the grand vin is almost entirely unregulated).

Second wines are not, in fact, a new phenomenon, but have existed at the top châteaux for at least 250 years. In the mid 18th century, all four of the "first growths" of the period (Lafite, Latour, Margaux, and Haut Brion) produced "second wines."[4] We do not know much about their nature, but there is some evidence from the early 19th century that they could have played an analogous role to the second wines of today, with lots being directed to either grand vin or second wine according to the vintage.

The basic issues have not changed. In 1810, Lamothe, the régisseur at Château Latour noted: "I abandoned to the second wine some cuvées that were intended for the first wines, but which did not please me... The second wines benefited from 10 tonneaux of first wines that I sacrificed because they did not reach my standard."[5] The opposite policy was followed at Château Lafite in the 1815 vintage and in subsequent years, when the régisseur, Joseph Goudal, redirected into the grand vin some of the best cuvées that would have gone into the second wine: "when the grapes achieve a good maturity, I can augment the volume of the first wine to the profit of the proprietors"[6]. As today, there were also differences in the encépagement (the mix of grape varieties) of the grand vin and second wines, with cabernet more prominent in the grand vin; and there were differences in the use of oak, with barriques of higher quality used for the grand vin.[7] And already wine from some inferior plots of land was being used for the second wine.[8]

Second wines in the mid 19th century typically represented about a quarter of total production, and sold for about a third of the price of the grand vin.[9] The grand vin showed the same sharp increase in price in great vintages that has been characteristic in modern times, so the price of the second wine fluctuated from 90% of the grand vin in a poor vintage to 20% in a great vintage.[10] Sometimes wine was labeled explicitly as a second vin (Figure 95). At the end of the century, the châteaux in the next tier were also producing second wines, according to records at Brane Cantenac and Rauzan-Ségla showing around 25-30% of production.[11, 12]

The importance of second wines diminished during the 20th century. Although all the first growths were regularly producing second wines, the volume was reduced to 10-20% of production.[13] In this period, they sold for higher prices relative to the grand vin, generally about half. This

Figure 95

Some wine from Château Lafite was labeled as second wine in the difficult conditions of the 1895 vintage.[14]

Photo courtesy of Zachys wine auctions.

was a terrible period during which it was difficult enough to sell the grand vins, and second wines did not become generally important again until the 1980s.

The New Second Wines

In the past 20 years, second wines have spread through most of the better properties of Bordeaux.[15] There were relatively few second wines before 1970, a steady rate of establishment until 1980, and then an explosion (Figure 96). In fact, the majority of second wines have been established since the 1980s.[16] Second wines now occur in all appellations of the Médoc and the Graves (Figure 97). On the right bank, they are most prominent in the Libournais.

Figure 96

Establishment of second wines surged in the 1980s and 1990s.

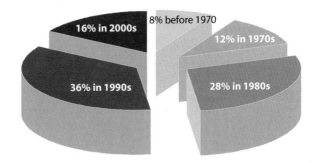

Figure 97

Second wines are widely distributed on both the left bank and right bank.[17]

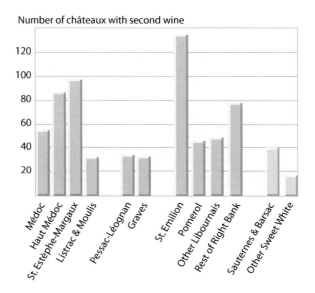

Number of châteaux with second wine

Second wines spread "top-down" through the Médoc. Before the 1980s, 50% of the first growths had established second wines. By the late 1980s, the second growths had reached this stage, then the other classes followed in the 1990s. The top ranks of Cru Bourgeois (Exceptionnel and Supérieur) reached it around the turn of the century; the Cru Bourgeois are still below 50%.

In the Médoc, the proportion of châteaux making second wines increases with the reputation of the commune. They are less than a quarter in the Bas-Médoc, rise to over a third in the Haut-Médoc, and reach a peak of about 60% in the communes of Pauillac, St. Julien, and Margaux.[18]

Not surprisingly, it is the more expensive wines that have second labels: of the 200 most expensive wines on the Bordeaux market (excluding garage wines), more than 120 have second labels (and many of those that do not are the smaller estates in Pomerol or St. Emilion). Most of the wines outside of the top 200 that do have second labels are at the level of Médoc Cru Bourgeois (usually quite close in price to the top 200).[19]

Declassification versus Special Parcels

Châteaux are quite forthcoming these days about the assemblage of cépages that goes into the grand vin, how it changes from year to year, what proportion of their total production is used for the grand vin, how much use was made of new oak, and what maturation protocol was followed. The châteaux tend to be rather less informative, one might even say quite cagey, about the origins of the grapes in their second wines. But there is an implicit understanding that the very selection of the second wine will have improved the quality of the grand vin.

The general perception is that a second wine is produced by declassifying those lots that are deemed not quite good enough for the grand vin. Actually, however, second wines range from those produced exclusively by declassification at assemblage of the grand vin (the stage when all its components are blended together) to those representing production of a separate vineyard. Most second wines represent an intermediate between these extremes. The second wine is usually made in a more approachable style, supposedly offering an opportunity to sample the style of the château sooner (and at lower price) than the grand vin.

Lack of precise definition for "second wine" allows for significant variety in its relationship with the grand vin (Figure 98). Altogether, just over half do not use specific parcels and therefore represent the same terroir as the grand vin. The wine may be declassified from the grand vin or may use production from young vines (which are generally felt to produce wine of lower quality, although the appropriate age for use in grand vin depends on the producer's judgment). Indeed, the most common use of a second wine is to absorb production from young vines.[21]

A small minority of second wines are made exclusively by declassifying lots from the grand vin. An extreme case of a second wine produced by declassification is at Domaine de Chevalier in Pessac-

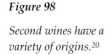

Figure 98

Second wines have a variety of origins.[20]

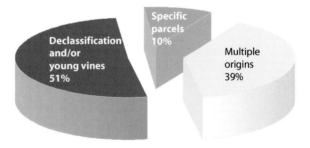

Léognan. For both the white and red wines, every barrel is tasted individually soon in the new year after the vintage by a committee of five tasters. Every taster has a veto power on each barrel: only barrels selected by unanimous vote can go into the grand vin.[22]

Overall about 75% of second wines are basically related to the grand vin, while 25% come mostly from separate terroir. In this latter class, 10% of second wines come exclusively from specific parcels (irrespective of vintage), and therefore are really an independent marque of the same producer rather than a second wine related to the grand vin. This rather undercuts the concept of the second wine, at least insofar as it may be used to improve the quality of the first wine.

The most famous second wines largely coming from distinct plots are Les Forts de Latour (of Château Latour) and the Clos du Marquis (of Léoville Las Cases). The main source of grapes for Les Forts de Latour (probably the best second wine in Bordeaux) is a separate vineyard to the west of the "Grand Enclos" around the château (Figure 46). But the second wine also includes production from vines that are under 12 years old within the Grand Enclos, and (depending on the year) some individual lots that are not thought good enough for the grand vin. Clos du Marquis is a separate plot of land within the estate of Léoville Las Cases, and was used to make a separate wine at the start of the 20th century; now it is the basis of the second wine.

Relative proportions of second wines to grand vin vary widely. The vast majority of châteaux put most of their production into the grand vin (Figure 99). However, the increasing trend towards second wines means that a fair number of châteaux routinely use less than half of production for the grand vin, therefore making their "second wine" the major product! Of course, proportions vary significantly with vintage. The range at some leading châteaux varies as much as 2-fold, depending on the vintage. In 1997, the worst vintage of the past decade, many châteaux

Figure 99

Percent of château with different proportions of grand vin in 2006.

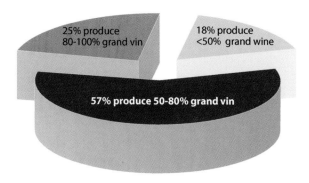

25% produce 80-100% grand vin

18% produce <50% grand wine

57% produce 50-80% grand vin

used less than half of their production for the grand vin. In the more normal 2006 vintage, second wines on average accounted for one third of production at châteaux that have them.[23]

Most châteaux produce their second wine every year. Larger châteaux have almost inevitably accumulated some plots of lesser terroir over the years, so they need to find a use for the inferior lots of wine. Indeed, second wines offer châteaux an opportunity to hide the mistakes of previous proprietors. In really terrible years, a château might declassify its entire crop to the second wine, but this has not happened for quite a while. Some smaller châteaux put their entire crop into the grand vin in really good years.

A Confusion of Names

You can certainly see increased consciousness of the marketing value of the château name on the labels of second wines. Many of the older second wines originally had names reflecting some subsidiary château owned by the same proprietor (Figure 100). Prior to 1970, second wines were pretty obscure, and only a third had a name that could easily be identified with the château.

Many second wines were renamed in the 1990s to reflect the name of the château. New second wines almost always show a close relationship. Most second wines now have a description such as Moulin, Petit, Pavillon, Fleur, Chapelle, Cadet, Benjamin, Dauphin, accompanied by some play on the château's name (Figure 101). [24]

One factor in naming second wines has been the tightening of regulations concerning nomenclature. The regulations are not without

Figure 100

The label gives no indication that Haut Bages Averous is the second wine of Château Lynch Bages.

2005

CHÂTEAU
HAUT-BAGES
AVEROUS

PAUILLAC
APPELLATION PAUILLAC CONTROLÉE

A CAZES PROPRIETAIRE À PAUILLAC

Figure 101

The second wine of Château Margaux flaunts its connection with the grand vin.

ambiguity, but terms such as "château" are reserved for an "exploitation viticole," which is interpreted by the FGVB (Fédération des Grands Vins de Bordeaux) to exclude second wines. Grandfathering provisions allow continued use of these terms where they were in regular use more than ten years before the new regulations. The regulations do not distinguish between second wines, third wines, or commercial marques, but in principle, when you see "château" on a label, it should mean that the wine is really the principal product of the producer.[25]

Châteaux may have commercial marques for wine produced from grapes sourced from outside of their appellation. By far the most successful of the commercial marques is Mouton Cadet, which with annual sales of 15 million bottles far outpaces Château Mouton Rothschild's 250,000 bottles, let alone the tiny production of the second wine, Le Petit Mouton.[26] In terms of contribution to the cash flow of Groupe Baron Philippe de Rothschild, this makes Mouton Cadet by far the most important, with close to two thirds of revenues. Mouton Cadet is an unusual case, however. Long established, since it began as a declassified second wine in 1934, it now even has brand extension into other products (i.e., cigars), a unique situation for a Bordeaux brand.

Confusion reigns where château names are concerned. Emphasizing the fact that a château is a brand, most have protected their marques by registering the names that they use. More than 12,000 names appear on Bordeaux labels, although the number of actual properties is somewhat less. Châteaux are no longer supposed to sell the same wine under different names (often enough a separate name will be used to supply a supermarket to make it appear that the wine is unique), but the rule is honored as much in the breach as in the observance.

A rough count suggests that more than 10% of labels purporting to be châteaux may really be no more than subsidiary marques or alternative bottlings. Out of 7000 "châteaux" listed by the FGVB, more than 1000 have addresses and phone numbers that belong to another château.[27] In some cases, as many as 10 or 20 "châteaux" all have the same address and phone number! Of course, some of these could simply be multiple properties all owned by one proprietor but managed from a single address; but one wonders how many of these "châteaux" are really phantom names used for bottling the same wine for different markets.[28] And this could just be the tip of the iceberg.

The FGVB is supposed to be auditing names to restore some validity to the notion that a wine labeled Château Quelquechose is in fact a unique representation of the vineyards of that château. In the meantime, no one really knows exactly how many châteaux there really are. Mythical château have been damaging the reputation of Bordeaux for more than a century, and it's really time to clean up the mess.

The association of "château" with quality is deeply rooted in Bordeaux, and there are very few wines from the prestigious appellations that do not use the description. The glow of their success created a halo effect in which even common AOC Bordeaux tended to be sold under a château name. (During the 1970s, the term "châteaumania" was used to describe the negociants' difficulties in selling Bordeaux brands as opposed to wines labeled "Château."[29])

During the 1990s, château-labeled wines represented about 50% of all AOC Bordeaux. They began to decline as sales increased in supermarkets at the expense of specialist stores. Things are now quite different at the level of generic Bordeaux, where only about 25% is sold under the name of a château, with the rest divided roughly 2:1 between brands developed by negociants and house brands produced specifically for supermarket chains.[30] At least with the brands it is pretty clear what you are getting, but it remains true you have only a relatively small chance that a generic Bordeaux labeled Château Quelquechose really represents the sole product of an individual château.

Forward and Fruity

Market forces have propelled the growth of second wines. As one proprietor said: "What we heard from Bordeaux wine merchants [about 5 years ago] was that traditional wines capable of withstanding 20 years [of maturation] were pretty unsellable, the times and customer taste having changed... We decided to take half of the crop and make out of it a product more suited to the supposed market. Easier to drink, lighter, less wood, ready to drink sooner."[31]

Figure 102

Comparison between content of Merlot in grand vin and second wine for the 2006 vintage on the left bank.[33]

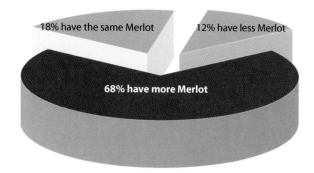

18% have the same Merlot   12% have less Merlot

68% have more Merlot

The most important difference in production of second wines versus grand vins is in the oak régime. Almost all châteaux use more new oak, and give grand vins longer maturation in oak, than for second wines.[32] Second wines are therefore ready to bottle (and to release on the market) quite a bit sooner.

The mix of grape varieties is another significant difference between grand vins and second wines. The wines of the left bank usually have Merlot as a minority component, with the more austere Cabernet Sauvignon as the dominant variety. Most left bank châteaux use more Merlot in the second wine (Figure 102). This gives the wine a fruitier, more forward and approachable style, meeting the objective of making the second wine easier to drink sooner. (The situation is different on the right bank, however, where Merlot is the dominant variety in both grand vins and second wines.)

Putting the change in cépage makeup on to a quantitative basis, the grand vins of the left bank on average have 52% Cabernet Sauvignon, but second wines have 44%.[34] This casts some doubt on how far the left bank second wines really represent the style of the grand vins. Indeed, although the proportion of Cabernet Sauvignon in the vineyards of the Grand Cru Classés has decreased in the past twenty years, the average proportion of Cabernet Sauvignon in their grand vins has changed much less.[35] The change in plantings at the Grand Crus may reflect the increased focus on second wines more than comprising a change in the grand vin.

More Is Less

The majority of châteaux with a wine selling above $15 and with production levels above 10,000 cases per year produce a second wine, but a significant minority chooses not to do so. Their reasons are sometimes practical and sometimes philosophical.

Châteaux without second wines tend to have lower production levels. Indeed, one common reason for deciding against a second wine is that production is too small. François Mitjavile at Château Tertre Rôteboeuf in St. Emilion argues that second wines are useful for properties where there is significant heterogeneity in the terroir; but where the terroir is relatively homogenous "it is more interesting not to make a selection for a second wine, because production of a single wine best expresses vintage character."[36]

The most common argument against producing a second wine is that a proprietor wants to concentrate on producing the single best wine possible. Along these lines, some argue that a second wine would diminish the reputation of the grand vin. Indeed, there is some vigorous dissension from the prevalent concept of second wines. A typical dissenting view: "how can a professional make wine that is only partly good. There can be multiple châteaux or different crus, but second wine? It is sure that second wines are a trick." Skepticism about motives is not uncommon: "Second wines originated when Grand Cru Classés found a means of diversifying their line while simultaneously rarifying production of the grand vin... the subject may be taboo at the grand properties." Derision about third wines is common: "Officially the best properties speak only of their second wines, but the majority utilize two or three commercial marques with the name of the château... When one speaks of a second wine today, one speaks also of third and fourth labels, which is somewhat astonishing, especially at the top properties."[37]

A decision against producing a second wine does not necessarily imply that all production goes into the single wine. Two thirds of châteaux that have no second wine routinely declassify some lots, generally to be sold off in bulk, but in some cases to be bottled although not sold under the name of the château.[38] So declassification is not a determinative factor in distinguishing châteaux that do or do not have second wines. In fact, some part of the increase in second wines may have come not at the expense of the grand vin, but as a more profitable use for lots that otherwise would have been sold off in bulk.

The substantial increase in second wines since 1980 should be seen against the context of an ~50% increase in overall production in Bordeaux over the period. The production of the second wine has limited the increase in production of the grand vin rather than resulted in any decrease.

Are Second Wines Second Best?

I remember once reading a book on wine that stated, "taste is the least important feature of wine." Whatever point the author was trying to make quite escaped me. Certainly there are other important features—aroma is no doubt of equal importance—but when we are talking about wine, the crucial thing is what we experience when we drink it, however that is described. Taste will do just fine as a descriptor. So how do second wines fare, or to be more precise, how does the taste of second wines compare with that of other wines at the same price level?

Opinions vary widely. Skepticism is common. "Second wine… is sadly too often the dumping ground for… unsuccessful cuves," Ginestet remarked in his book on Pauillac.[39] Similarly the Revue du Vin de France commented that "tasting has demonstrated that many proprietors have little respect for their second wines. Many suffer from lack of maturity, dilution, and faults." 47 out of 105 second wines tasted were judged "mediocre… …and should have been declassified as generics"[40]. On the other hand, second wines have become virtually a necessity in order to maintain credibility for the quality of the grand vin: "All large, ambitious properties now produce second wines… The hallmark of mediocre Bordeaux properties of any size is the refusal to make a second wine… [second] wines often offer excellent value."[41]

At the end of the day, irrespective of the origins of the grapes in the second wine, the question becomes whether the wine genuinely offers the consumer a chance to experience the style of the grand vin at a cheaper price and earlier stage, or whether the second wine is effectively trading on the reputation of the grand vin, possibly selling at an inflated price without offering any special value. Second wines tend to trade at a price level one or two notches below the grand vin; for example, the second wines of the first growths are usually available at price levels corresponding to the second growths, the second wines of the Deuxième Crus sell with the third or fourth growths, and so on.

At tastings I held specifically to compare second wines with other wines of the same price from the same commune, both professional and amateur tasters concluded that most often they preferred the other wine.[42] There was a slight, but not very significant difference, in second wines being regarded as just a little readier to drink than alternatives. The moral is pretty clear: if you want a wine at a certain price from a given appellation, you are usually going to do better to avoid a second wine, whose price reflects the glory of the grand vin.

A Sheep in Wolf's Clothing?

The expansion of second wines has created a new significant economic factor in Bordeaux. On average a second wine sells for a third of the price of the grand vin (with a wide spread from 20-70%), and accounts for roughly 15% of revenue to the château.[43]

An economic breakdown of Bordeaux shows that red AOC Bordeaux accounts for half of production, but because of its low price, only a third of revenues (Figure 103). The Médoc and Graves are much more important in terms of revenue than production. White wines have a small slice of the cake by either criterion. Second wines occupy quite a large proportion of production on both left and right banks, and have an economic significance greater than white wines.[44] And increases in the prices of grand vins resulting from improvements in quality and (at the top level) from maintaining scarcity, may further increase the impact of second wines.

The creation of second wines peaked in the period 1985-1995 and may now be near exhaustion, since many of the châteaux who do not have second wines express a strong preference for their present modus operandi. And the high proportions of production of second wines at leading châteaux in recent years suggests there is not much scope for further increase. Second wines have therefore now stabilized in the Bordeaux wine market.

Figure 103

Comparison of production and revenues shows that AOC Bordeaux produces the most wine but Médoc and Graves generates almost as much revenue. [45]

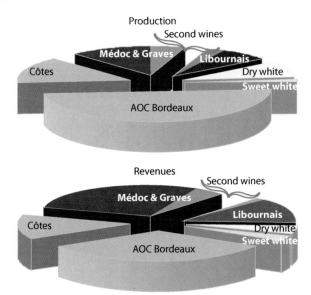

The growth of second wines as a new category has effectively occurred outside of the tight rules that govern the appellations, as indicated by the lack of distinction between second wines, third wines, or commercial marques in naming regulations. Although an attempt has been made to prevent confusion with grand vins, the consumer would certainly benefit from a clearer distinction between second wines and other products. It would be good to limit a château to using its name on only its grand vin and second wine, and excluding its use on wines that come from lesser appellations (such as an Haut-Médoc produced by a château in one of the communes). And it would be helpful to distinguish second wines that originate by declassification from those that are really second marques. Of course, this would require a more precise definition of "second wine," which is not a simple matter.

12

Plus Ça Change

IT'S AN AGE-OLD QUESTION IN FRANCE: is it more important for a wine to be authentic or for it to be good? The authorities come down resoundingly for the first option, but the response of those charged with fraud has stayed the same over the centuries: no one was cheated because the wine had been improved.

There's many a slip between barrel and bottle. Adulteration has always been a thorny issue in Bordeaux. In the 19th century it was the norm; indeed, part of the responsibility of negociants was to "adjust" their wine for the tastes of the market. What significance could the 1855 classification have had for a consumer who had only ever tasted the classed growths "improved" by the negociants' efforts? But by the start of the 20th century, it was recognized that there was a greater interest in maintaining authenticity. When the regulations of the Appellation Contrôlée came into effect, it was a criminal offense to blend in foreign wine or indeed to label any wine as having an origin other than the stated appellation.

In spite of the most intense welter of regulations in the world, Bordeaux (and other AOC regions also, of course) have long had problems with fraud. The most egregious go far back into the history of winemaking: passing off the wine of other regions (or countries) as coming from Bordeaux itself. The major frauds have been more subtle: presenting wine from an inferior appellation in the region as coming from a better appellation. This has been a perennial problem in both Bordeaux and Burgundy.

Most recently, driven perhaps by the fantastic rise in prices for the top wines, outright frauds have been committed by sticking prestigious labels on bottles of plonk, and (it is alleged) faking very old bottles of wine to sell at high prices at auction. But these frauds affect only a small number of purchasers of very expensive wines; more worrisome for the general consumer is the continued occurrence of the habitual fraud, when wine is either adulterated or given a better label. As recently as the 1950s, when Beaujolais was producing less than 500,000 hl per year, it was estimated that the Paris region alone consumed more than 2 million hl annually.[1] One recent estimate is that "probably about one third of wine sold since the 1920s has been fraudulent due to illegal additives, and it is highly unlikely that it is ever detected."[2] Fraud is not exactly a new problem; Pliny the Elder complained in 77 C.E. that "genuine, unadulterated wine is not to be had now, not even by the nobility."[3]

Hermitaging the Wine

Today Hermitage is one of the top appellations of the Northern Rhône, producing wonderful, long-lived wines from the Syrah grape. The best are cult items selling at auctions for hundreds of dollars. But a century ago it had a very different reputation and significance. To "hermitage" the wines of Bordeaux (or Burgundy) described the practice of adding wine from the Rhône to increase color and alcoholic strength.

Adding foreign wine to the local production was for long the established practice; remember that wine was not bottled by the producers, but was bought in bulk and then matured by the negociants, who prided themselves on their ability to suit the wine to the customer. The wine was said to be "travaillé" (worked). Blending was important enough for trade disputes to occur over who had the rights to perform it.

Arguments about the legitimacy of the process have been more or less continuous. As early as the 17th century, laws were passed to prevent even the blending of wine from the Haut-Pays (the surrounding region) with those from the environs of Bordeaux itself. Over the next three centuries, at various times such laws were repealed (as restricting the freedom of the merchant to produce the best wine) and reinstated (to protect the reputation of the region).

Following an argument about blending wines from outside Bordeaux with the local production, Colbert (the minister of finance under Louis XIV) tried to ban the practice in 1683, but then, following protests from the merchants, concluded that "given that the blending satisfies the tastes of the English and the Dutch, the merchants may have better reason than the lawyers."[4]

In the 18th century, the Irish merchants, the forerunners of some of the important negociant firms, tried to insist that only unblended wines could be exported, so that they could perform the blending upon receipt in Ireland. This resulted in an edict against blending in 1764,[5] which interestingly referred to previous regulations going back to the 1600s and even earlier. This battle was not finally to be resolved until into the early years of the 20th century.

A commentator in Bordeaux in 1744 noted, "everyone knows that Spanish wine is a great resource because its qualities of vigor, body, color complement the wines of Bordeaux and the English have always used it, obtaining it directly from Spain in times of peace in order to mix a small amount with the wine of Bordeaux according to the English taste."[6] When the English-Spanish war prevented such imports, the merchants turned to importing the wine from Spain directly to Bordeaux; it is possible that the practice of blending Spanish wine in Bordeaux itself dates from this period.[7]

In the 18th century, the wines used to improve the local production were called "vins médecins" or "vins d'aide" and typically came from Alicante or Benicarlo in Spain. When vintages were good in the South of France, wine from Rivesaltes (close to the Spanish border) might be used instead. By the 19th century, the source of foreign wine had shifted to Hermitage, and according to one writer in 1827, 80% of the production of Hermitage usually was bought by the Bordeaux wine trade.[8] And it was by no means the lesser wines of Hermitage that were sent up to Bordeaux. "The first growths are sent to Bordeaux to be mixed with the clarets which are made up for the English market, and only the second growths are sold in the trade as Hermitage," according to a popular report in 1874.[9]

One contemporary description of a recipe for production in 1765 was this: "I have always altered my quantities of the mixture in proportion to the years, and body, color etc. of my wines. I have given from 4 or 5 to 7 or 8 of Spanish in a middling year; or as far as 15 or 16 gallons to the hogshead [46 gallons] when the season was very bad and the wine thin and green."[10] The same commentator, however, noted that although wines of the Médoc and Graves might be mixed, vintages were usually kept separate!

Views about these practices varied. Lamothe noted in 1809 that "the knowledge that the wine has been matured without fraud in the cellars at Latour must count for something with the purchasers."[11] Not everyone was so concerned: at Château Margaux, the wine of a poor year was blended with wine from a property in the palus owned by the same proprietor. However, irrespective of details, the practice of improving the wines in poor vintages seems to have been universal, even at the first growths, at least through the first half of the 19th century.

Adulteration was no secret. A well known English wine writer, Cyrus Redding, remarked in 1833 that "Bordeaux wine in England and in Bordeaux scarcely resemble each other. The merchants are obliged to "work" the wines before they are shipped, or, in other words, to mingle stronger wines with them, such as Hermitage, or Cahors, which is destructive almost wholly of the bouquet, color, and aroma of the original wine."[12] Thomas Jefferson was highly skeptical of the negociants' activities: "The vigneron never adulterates his wine, but on the contrary gives it the most perfect and pure care possible. But when once a wine has been into a merchant's hands, it never comes out unmixed. This being the basis of their trade, no degree of honesty, of personal friendship or of kindred prevents it."[13]

Adulteration by no means stopped with blending wines: "[Each negociant] had his own recipe. One used an extract of elderberries, another grew blackberries, a third had recourse to an infusion made from hollyhocks or other herbal flowers."[14]

From Fraud to Regulation

The decade of devastation after phylloxera arrived in France increased the stakes enormously. Production in France overall fell by more than half between 1870 and 1880.[15] Production in Bordeaux collapsed by about the same proportion.[16] Lost production was replaced by cheap wine imported from elsewhere in Europe, more than 90% of it from Spain. Adulteration became so blatant as to become a matter of public comment and news reports. All the way across the Atlantic, the New York Times headlined an article in 1881 "French Wines of Today: A great deficiency supplied by adulteration."[17] The United States Vice Consul in Bordeaux commented, "the Bordeaux cheap wine importers mix, fix, flavor, color, and perfume [imported wines], adding water or alcohol as the case may require. This fraudulent operation is carried on without any doubt, and even *sans gène*... Cargo wine is generally mixed and 'doctored' on the wharves or near the railway station, where the wines from Spain and Portugal are discharged."

A striking change in the relative values of exported and imported wine indicates the scale of the problem for France as a whole. Between 1870 and 1879, the value of exported wine stayed quite steady, in spite of the fall in production. But the value of imported wine rose sharply.[18] Imports of Spanish wine into Bordeaux doubled in a single year between 1879 and 1880. As the New York Times commented, the figures provided "the most striking proof of the manner in which 'French' wines are now made in other European countries". The quality was pretty miserable: the Consular clerk to the embassy in Paris referred to "the abominable mixtures now exported to the United States".[19]

So long as vineyards in France were decimated by phylloxera, but the plague had not reached elsewhere in Europe, the pattern was set for substitution with cheap imports. Many of these wines entered through the port of Bordeaux. Often enough they left Bordeaux relabeled as wines of the Médoc. A vigneron protested, in an epic poem of 1600 verses:

"Fraud is everywhere…
At Pauillac, the crooks unload by hundreds
with cargoes from overseas…
The exotic wines are baptized at Bordeaux
and all depart as wines of the Médoc"[20]

Annual exports from Bordeaux were vastly in excess of the average local production, a situation that persisted through the first decade of the 20th century. Nathaniel Johnston, an important negociant and owner of Château Ducru Beaucaillou, commented in 1901 that "the Gironde produces an average of 2.5 to 3 million hectoliters [but] the quantity sold by the Département is 6-7 million hectoliters."[21] Château proprietors and honest negociants denounced the unscrupulous, but to little avail. The frauds went so far as to invent imaginary châteaux on the labels. (Not that much has changed. Even today, the authorities are still trying to stamp out the use of non-existent château names on labels.)

Coupage (blending the local wines with foreign wines to increase the volume) was common. "Coupage," literally meaning cutting, came to mean blending in the pejorative sense of dilution or adulteration, as opposed to "assemblage" which refers to the blending of the different varieties grown locally (such as Cabernet Sauvignon or Merlot) before a wine is bottled.

The fraud did not confine itself to mere substitution of foreign wine, but sometimes used "wines" that were no more than industrial fabrications from alcohol, tartaric acid, flavoring, and so on. There were substantial sales of "sugar wine," an appalling product made by fermenting sugar and adding flavoring compounds. At the peak of the crisis caused by the loss of production resulting from the phylloxera devastation (1885-1890), as much as 10-20% of total wine production in France[22] may have come from fermenting dried raisins that had been mixed with water and a little sugar (a large part from industrial establishments in the Parisian region; if you weren't going to grow grapes, why not eliminate the costs of transport to the consumers).[23] There seem to have been no limits to the fraud, and little legal restraint

Figure 104

Vignerons protested in Montpellier in 1907. The slogan on the barrel says "war on fraud, keep wine natural."

unless there was direct imitation of an important château—one court case resulted from counterfeits of Mouton Rothschild.

These local difficulties, coupled with the appearance of faked wine from the classified growths on foreign markets, led to the creation of the Syndicat des Grands Crus Classés du Médoc in 1901. The Syndicat urged the negociants (who were bottling most of the wine in this period) to use corks and labels clearly identifying the château to give a mark of authenticity. The Union of Negociants responded with a request that bottling at the château should be stopped. The issue went to and fro for some years, in the end settled by an agreement that when wine was bottled at the château, the labels, capsules, and corks would carry the legend "mis en bouteilles au château," but without any other compulsory steps to ensure authenticity.[24]

The problems were not confined to Bordeaux, of course, and the most vehement protests occurred in the revolt of the vignerons in the Languedoc in 1907 (Figure 104). By then, the problem was that, although production had recovered in France, the wines could not compete with the cheap European imports (to which considerable quantities from Algeria had been added in the past decade) or fraudulent products. Badly managed by the authorities, deaths resulted from police action against the protesting vignerons.

Economic pressure led to rising concern about fraud at the start of the 20th century. The first law on the repression of frauds was passed in 1905, defining types of fraud for food products, especially with regards to wine. The law depended on the subsequent establishment of local regulations, on which it proved difficult to obtain consensus. The Syndicat of Grand Crus argued for a regulation that would require wines labeled as Bordeaux to be produced only in the Departément of the Gironde. The negociants opposed the idea, ostensibly because of practical difficulties in tracking their stocks.[25] They succeeded in delaying its implementation until 1912, when finally the law restricted the name Bordeaux to wines from the region.[26] An era of fraud ended in 1913 when the first negociants were sent to prison for adulterating wine under the new regulations.

As the result of an initiative by Baron Philippe, château bottling became the norm at Mouton Rothschild, d'Yquem, and the Premier Grand Cru Classés over the period 1923-1925. They agreed that "purchasers must leave the wines in the chais of the château, at their expense, risks, and perils, including that of fire, until the moment of bottling, which will be obligatory at the château for the entire harvest."[27] This was the beginning of the en primeur system, with wine sold after the harvest but not released by the châteaux until it had matured. Slowly château bottling extended down the hierarchy, although it was not until 1967 that it was made mandatory for the cru classés, and not until 1990 that it became generally compulsory.[28]

The WineGate Scandal

The heart of the Syndicat's proposal in 1905 was that each lot of wine should be accompanied by a certificate of origin. Certificates identifying wines with a source in the Département of the Gironde would be white, to distinguish them from certificates for other wines, which would be red. Proprietors would declare their harvests in order to obtain the acquit blanc (white certificate). The certificate would have detachable coupons that could be used to identify a lot of wine when it was transported.

Half a century later, certificates of origin accompanied all wines in France. AOC wines had an acquit vert (green certificate), while table wines had a white certificate. The certificate was issued by the producer's local tax office, where the original remained. A copy of the certificate with detachable coupons travels with every lot of wine. When the wine is moved from one location to another, for example from a grower to a negociant, an approved shipper can stamp a coupon, detach it, and return the copies to his local tax office and to INAO.

The authorities thought the system was infallible. "Our system of control has been perfected so that [fraud] is impossible. All these stories of coupages [blending], of wines from the Midi that are sold as Beaujolais or Bordeaux, are nothing but a tissue of ridiculous lies," said Pierre Perromat, the President of INAO in 1973.[29] But there was a fatal flaw in the system.

The AOC of the wine is noted on the coupons, but the color of the wine was stated only on the original that remained in the originating tax office. This was to be the basis for an ingenious fraud that convulsed Bordeaux in the 1970s. The Affaire Bert started with a small time negociant, Pierre Bert, and spread to one of the oldest and most prestigious negociants, Cruse et Fils.[30, 31]

Pierre Bert was a broker who, after a history of wine frauds, early in 1973 set up a small negociant business that he called Balan et cie (after the name of his driver, Serge Balan). Like many others, he was under financial pressure because in 1972 he had sold wine that he did not actually possess, expecting prices to fall before he needed to deliver. Confounded by the rising market, he was faced with a ruinous situation in the form of a deficit of 300,000 francs.

Balan et cie obtained a franking machine from the local tax office. (Machines were routinely available to reliable negociants.) The secret of their success was that they simultaneously purchased red table wine and white AOC Bordeaux. The white wine came with an acquit vert, and the red wine came with an acquit blanc. By swapping the acquits, that is by stamping the acquit vert when the red wine was sold and by using the acquit blanc for the white wine, Bert could sell the red wine as AOC Bordeaux and the white wine as table wine (Figure 105).

Figure 105

Bert bought white Bordeaux AOC, which he sold for a loss as table wine. But he made a profit by buying red table wine that was sold as Bordeaux AOC.

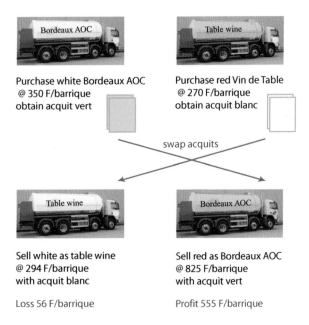

Purchase white Bordeaux AOC
@ 350 F/barrique
obtain acquit vert

Purchase red Vin de Table
@ 270 F/barrique
obtain acquit blanc

swap acquits

Sell white as table wine
@ 294 F/barrique
with acquit blanc

Loss 56 F/barrique

Sell red as Bordeaux AOC
@ 825 F/barrique
with acquit vert

Profit 555 F/barrique

The price differential between white AOC Bordeaux and white table wine was small, about 10%, and Bert took a corresponding loss on that transaction. But the differential on the red wines was much larger, with AOC Bordeaux selling for about 3 times the table wine. So Bert trebled his money on that side of the transaction. A single tanker trundling from warehouse to warehouse where the switches were made was sufficient to move the equivalent of 4 million bottles and make several million francs of profits in a period of four months.

The stakes increased when Bert recruited Cruse, a major negociant, as a client. They set up a trade in which Cruse purchased the fake red AOC wine at a price some 15% below market, while simultaneously selling the same amount of vin de table (of which they had an excess) to Bert. "We will deal with you," the Cruses said to Bert, "on condition that we can exchange wines for current consumption [table wines] for the appellation wines that you deliver to us"[32]. In due course, the system was simplified to the extent in which no wine actually changed hands, although for the sake of appearances a single tanker load of wine made the rounds from Balan to Cruse and back again. Essentially, Cruse received an acquit vert from Bert in exchange for an acquit blanc, but the wine stayed in the tanker. This enabled Cruse directly to sell their excess of vin de table as AOC Bordeaux.

The fraud was uncovered quite rapidly, it was claimed as the result of a tip to the tax authorities, who then inspected Bert's records. Nothing quite like this had ever been seen before; although they knew there was a fraud, it took several months before they were able to disentangle the details. The question of whether there was complicity or whether the Cruse's (and others) were innocent victims was resolved for the tax authorities by Inspector Destrau: "Bert sold Bordeaux red wine that was not in his chai, which at that time mathematically could only have contained white wine. Consequently, clients having bought these red wines could not [claim to] be exploited in receiving the white wine. Therefore, they could only be perfectly consenting accomplices. Q.E.D."[33]

In the meantime, the situation descended into farce when the tax inspectors appeared at Cruse headquarters on June 28 and demanded to take an inventory. There had for years been a gentleman's agreement between the negociants and the tax authorities that due notice would be given of inspections, and on these grounds, Cruse refused to allow the inspectors entry to the cellars. It took another two months before the inspectors were able to check the records, starting on August 28, when it soon became apparent that the fraud practiced by Bert was only a small part of the problem, and that Cruse had habitually sold the wine of one appellation as coming from another, labeled the same wine as coming from different appellations, sold the same wine under different château names, or had changed vintages, as well as promoting vin de table to AOC.[34] There were also accusations of chemical adulteration. Descriptions of vats were give-aways, such as "could be Beaujolais for the American market."

As so often the case in France, politics were never far from the surface. At that time, the contenders for the succession to French political leadership were Jacques Chaban-Delmas, a major figure in Bordeaux politics, to whom the Cruses were close, and his rival Valéry Giscard-d'Estaing. In connection with their rivalry, the story of the investigation was leaked to the press, and (with Watergate in mind) rapidly became known as Winegate. The investigation moved to the national level and in due course (with Giscard d'Estaing now Président of France) to a prosecution.

The trial started in October 1974, with Bert and the Cruses as the principal targets. Bert was accused of adulterating wine as well as changing its appellation. He defended himself vigorously on the grounds that, whether his actions were legal or not, they were no more than accustomed practice in improving the wine—"baptizing" was the term he used. He took the classic defense that he had never received any complaints from any of his customers. In one exchange that became famous, Bert conceded that he had mixed white wines with red, because "a little white wine does not harm the quality when there is too much tannin in the red." "Yes, but it's not legal," said the judge. "No, but it's good," Bert answered. When the verdict came in December, only Bert received a jail sentence jail; the Cruses were given suspended sentences. With typical insouciance, when the sentence was handed down, Bert turned to the tax inspectors and said, "you've won, let me buy you a glass of champagne."[35]

The fraud occurred in the context of an overheated, speculative market. Prices rocketed in 1972 to 1973 and then collapsed in 1974 (Chapter 7). Many negociants were faced with the need to purchase wine at inflated prices in order to fulfill commitments made previously to sell at lower prices. The collapse of the negociants owed more to these fundamental economics than to the fraud, but the question has never been answered: was the fraud unique or was it the tip of the iceberg?

The Belgian Connection

The end of February 2002 was a black week for Bordeaux. Three alleged frauds occupied the local newspapers, which were full of headlines such as "Bordeaux in Torment."

The first was the ancient problem of mislabeling: no fewer than six negociants were accused of selling wines that were falsely labeled "mis en bouteilles au château." Between 1994 and 1998, the houses of Cordier, Ginestet, GVG, CVBG, Mestrezat & Domaines, and Dulong were alleged to have bought wines from a small negociant in Pian-Médoc that were sold as Cru Bourgeois, but actually had been blended with wine from the Languedoc. The large negociants did not directly participate in the fraud, but had been negligent in supplying the labels and corks without making any further checks on their use.

Déjà vu all over again: a small negociant provided mislabeled wines to large, reputable negociants; the tax authorities received a tip off from an unknown source; the small negociant, Jacques Hemmer, defended himself by saying "I have never had any complaint from negociants on the quality of the wine"; and the case took the best part of a decade to come to court. Jacques Hemmer received a prison sentence of 18 months; the larger negociants received derisory fines.[36, 37]

Much further down the wine chain, the second fraud concerned fakes of old vintages of Pétrus. This was the least significant in terms of the amount of wine involved, but high profile given the nature of the wine. Early in 2000, Sébastien Laffitte, the young owner of Laffitte Grands Vins, had purchased a lot of false Pétrus (vintages 1982, 1989, 1990) for €131,000. The wine was sold to a dealer in Paris, who then encountered suspicion when he attempted to sell the wine in London. An investigation was started, at which it emerged that Laffitte had purchased the wine "from a man he met in the street." Curiously the investigation then stopped. It revived in 2002, when it turned out that the wine had in fact been Spanish.[38]

The third was the start of the Geens scandal. Under Belgian ownership, Geens was a sizeable player in Bordeaux, with direct ownership of 800 hectares of vineyards and 16 châteaux, as well as owning vineyards in the Aude and Herault. The affair started with a falling out between the company and its former manager, Isabel Teles-Pinto, who had been fired in January. Her allegations that there had been fraud in selling the wines from one of Geens' subsidiaries, Vignoble Rocher Cap de Rive, were met by counter-allegations that she had been involved in financial improprieties.

The accusations were that Geens was involved in selling wine that had been marked for distillation, changing appellations, and using false names of châteaux. The fraud was alleged to go right to Roger Geens at the head of the company, who remained untouchable in the refuge of Monaco (not that any effort was made to reach him anyway). Most of the mislabeled wine was exported to Belgium. Support for the claims was provided by other former employees, implying that several millions of bottles were involved. According to the local newspaper, no fewer than 200 agents of the customs, the wine authorities, and the police were milling about in the chais of Geens, but by 2006 virtually nothing had been established by judicial investigation, let alone any action taken.[39]

While the French authorities were still proceeding with their usual speed (electrons moving at the speed of sound), action finally occurred in Belgium in 2007, when a large investigation was launched in the home location of the Geens group at Aarschot. Sixty policemen invaded Geens headquarters, among other activities seizing chemicals from a well-equipped laboratory. Some of the chief officers of the company were held in prison for three months, the company was placed in liquidation, and an administrator was appointed to run the group.

The Belgian investigation finally provoked a flurry of activity in France. In February 2007, the FGVB (Fédération des Syndicats des Grands Vins de Bordeaux) brought a civil lawsuit. There was an interesting justification for the delay: "At this time [of the original fraud], the wine industry was going through an economic crisis which relegated the fraud to secondary importance," according to Yann Le Goaster, its Director.[40] The consumer group Que Choisir brought an action in September 2007, finally joined by INAO in November.

But how much wine was faked? Exactly what found its way on to the market in what form? We still don't know. Sound familiar?

The Ineffable Touch of INAO

The concept of appellations originated with the law of 1905 that attempted to suppress fraud in food and wine production. An organization was created in 1935 to administer the appellation laws, and this developed into INAO in 1947. INAO is responsible for defining specific regulations for each appellation: what land is included, what grapes may be grown, how the grapevines are tended, what treatments are permitted for the wine, and how it may be described. It is INAO, for example, that has determined whether French AOC wines are allowed to state the names of the grape varieties on the label.

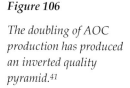

Figure 106

*The doubling of AOC
production has produced
an inverted quality
pyramid.*[41]

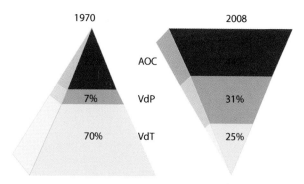

Even the original regulations went beyond guaranteeing authenticity into attempting to ensure a certain basic level of quality and conformance to traditional local character. Slowly they became extended to control every aspect of viticulture and vinification, sometimes with beneficial effects on quality, sometimes inhibiting necessary innovations. To be sure, we can argue whether INAO got the balance right, but at least you can say now that, unless outright fraud has occurred, an AOC wine comes from where it is supposed to.

The system has expanded greatly, from 70 AOCs at its inception to 467 today. (So right now there are almost as many AOCs in Bordeaux alone as there were in whole system when it was introduced.) In 1950, AOC wines accounted for 14% of French production; today this has grown to 44%. In fact, the pyramid of quality from AOC to Vin de Table has been completely inverted in the past half century. Compare the situations in 1970 and today (Figure 106). Vin de Table has shrunk from 70% of production to 25%, Vin de Pays has increased from a negligible proportion to one third, and AOC has doubled to become the largest single category of wine produced in France!

Nowhere are the effects more evident than in Bordeaux. Things seem to have been a bit erratic after the concept of appellations was introduced, with the declared proportion jumping from an initial 40% in the early 1920s, to around 80% in the early 1930s, and then reducing sharply after the second World War,[42] perhaps due to the more precise restrictions that had been introduced with the formal AOC system in 1936. From 1950 to the present, the proportion of AOC in Bordeaux has increased steadily, from just over 50% to essentially 100% (Figure 107).

The consequences of this enormous growth have been caricatured by Michel Bettane (one of France's most respected tasters): "When the AOC represented 10% of the volume of wine produced in France, there was an equivalent 10% of the population interested in the cultural and historic

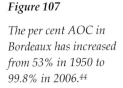

Figure 107

The per cent AOC in Bordeaux has increased from 53% in 1950 to 99.8% in 2006.[44]

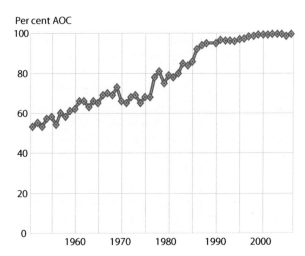

elements of wine. But the immense farce which consisted of transforming the entire wine-producing territory of France into AOC areas lead to the creation of false AOCs. Because a certain amount of professional discipline is required for a wine to genuinely deserve this label. Paying the producer less than €2 per bottle is not sufficient to maintain this discipline. So 90% of French wines carry an AOC label, but the products do not meet the label's criteria."[43]

Others question even more harshly the way INAO is run. Kermit Lynch, the well-known American importer of French wines, remarks: "At its inception, the system of appellation contrôlée was elaborated with admirable rigor. Here was a noble idea. But when they set their minds to it the French can outwhore anybody. Imagine someone trying to convince you that red is green, or a square, round. The current bunch in control of the INAO would have us accept the notion that a slope is flat. This is more than preposterous, it is legalized fraud."[45]

Part of the decline in the popularity of French wine is no doubt due to the complexity of the AOC regulations. Yet INAO's most recent attempt to modernize the system took the form of a proposal from its late President, René Renou, for the introduction of yet further complexity, by introducing a new classification of elite wine regions to be called the AOCE (Appellation d'Origine Contrôlée d'Excellence). Will the real AOC stand up, please! As a newsletter from the Rhône producer Vieux Télégraphe commented sarcastically, it would be more to the point to enforce existing regulations.

In 2007 INAO changed its name to Institut National de l'Origine et de la Qualité, to emphasize its role in determining quality. Up to the present, quality has been more implied than enforced: while INAO determines the potential quality of each wine-producing region, it does little to prevent wine that fails to meet the standard from being sold under the label of the appellation. It is more concerned with setting a basic minimum standard (although even that can be risible in some cases) than with encouraging quality.

Part of the procedure involved in describing a wine as AOC is the need to obtain an *agrément* (an official form stating that the wine conforms to AOC standards). The French consumer organization, QueChosir, pointed out sarcastically that it is hard to believe this confers the supposed guarantee of authenticity and quality, given that 98% of submissions were approved in 2004 and 99% in 2005.[46] Wines have sometimes been turned down for being too good, however, such as Pinot Noirs from Alsace which achieved real weight in a hot vintage, thereby failing to achieve the "typicity" of the usual rosé imitations.[47] Could it be that wines showing up the others are more of a threat to the system than those of low quality?

INAO is responsible for enforcing the regulations, although cases of fraud go to the tax and customs authorities for prosecution. Actions vary from surprising spurts of energy in the most trivial cases to violent lethargy in the most serious. The wine bureaucracy seems mostly to take its policy from the motto "don't scare the horses." It's unusual for large negociants or producers to be brought to task for abuse of the system; this could lead to the impression that abuse is widespread. It's more common for trivial misinterpretations of the regulations to be punished.

Compare the lethargy of the *affaire Geens* with the enthusiastic prosecution of Georges Duboeuf in Beaujolais. Geens may have mislabeled millions of bottles, but after six years the details are unclear. Georges Duboeuf single-handedly revitalized Beaujolais with his terroir-based quality bottlings of its best Crus, but in 2005, an error in his new computerized winery led to some Beaujolais Villages (a lower quality appellation) being mixed with some of the Crus. The employee who made the mistake was suspended, and the wine was not bottled. When the local tax and customs authorities heard about this, however, they rushed to prosecute, and a fine was imposed for "trickery and attempted trickery."[48] Duboeuf was a safe target: his record for quality is unimpeachable and little damage will be done to the reputation of French wines given the nature of the mistake. But to track millions of bottles mislabeled by a major negociant: that might cast doubt on the reliability of the system.

The Jefferson Scandal

At the time, it was the most expensive bottle of wine in the world. Sold at a wine auction at Christie's in 1985 for a bid of £105,000, it was hand-blown in dark green glass, and had no label, but had etched into the glass "1787, Lafitte, Th. J." (Figure 108). This was one of a cache of bottles supposedly discovered in a bricked-up cellar in Paris that had been bottled for Thomas Jefferson, who had become a collector of top Bordeaux during his period in Paris as America's Minister to France.

Several of these bottles were later purchased by Bill Koch, an American tycoon. Koch became suspicious about their authenticity when the Thomas Jefferson Foundation cast doubt on the provenance of the bottles. Investigations of the wine itself, using techniques such as carbon dating, were inconclusive in most cases (although they did suggest that at least some of the bottles contained wine one or two centuries younger than claimed), but an examination of the bottles suggested that they had been engraved using 20th century power tools.[50]

The seller of these, and many other old wines, was Hardy Rodenstock, a German living in Munich, who was originally a manager of pop music groups. Interested in wine as an amateur, he was a regular contributor to one of Germany's wine magazines (Alles über Wein) and a regular buyer at the London wine auctions. He acquired an almost mystical reputation for his ability to sniff out caves of old bottles. The

Figure 108

A bottle supposedly of Château Lafite from 1787 that was engraved for Thomas Jefferson. (Artist's impression.[49])

Jefferson collection, supposed to have been revealed when a hidden cellar was exposed during the destruction of an 18th century house in Paris, was only one of these. Other included a supply of Pétrus in large format bottles, reported to be from an English cellar, a cache of old Bordeaux in Venezuela, and a cellar in Russia of first growth Bordeaux that was claimed to have belonged to the Tsar. By the 1980s, Rodenstock had become a professional wine trader, and hosted a series of high-end tastings at which a seemingly endless series of extraordinary old bottles appeared. One of these tastings went through 125 vintages of Château d'Yquem.

The Jefferson cellar supposedly contained about a hundred bottles, including many of the first growths, and a couple of dozen bottles engraved with the initials "Th. J." Rodenstock has never revealed the source of the bottles, in spite of considerable pressure after the problems emerged. Believing that the bottles were fakes, Koch started an extensive investigation, not only to analyze the bottles, but also to search into Rodenstock's background. The investigation discovered that Rodenstock had changed his name, revealed various legal problems in Rodenstock's past, and culminated in a lawsuit in New York. There was of course an argument as to whether this was the appropriate jurisdiction, and to date the lawsuit has not brought any final resolution to the question of authenticity.

Several collectors have been burned by buying very expensive old bottles that could be traced back to Rodenstock and which now have dubious value. Bottles from Rodenstock were sold by Farr Wine Merchants in London, The Wine Library in California, and at various auction houses in London and New York. Finally this has led to sensitivity on the question of fraud, and the auction houses are refusing to accept suspect bottles. Is the apparent increase in the number of fakes due to fraud becoming more profitable with the rise in prices or has it been going on all along and only now is anyone paying attention?

Provenance has finally become important in wine, as it has always been in the art market. I remember that when I asked Christies in London about the provenance of some wine in an auction in the early 1980s, initially they did not understand the question, and then they were surprised if not slightly insulted. Today it's the first question anyone asks when an old wine is offered for sale. Where did you get it, and how far back can you trace it?

Sometimes a fraud comes to light only because a bottle appears that could not have existed. Laurent Ponsot was surprised to discover vintages of the grand cru Clos St. Denis from the 1940s through the 1960s offered for sale at the Acker Merrall auction in New York in April 2008;

the wine supposedly originated from Domaine Ponsot in Burgundy, but this was impossible since the domain did not produce this wine until 1982.[51] That wine was withdrawn from the auction.

Producers are turning to special bottles and labels to prevent their current offerings from being faked, but what is to be done about old vintages? Taking a leaf from the fine art market, techniques are being developed for authenticating wine by using ion beams to measure the radiation spectrum. Of course, you have to be able to distinguish between the bottle and its contents, and the technique is only as good as the basic reference source: it's no use unless you have a wine that is guaranteed to be authentic to use for comparison.

With the very old wines, more is at stake than the authenticity of the particular bottles. Over the years, Rodenstock's supply of rare bottles included a significant number from the 18th and 19th centuries. Indeed, one writer pointed out that much of our knowledge about the supposed taste of these rare old wines depends on bottles provided by Rodenstock.[52] It now seems that, at the very least, the basis for all this knowledge is highly questionable. In fact, do we really know anything now about the taste of 19th century wines?

13

Rational Classification

No subject is more controversial, not to say inflammatory, in Bordeaux than the 1855 classification. Witness the reaction of Jean-Hubert Delon, proprietor of second growth Léoville Las Cases, when his château was omitted from a coffee table book commissioned by the Conseil des Grands Crus Classés to commemorate the 150th anniversary of the classification.[1] Château Léoville Las Cases was not included in the book because M. Delon (well known for his view that Léoville Las Cases was producing wine at first growth level) had withdrawn from the Conseil in 1998, "because it had become a means for commercial promotion of a disputable classification, and thereby for misinforming the consumer."[2] All the same, to be left out of the book of Grand Cru Classés, well that was serious enough for M. Delon to threaten legal action. (The symbol of Léoville Las Cases is a lion, with the motto "I do not attack unless provoked." Evidently the omission was sufficient provocation.)

Is the 1855 classification the most effective marketing tool ever? After a century and a half it has its admirers and its detractors, it is controversial, but still it looms over the reputation of the top châteaux of the Médoc. What is its contact with reality, whom has it benefited, whom has it damaged?

A Clash of Cultures

Whether they admit it or not, everyone knows the 1855 classification is hopelessly out of date, but views on its existing value vary widely. It is most vigorously propagated for marketing. It is almost comical how the fact that there has only ever been a single modification, which might be taken as evidence of irrelevance, is quoted in support of its validity. Berry Bros, the old established London wine merchant, comment: "The five tier ranking for the Médoc was based on the current market values of the wines at that time… Although some châteaux no longer exist the classification remains surprisingly accurate, and there has only ever been one change."[3]

Albeit with some notable exceptions (such as M. Delon), proprietors of the Grand Cru Classés are the staunchest defenders (surprise, surprise!) "Basically the classification remains sound, for it is based on the soil and sub-soil, and this has not changed. Given equal conditions a second can still, and will normally, produce a better wine than a third, a third than a fourth, and so on. The perfect proof of this is to be found in the vineyards of Léoville Barton and Langoa. The two vineyards are run as one property and equal care is bestowed on both. And yet it can be said that always, whether the wine be good, bad or indifferent, the Léoville turns out to be the superior of the two," Ronald Barton maintained.[4]

Well yes: but this is an unusual case, where two adjacent châteaux are under the same ownership and have experienced little change since 1855. Indeed, *only* the two Barton châteaux, together with Mouton Rothschild, remain under the same ownership as in 1855. The difference between Léoville Barton and Langoa makes a powerful case for the role of terroir where no other relevant factors have changed, but the stability of the relationship between these two châteaux is unique.

Defense of the classification usually takes the view that, whatever the problems of a château might be at the moment, if only it could be brought under proper management, it could be restored to the glories of 1855. Indeed, there have been several attempts to do just that with châteaux that had fallen below the expected level of their classification, giving powerful force to the practical (and self-fulfilling?) benefits of the classification. But this presupposes that all châteaux were performing at their optimum level in 1855. No doubt then as now, some were performing below standard, and were therefore under-rated. Others may have been over-rated. And, of course, most châteaux have changed their terroir in the last 150 years.

And while the brokers may have done a good job in producing a classification reflecting the commercial reality of 1855, still you have ask how accurately prices reflected quality? Nicholas Faith points out one source of bias: before the railway was constructed up the Médoc (in 1860), châteaux nearer to Bordeaux were valued more highly because of their lower transport costs.[5] Other distortions could have arisen from effective promotion efforts or from the individual relationships between proprietors and negociants.

Criticism of the survival of the classification is widespread both outside of and within France. Kermit Lynch, noted for pioneering the export of wines from artisan producers all over France commented: "As a Bordeaux proprietor, you do not even need a good winemaker... You need only to have been included in the classification of 1855, 130-some years ago. Your vineyard might now be ten times larger than it was in 1855, your production per acre five times larger, your grape varieties blended in different proportions, your vinification new fangled (but concealed behind a façade of varnished oak vats)... No matter. If your château's name was included in the classification of 1855, you are on good terms with your banker. You may even be a banker."[6]

(Actually there is quite a long history of bankers *purchasing* châteaux, from Pillet-Will purchasing Château Margaux in 1879 to Clarence Dillon purchasing Haut Brion in 1934, although since then the outside buyers of important châteaux have tended to be industrialists rather than bankers.)

Alexis Lichine was more concerned with the damage done to the reputation of Bordeaux: "Other classified châteaux, including some second and third growths, no longer make any wine; the names stand for Great Growths of 1855 as a Roman ruin may persist as a reminder of a vanished monument of classical times. This absurdity does harm to the Bordeaux wine trade; and the reverse case, of a vineyard classified as a fifth or even a bourgeois growth, when it deserves to be sold as a second or third growth deprives both grower and customer (who is misled by the wine's rating) of a satisfactory transaction."[7]

Bernard Ginestet, of the negociant house Ginestet, and at one time owner of Château Margaux, who was always somewhat of a gadfly in Bordeaux, made similar comments: "[The 1855 classification] was in reality a formidable injection of formalin. From the top of the monumental pyramid of the 1855 classification, we can view a century of economic immobility. The grand crus have transformed themselves into venerable mummies, untouchable, frozen in a glorious eternity. With the exception of Pomerol, which has more sense, the other regions also wish to introduce classifications in order to reach petrification in their turn."[8]

A measured, albeit qualified, defense was mustered by Dewey Markham in his book on the history of the classification: "Calls for altering the 1855 list are largely rooted in a misunderstanding of the classification's origins, a belief that the brokers based their rankings on the properties' commercial performance in 1854 alone, or for the five or event ten years previous to 1855... In reality... the 1855 classification was the result of a much longer period of assessment by the brokers, almost half a century... To demand a property's demotion in the hierarchy after even a decade of producing disappointing wines is unjust, when it may have taken at least five times as long for it to have reached its given level of the classification... The 1855 classification is very much a vital part of the current Bordeaux wine world in bearing testimony to the high level of quality of which its vineyards are capable."[9]

The First Classifications

The classification of 1855 did not come out of the blue. Classification was already an engrained habit in Bordeaux. Developed as tools for the commercial purpose of more easily handling each new vintage, the classifications reflected the reality of the marketplace. Grouping the châteaux into first, second, third growths, and so on, enabled the brokers more rapidly to set the prices for individual châteaux. By the middle of the 18th century, a hierarchy based on price was already developing. One of the earliest de facto classifications is found in the records of the old established courtier, Tastet & Lawton.[10] Out of 37 Crus shown in the price records from 1741 to 1774, 26 can be recognized as properties that were classified as Grand Crus in 1855, and another 7 today are Cru Bourgeois (Table 19).

The 18th century hierarchy is recognizable in terms of today's châteaux.[11] The first growths are well separated at the head of the list. After that, there is more or a less a continuum of prices, with much less distinction between groups, but most of the remaining growths classified in 1855 are within one level of their subsequent ranking. Léoville is at the head of the second group; the future Mouton Rothschild is only in the middle. Two of the most important second growths, Châteaux Montrose and Cos d'Estournel, had not yet been planted. Château Palmer did not yet exist, although some of the vineyards that it was to incorporate were listed as a third growth. Several wines that are today in the Cru Bourgeois classification were clearly much more important in the 18th century than they are today. The wines of the Libournais were mostly sent for distillation.

Table 19 Relative prices between 1741-1774 identify a hierarchy of four classes.

Château	Class in 1774	Class in 1855	Price
Haut Brion		1st	111.6%
Lafite	Firsts	1st	97.8%
Margaux	Firsts	1st	97.6%
Latour		1st	93.0%
Léoville		2nd	62.0%
Brane St Julien		unidentified	61.2%
Calon Ségur		3rd	59.3%
Lascombes		2nd	58.8%
(Marquis) de Terme		4th	58.6%
Gruaud (Larose)		2nd	56.2%
Brane-Mouton (Mouton Rothschild)	Seconds	2nd	54.8%
Gorse (Brane Cantenac)		2nd	52.5%
Malescot		3rd	51.3%
President Kazoo		unidentified	50.9%
Puget		4th	50.1%
Pontac		CBS	46.3%
Rauzan		2nd	46.2%
Desmirail		3rd	41.3%
Nissan		3rd	41.1%
Pichon Longueville		2nd	40.9%
Giscours		3rd	38.7%
de Gassy (Palmer)		3rd	37.8%
La Chesnee		CB	37.7%
La Colonies		sold	37.4%
Bergeron (Ducru Beaucaillou)	Thirds	2nd	37.0%
Gouda		unidentified	35.1%
Beychevelle		4th	33.7%
La Tour de Moons		CBS	32.9%
Citron		CBS	32.2%
Lynch Bages		5th	30.6%
Duluc (Branaire Ducru)		4th	30.2%
Pontet Canet		5th	27.9%
Le Pavie		CB	27.6%
Pontet St Julien (Langoa)		3rd	27.6%
Ponies	Fourths	CB	26.2%
Lafon Rochet		4th	25.4%
Holstein		CBS	23.7%

Wines that can be identified with modern châteaux are shown in terms of the 1855 classification or as CBS (Cru Bourgeois Supérieur) or CB (Cru Bourgeois). Some vineyards have been amalgamated into other châteaux (sold). A few châteaux cannot be identified.[12] Prices in 1774 are shown relative to the first growth average.

The Solidifying Effect of 1855

By 1855 the hierarchy had been fairly static for almost 50 years, as witnessed by various classifications published by authorities of the period.[13] For this reason (and perhaps also because it rapidly acquired, no matter how inaccurately, an official mantra), the classification for the great exposition attracted little controversy. This was reinforced by its usage in Cocks & Féret in 1868, which, after all, carried the title "Bordeaux et Ses Vins: Classés par Ordre de Mérite."

While describing it as an official classification, Cocks & Féret noted that "like all human institutions, it is subject to the laws of time, and certainly will need to be revised depending on progress. In changing proprietors, the Crus are often modified. Any Cru, neglected by a proprietor who is negligent or indebted, can fall into the hands of a man who is rich, active, and intelligent, and may then produce better wine. The contrary can also arrive, in the manner in which it was necessary in 1855 to modify the old classifications."

This statement was repeated in editions until 1949, but in 1969 (a century after the classification!) was replaced by the note that "Since 1855, many things have changed. Many properties no longer belong to the family that owned them in 1855… It is evident that conditions of culture, care taken with the harvest and with vinification, methods of commercialization are not what they were… It is probable that if a reclassification were made today, it would not be exactly the same as in 1855, some Crus would have progressed in the hierarchy, while others would have fallen…We have respected the classification, but noted for some Crus that quality now is superior to the level that was recognized in 1855." (They did not note cases where the level was inferior!)

A snapshot of prices in 1943 exists in legislation passed by the Vichy government in an attempt to stabilize prices. As unearthed by Markham, this list not only ordered the châteaux of the Médoc, but also included châteaux in St. Emilion and Pomerol.[14] The list needs to be treated with some caution as an assessment of hierarchy, because the order is not entirely borne out by available en primeur prices. It divides the châteaux into six groups, with prices ranging from 100,000 to 60,000 francs per tonneau, and its list for the Médoc essentially follows the 1855 classification except for the promotion of a group of fourth and fifth growths into the central groups (75,000 and 70,000 francs/tonneau). Since we do not know how the list was compiled, it would be a mistake to attribute too much significance to it, but it does suggest a relatively static situation for the first half of the 20th century.

A Foiled Attempt at Reclassification

Things were stirred up in 1959 when Alexis Lichine (the proprietor of Château Prieuré Lichine) published his own classification. This was only distributed privately at the time, but was made public in his Encyclopedia of Wines in 1967. Lichine divided the wines into five groups. The first group included the first growths of the Médoc plus Pétrus, Ausone, and Cheval Blanc from the right bank. Although noting

Figure 109

INAO's proposal in 1961 to replace the 1855 classification.[15]

Colors indicate positions in earlier classifications.

Purple = first growths

Red = second growths

Brown = third growths

Blue = fourth growths

Green = fifth growths

Black = cru bourgeois

Premiers Grands Crus Classés Exceptionnels

Lafite Rothschild
Latour
Margaux
Mouton Rothschild

Premiers Grands Crus Classés

Beychevelle
Brane-Cantenac
Calon Ségur
Cantemerle
Cos d'Estournel
Ducru Beaucaillou
Gruaud Larose
Lascombes
Léoville Barton
Léoville Lascases
Léoville Poyferré
Lynch Bages
Malescot St. Exupéry
Montrose
Palmer
Pichon Baron
Pichon Lalande
Pontet-Canet
Rauzan Gassies
Rauzan-Ségla
Talbot

Grands Crus Classés

Batailley
Bel-Air-Marquis d'Aligre
Boyd Cantenac
Branaire Ducru
Cantenac Brown
Chasse-Spleen
Cos Labory
Duhart Milon Rothschild
Dutruch-Grand-Poujeaux
Giscours
Gloria
Grand Puy Ducasse
Grand Puy Lacoste
Gressier-Grand-Poujeaux
Haut Batailley
d'Issan
Kirwan
Labergorce
La Lagune
Lanessan
Langoa Barton
La Tour de Mons
Prieuré Lichine
Marquis de Terme
Meyney
Mouton Baronne (d'Armailhac)
de Pez
Phélan-Segur
Poujeaux
Siran

Dropped from Classification

Belgrave
Camensac
Clerc Milon
Croizet-Bages
Dauzac
Durfort Vivens
Ferrière
Haut Bages Libéral
Lafon Rochet
Lagrange
Lynch Moussas
Marquis-d'Alesme-Becker
Pédesclaux
Pouget
Saint Pierre
du Tertre
Tour-Carnet

that a classification should be planned only every quarter or half century, he made significant revisions in his edition of 1974.

In Lichine's classifications of the Médoc, most of the second growths retained their position, but the third through fifth categories were quite changed relative to 1855. In the revised edition, Lichine significantly increased the size of the fifth group, bringing the overall number of classified château to 79.[16] This avoided the need to demote any châteaux entirely from the list, which therefore included all of the classed growths of 1855 (except Desmirail which at that time had been incorporated into Palmer). The additional 18 châteaux from the Cru Bourgeois classification were almost all classified in the fifth category.

Lichine, no matter how well respected, was of course no more than an individual giving his opinion. A much greater threat to the status quo occurred when INAO agreed to make a reclassification in 1961. INAO divided the châteaux into three groups, and removed 17 of the original châteaux while including 10 new châteaux (Figure 109). When the results were leaked to the local newspaper in Bordeaux, Sud Ouest, the ensuing furor killed all prospect of any official reclassification.

The Chamber of Commerce in Bordeaux went so far as to obtain a judicial opinion that questioned INAO's authority to make a new classification.[17] Baron Philippe Rothschild denounced INAO's reclassification in Sud-Ouest.[18] In 1962 the Minister of Agriculture decided "not to follow up on the classification that had been made," recognizing the need for further study in order to make a "classification of these wines in a manner that would be judicially sound."[19] Needless to say, this never happened.

The Rise of Mouton Rothschild

Only two changes have ever been officially made in the classification. In the year after publication, Château Cantemerle was included following a protest about its exclusion from its proprietor. Then the classification remained quiescent for more than a century, until in 1973 Château Mouton Rothschild was promoted from second growth to first growth.

Mouton had been rising steadily in the hierarchy ever since the first classifications. In Thomas Jefferson's classification of 1787, it was placed in the third growths, just behind Calon-Ségur. In some earlier classifications it was even lower in the third growths. By the time of Lawton's classification in 1815, it was at the head of the second growths, and in subsequent classifications it moved lower down the seconds and then back up again.

By 1855, Mouton had become somewhat of an anomaly. At the time of the 1855 classification, it had been owned by its new proprietor, Nathaniel Rothschild, for only two years. It was clearly recognized as achieving a price at the head of the second growths, but at a level well below the first growths. (Just before the sale, the régisseur had written to the current proprietor that "your intention to place Mouton between the premiers and the seconds is half accomplished."[20]) In the decade leading up to the 1855 classification, Mouton Rothschild sold at an average 68% of the price of the first growths, just ahead of the rest of the seconds, which varied in order from year to year, in a relative price range of 65-50%.

This remained the situation for the next half-century. In 1865, for example, the first growths sold en primeur at 5,600 francs the tonneau, Mouton was at 3,500, and the second growths were at 2,500-2,600, a clear enough distinction.[21] It is not evident therefore why there should have been any sense of grievance about the classification, but when Baron Philippe Rothschild took over in 1922, it became his aim to move Mouton into the first growths. He devised the motto for Mouton:

Premier ne puis
Second ne daigne
Mouton suis

(First I cannot be, Second I disdain, I am Mouton.)

During the fifty years following the classification, Mouton Rothschild sold en primeur at an average of about 80% of the price of Lafite Rothschild. Only after 1910 did it increase to achieve parity, so at the

Figure 110

The price of Mouton Rothschild en primeur was significantly below the Lafite Rothschild until it increased to achieve parity after 1910. (Lafite Rothschild represents the average of first growth prices for the period.)[22]

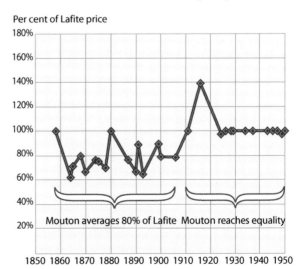

time when Baron Philippe took over, there was only a decade of records to justify a place for Mouton among the first growths, although by then its reputation was established as comparable to the first growths.[23] Since the 1920s, its position has been easily maintained (Figure 110); in fact, what were effectively now five first growths marched in lockstep until 1945, all selling at essentially the same price.

"Mouton Ne Change"

Everyone knows that Mouton Rothschild is the only case where a change has been made in the 1855 classification. When I started researching the classification, I assumed that it would be simple routine to check its promotion by looking at the announcement. But far from it. The actual events are shrouded in a baffling obscurity and only some friendly archivists saved me from total defeat. Why should there be such secrecy?

Baron Philippe spent half a century after he took over Mouton Rothschild battling for its promotion to first growth, but all attempts to revise the 1855 classification were lost in an administrative labyrinth, not to mention opposition from the other first growths. A major source of opposition came from his cousin, Elie de Rothschild, at neighboring rival Château Lafite Rothschild. The two proprietors were continuously sniping at one another, each fighting to push their price above the other, or comparing a poor vintage of their rival's wine with a better one of their own. It's never been quite clear why after all these years Elie withdrew his opposition and made it possible for Mouton to be promoted.

One tactic almost succeeded when Baron Philippe, together with a group of proprietors of other classed growths, revitalized the Syndicat of Grand Cru Classés, which in 1959 adopted a resolution calling for revision of the classification. This was the impetus for INAO's abortive reclassification of 1961. But following the debacle, the authorities washed their hands of the job.

The next phase of the campaign was to obtain a decree describing the conditions under which the classification could be revised. Baron Philippe must have worked furiously behind the scenes to obtain agreement that a "concours public" would be organized under the aegis of various interested bodies and would submit its recommendations for ratification by the Minister of Agriculture.

This was no mean feat to organize in the face of opposition from some of the very organizations who were supposed to sponsor it, but in 1969 the Chamber of Commerce declared the concours open, specifically with the purpose of considering the status of Mouton Rothschild and Pétrus (the top wine of Pomerol, and indeed of the right bank). But once again the process evaporated under administrative bureaucracy.

In June 1972 the Minister of Agriculture asked the Chamber of Commerce to organize another concours public. No more was heard of the candidature of Pétrus, but Mouton Rothschild renewed its claims. (Château Gloria is also supposed to have entered a candidacy, but no more was heard of that either.[24])

The "concours public" does not seem to have been at all public; I have been unable to find any public record of its meeting, let alone details of its deliberations. However, buried in the archives of the Chamber of Commerce of Bordeaux is a statement that a jury was convened at their headquarters on February 23, 1973.[25] The jury included five of the leading courtiers and various other distinguished personages. Although it included the Managing Director of Sud-Ouest, the local newspaper, no report seems to have been made public. The jury was informed that it should consider the question of classification, but nothing is known of any deliberations. Consideration seems to have been awfully quick, not to say cursory, for such a serious matter. The jury met briefly only on the single occasion, and immediately after, on February 27, the Vice-President of the Chamber of Commerce wrote to the Minister to recommend that the list of first growths should be presented in alphabetical order with five names that now included Mouton Rothschild. The long campaign to promote Mouton culminated in the pronouncement in the form of an Arrêté Ministeriel (a formal declaration by a minister of the French government) by the incorruptible Jacques Chirac in his capacity as Minister of Agriculture on June 21, 1973 that Mouton was included in the first growths.

Usually such declarations are published in the Journal Officiel[26] to give them legal force, but there is no record of this happening in this case. The actual content of the official declaration is curiously difficult to pin down. It seems scarcely credible, but even Château Mouton Rothschild denies all knowledge of the original text![27] (Although the Chamber of Commerce wrote to Baron Philippe on June 27, 1973 and sent him a copy of the Arrêté.[28]) Apparently only a single copy exists in the archives of the French government,[29] and that is not even an official declaration but is merely a clipping from the local newspaper (Figure 111).[30] All of this reflects the reality that the entire notion of the concours public was no more than a fig leaf to cover Baron Philippe's success in persuading the authorities to move Mouton into the top category.

But did the government really have the authority to do this? The text of the arrêté is evasive about the basis for the authority to promote

Mouton. It refers to a décret on the repression of fraud of June 1964 that slightly modified the original décret of 1949 restricting use of the term cru classé (Figure 21). Other references go back to the original law of 1905 that was the forerunner for the introduction of the appellation system. Then it gets to the point, referring to an appeal of the Minister of Agriculture in 1972 for organizing a concours public (which can't be found in the Journal Officiel either) and to the results of the concours in 1973. But do the previous laws, all of which are concerned with preventing the use of misleading nomenclature, really give authority to the Minister to revise what was originally an unofficial classification (Chapter 3)?

There is a fascinating elision from the law of 1949, which restricts use of the term Cru Classé, to the modification of 1964 which allows for "Cru Classé" also to be used for wines of Bordeaux selected by a concours public, to an acknowledgement *en passant* that cru classés may have a hierarchy,[31] to an actual change in the *level* of a château within the classification.[32] There does not seem to be any precedent or authority for this change within the law. None of this is to deny that Mouton deserves promotion (as indeed do others, of course), but one is left wondering whether the obscurity of the process was intended to disguise a lack of proper authority.

Any other attempts to revise the classification have been seen off easily, and no more has been heard of proposals to revise other levels of the classification, the moving force, Baron Philippe, having oddly lost interest after 1973. His last word was to change Mouton's motto:

Premier je suis

Second je fus

Mouton ne change

(First I am, Second I was, Mouton does not change).

What difference did its promotion make to Mouton Rothschild? By the time M. Chirac signed the declaration, Mouton had been showing parity in price with its new group for half a century. This did not change. The promotion was no more and no less than a (long overdue) recognition of the situation in the market, very satisfying for Baron Philippe, but without practical consequences. There's an interesting contrast between Baron Philippe's ability to muscle his way to the top fifty years ago and the inability of the super-seconds to do the same in the last twenty years.

Figure 111 (Opposite) The official declaration of the Ministry of Agriculture promoting Château Mouton Rothschild to first growth status in 1973.[33] The poor condition reflects the fact that this is the only copy in the government archives.

ANNEXE 6

Jeudi 28 juin 1973   / SUD-OUEST

Voici le texte officiel concernant
le nouveau classement des premiers crus

NOUS avons annoncé, dans nos éditions d'hier, l'imminence d'un communiqué officiel de la Chambre de commerce et d'industrie de Bordeaux, au sujet du nouveau classement des premiers crus du Médoc, avec aussi la mention, par assimilation, du château Haut-Brion, dans les graves.

Voici le texte en question, tel qu'il vient de nous être transmis par la compagnie consulaire.

Le ministre de l'agriculture et du développement rural:

Vu le décret n. 64-663 du 27 juin 1904 portant règlement d'administration publique et modifiant l'article 13 du décret du 19 août 1921, pris pour l'application de la loi du 1er août 1905 sur la répression des fraudes;

Vu l'arrêté du ministre de l'agriculture du 27 juin 1972 portant approbation du règlement d'organisation d'un concours public pour la sélection par ordre

de mérite des crus du Médoc, modifié par l'arrêté du 10 août 1972 du ministre de l'agriculture et du développement rural;

Vu la décision du jury de concours en date du 20 février 1973, présentée à l'homologation par lettre du président de la Chambre de commerce et d'industrie de Bordeaux du 27 février 1973;

Vu les consultations en date du 10 avril 1973, faites en application de l'article 1 du règlement d'organisation du concours; de l'Institut national des appellations d'origine des vins et eaux-de-vie, des syndicats locaux A.O.C. du Médoc et Haut-Médoc, de Saint-Estèphe, de Pauillac, de Saint-Julien, de Margaux, de Moulis et de Listrac ainsi que du Syndicat viticole des graves et autres crus;

Vu les avis reçus des organismes ci-dessus visés dans les délais de réponse qui leur avaient été impartis;

ARRETE

Article premier. - Est homologuée la décision du jury de concours susvisée et ainsi formulée:

Le jury de concours, lors de sa réunion du 20 février, a confirmé à l'unanimité les crus suivants au titre de « premiers crus classés, 1973 », ces crus étant nommés par ordre alphabétique:

Château Lafite-Rothschild, château Latour, château Margaux, château Mouton-Rothschild, par assimilation: château Haut-Brion.

Art. 2. — Une ampliation du présent arrêté sera adressée à la Chambre de commerce et d'industrie, à la charge de celle-ci, éprouves successives au concours, d'établir une nouvelle présentation du classement par aire géographique correspondant à l'appellation contrôlée conformément aux dispositions de l'article 6 du règlement de concours.

Fait à Paris, le 21 juin 1973.

Pour le ministre et par délégation, le préfet chargé de mission: Edouard DUCHENE.

329

The Primacy of the First Growths

In 1855, each class of growths occupied a fairly narrow price range and
was distinct from the next group. The first growths typically sold for 15%
more than the second growths, the seconds for 15% more than the thirds,
and so on (Figure 19). The first effect of the classification was to reinforce
the position of the first growths, which increased their price advantage
over the seconds: this was a forecast of things to come.

A century later, after the retreat from the speculative prices at the
beginning of the 1970s, the first growths sold for 2-3× the average price
of the second growths (Figure 112). Since 1996 there has been a steady
widening of the difference, to a peak of almost 6× in the great 2005
vintage, when en primeur prices reached unprecedented levels.

The second growths as a group remain well ahead of the third
growths, with an average difference of about 1.5×. The classification then
begins to lose its validity at lower levels. The difference between the
thirds and fourths is less marked and more variable. And there is no
statistical difference between the prices of the fourth and fifth growths
taken as a group.

Figure 112

*The first growths have
been consistently well
ahead of all others in
price. Seconds are ahead
of thirds, and thirds are
ahead of fourths, but the
fourths have no
consistent advantage
over the fifths.*[34]

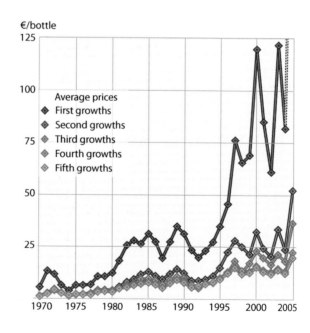

Separation of the Super-Seconds

A century after the classification, the relationship between the classes was fairly steady. Through the 1970s, the second growths were priced at an average level of about a third of the first growths. In most years the range was fairly narrow within the seconds, usually showing a 25% increase from cheapest to most expensive. As prices climbed steadily through the 1980s and 1990s, and the first growths became more clearly separated from the second growths, the seconds began to split into two groups. Léoville Las Cases, Pichon Lalande, Ducru Beaucaillou, Palmer, Cos d'Estournel, Montrose, and Lynch Bages (joined more recently by Pichon Baron) have usually been at the head of the second growths.[35] They have emerged as a subgroup of "super-seconds" that has become progressively distinguished from the other seconds.

The super-seconds are an extreme example of classification by price. Defined by this single criterion, they have a price below the first growths but distinctly above the rest of the seconds. The super-seconds really began to separate from the other second growths as a distinct group after 1995 (Figure 113). Another jump occurred in 2005 when the first growths increased dramatically and the super-seconds also increased more than the other seconds. The super-seconds now fetch as much as double the price of the other seconds. Their advance is shown clearly by the ratio of their average price to the rest of the seconds (Figure 114).

Figure 113

First growths have pulled away from the second growths, and the second growths have split into two groups.[36]

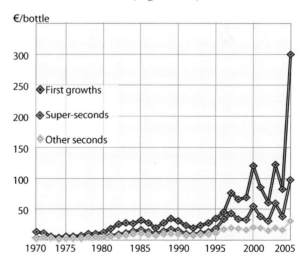

The increasing importance of the super-seconds is emphasized by the resemblance between their behavior and that of the first growths. In very good years, speculative fever tends to push up the prices of the first growths disproportionately. The super-seconds show the same pattern in increasing their lead over the other seconds in the best years (2000, 2003, 2005), but then falling back in the other years (2001, 2004).

Some super-seconds have long held ambitions to become first growths; at the forefront, Michel Delon of Léoville Las Cases was unabashed about trying to push his price to first growth levels. In the late 1990s, he came very close indeed,[37] but since then the stratospheric rise in first growth prices may have pushed the ambition out of reach.

Individual second growths sometimes have unusual successes, but, at least so far, this has become evident only well after the vintage; there is to date no case of a second growth actually penetrating the range of first growth prices en primeur. Palmer 1961, for example, is sometimes regarded as the best Médoc of the vintage, and for a period in the late 1980s reached prices at auction that were ahead of any first growth. Montrose had a great success in 1990 and now achieves an auction price just at the bottom end of the first growth range. But a vintage later, prices settle back into the usual relationship (Chapter 8).

Figure 114

In the 1970s there was no significant difference between the super-seconds and other second growths, but since then the super-seconds have become a distinct group, reaching a price level around twice that of the other seconds.[38]

A New Classification

Classification is not for the fainthearted. It can never be more than transient and is bound to offend as many as it pleases. Change today is far more rapid than it was during the more leisurely period leading up to the 1855 classification. Classification then represented 50 years of received wisdom. Today, the whole new class of super-seconds has emerged in the past 25 years. Even taking a more recent period, comparing the current price order of Médoc châteaux gives different results depending on whether the period is the past 20, 10, or 5 years. A 20 year period may not allow sufficiently for changes occurring during the period, but over 5 years a transient fad may over-influence results. On balance, a decade seems the right balance to strike between stability and change, as adopted by INAO for the classification of Saint Emilion.

Looking at the average prices achieved by the wines of the Médoc on the Place de Bordeaux over the past decade, only about one third of the classed growths would be in the same group today as they were in 1855 (Figure 115). The best relationship with the classification of 1855 is right at the top, where the first growths (now including Mouton Rothschild) remain unchallenged.

The old second growths, together with some newcomers, now fall into three subgroups. At the top, La Mission Haut Brion, Léoville Las Cases, and Palmer now occupy somewhat the position that Mouton Rothschild occupied in 1855: significantly below the first growths, but above the rest of the second group. (La Mission Haut Brion is the sister property of Château Haut Brion in Pessac-Léognan; although it is not usually included with the super-seconds of the Médoc, its price would put it at the head of this group.) The next six châteaux, headed by Cos d'Estournel, form the rest of the super-seconds. A price gap separates them from the following group, which includes most of the other second growths. A couple of the old seconds have fallen right down the list.

From this point on, there is a more or less continuous range of prices, making it difficult to divide the wines into clear groups. The dividing line between the last two groups is more or less arbitrary. Cutting off the number of châteaux arbitrarily at the number classified in 1855 would exclude 11 from the classification.

A distinct difference between this classification and those made in the 1960s is the appearance in the top 61 of some second wines. The second wines of three of the first growths (Latour, Lafite Rothschild, and Margaux) make it into the group immediately below the super-seconds. The close approach of Léoville Las Cases to the first growths is indicated

Figure 115

A new classification shows the top 61 wines of the Médoc ordered by average price for the period from 1996-2005. (Haut Brion and La Mission Haut Brion are also included.)[39]

Colors indicate positions in present classifications.

Purple = first growths

Red = second growths

Brown = third growths

Blue = fourth growths

Green = fifth growths

Black = cru bourgeois or unclassified
Gray = second wine.

Latour
Margaux
Mouton Rothschild
Lafite Rothschild
Haut Brion

La Mission Haut Brion
Léoville Lascases
Palmer
Cos d'Estournel
Pichon Lalande
Ducru Beaucaillou
Montrose
Pichon Baron
Lynch Bages

Rauzan-Ségla
Léoville-Barton
Gruaud Larose
Forts de Latour
Léoville-Poyferré
Grand Puy Lacoste
Pontet-Canet
Lascombes
Pavillon Rouge du Margaux
Langoa Barton
Clos du Marquis
Brane-Cantenac
Calon Ségur
Carruades de Lafite
Talbot

Beychevelle
Haut Marbuzet
Saint Pierre
Lagrange
Sociando-Mallet
Branaire Ducru
Clerc Milon
Prieuré Lichine
Giscours
Malescot-St-Exupéry
Kirwan
Duhart-Milon-Rothschild
La Lagune
d'Issan

Tourelles Longueville
Rauzan Gassies
Alter Ego de Palmer
Cantenac Brown
Ferrière
Haut Batailley
Dauzac
Phélan Ségur
Durfort Vivens
Lafon Rochet
Gloria
Pibran
Cos Labory
d'Armailhac
Haut-Bages-Libéral
Marquis de Terme
Du Tertre
Siran
Labégorce
Ormes de Pez

Below top 61

Grand Puy Ducasse
Lynch Moussas
La Tour-Carnet
Cantemerle
Desmirail
Boyd Cantenac
Croizet-Bages
Pédesclaux
Camensac
Marquis-d'Alesme-Becker
Batailley
Belgrave
Pouget

by the appearance of its second wine (Clos du Marquis) in this group. The second wines of two further super-seconds (Pichon Lalande and Palmer) appear at the head of the fifth group. Given the unregulated, not to say slightly irregular, nature of second wines, this would no doubt be a problem for any official classification.

The impossibility of being included in the 1855 classification means that there may be more to be lost than to be gained for unclassified châteaux in participating in any other new classifications. Sociando-Mallet was classified as a Cru Bourgeois in the original classification of 1932, but now by any standard would be well up the list of Grand Cru Classés if there were any reclassification. However, the château decided not to be included in the 2003 classification because in effect that would stamp the wine at the Cru Bourgeois level: "there are the Grand Cru Classés, there are the Cru Bourgeois, and then there is Sociando-Mallet."[40]

The wines that would be dropped from the classification are mostly the perennial under-performers from the old group of fifth growths, but a fourth and some thirds are found as well. Most of these wines in fact fail to make the top 61 by a fairly wide margin. Several Cru Bourgeois would be ahead of them if the classification were extended, as it probably should be, to include (say) 80 wines.

Terroir is For Ever

The changes in relative position among châteaux over such a short period as a decade question whether any classification remains in place long enough to be useful. There is more stability at the top than lower down. Although it would make no difference to the top two groups if the Médoc classification were based on (say) a twenty year period instead of a decade, there would be changes in all the other groups. The hierarchy of Saint Emilion also shows the inability of the classification system to keep up with changes in the marketplace (Table 17). Are these difficulties characteristic of all classification systems or are they specific to those based on price?

It's a fascinating contrast to look at the classification system in Burgundy, which is based exclusively on terroir. Established when the Appellation Contrôlée was defined for Burgundy in 1937, it has suffered only a couple of minor revisions since that date. How is the hierarchy of the Burgundy pyramid, going up from AOC (village) wines, through premier crus, to grand crus, reflected in the marketplace?

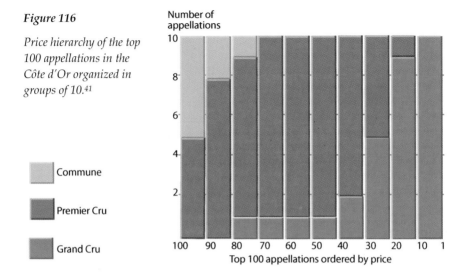

Figure 116

Price hierarchy of the top 100 appellations in the Côte d'Or organized in groups of 10.[41]

Commune

Premier Cru

Grand Cru

The great difference between Burgundy and Bordeaux is that many producers may make wine within any given appellation in Burgundy. Price in Burgundy in fact is influenced more by the producer than by the appellation: a great producer's Bourgogne may sell for more than a poor producer's premier or grand cru. However, the effect of appellation on price is revealed by comparing the prices for wines of different appellations from a single producer. The *relative* order of appellations by price should be the same for each producer. This hierarchy gives the market's view of the appellations (Figure 116).

This price hierarchy shows a much better correlation with the appellations than is shown by the corresponding comparison with the Cru Classés of the Médoc (Figure 115). The bottom 10 of the top 100 are a mix of communal appellations and premier crus, but as price increases, the premier crus take over. By the time we get to the top 20, there is only one premier cru in the list; and all of the top ten appellations by price are grand crus. (And all of the grand crus that fall below the top 30 represent one of two cases where a [relatively] large area was given a single classification: Clos Vougeot and Corton. It is in fact widely recognized that this was a mistake; had closer distinctions been drawn, parts of each of these grand crus would have been only premier crus or possibly even communal appellation.)

The classification does pretty well in showing the same relative price order for appellations among different producers, but comparisons between producers show they are far more important than terroir. A typical grand cru in the 2004 vintage showed a price spread from $90 to $480 per bottle, depending on the producer. As always, the marketplace recognizes the under- and over-performers by that harsh criterion: price.

What Price Classification?

How important is classification in the grand scheme of things in Bordeaux? Almost 500 châteaux are classified in the various schemes in the Médoc, Graves, St. Emilion, and Sauternes. Where do they figure in the ultimate hierarchy on which they are all based: market price? Far from dominating the rankings, actually only half of the châteaux in the top 250 by price in recent vintages are classified (Figure 117).

The unclassified châteaux fall into two groups. Just over a quarter of the top 250 are châteaux that are either in appellations without classification (mostly Pomerol) or that have chosen not to participate in the classification of their appellation. The rest are in those two new categories that have dominated developments of the past twenty years: garage wines and second wines.

Within the top 250 châteaux, two groups offer a revealing contrast. Half of the classified châteaux consist of the wines of the 1855 classification, now more than 150 years old and never revised. Half of the unclassified wines consist of châteaux (or second wines) that did not even exist 25 years ago, and that have altogether bypassed all classification. The ranking offers a compelling view of the ability of the new to coexist with the old.

No doubt the appellations that have established classification systems, and the châteaux that are classified, believe that they gain support in the marketplace from the classification. But neither in Bordeaux, where price is the basis, nor in Burgundy, where terroir is the

Figure 117

Only 125 of the top 250 châteaux by price in Bordeaux are classified.[42]

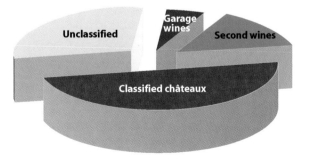

determinant, does classification offer the consumer any guidance as to whether the bottle is worth the price. So how useful is it?

Producers may gain more from classification than consumers. In Bordeaux, under performing châteaux may be protected from falling prices by their position in the outdated classification. Nowhere is this clearer than in the case of Premier Grand Cru Classés, clearly known to the trade to perform far below their potential in the 1960s and 1970s, but nonetheless still then sustaining a price significantly above the second growths. In Burgundy, lesser wines sometimes get a ride on the coattails of reputation; witness the boost to prices obtained for wines from the poorer plots in Clos Vougeot because it was classified in its entirety as a Grand Cru.

But producers may also lose, especially in Bordeaux where exclusion from the classification may prevent them from reaching their true price level. The difference between the classification and the present price hierarchy shows clearly enough that the market is able to see past the classification in extensively reordering prices in what would be the groups of third to fifth growths. But would some of the rising châteaux have risen even higher if not suppressed by the green glass ceiling of those assigned positions above them in the hierarchy? This is more true in the Médoc, and especially so at the prominent level of the first and second growths, than on the right bank. Even a free marketer must agree that price is not a wholly objective classification; prices can be distorted by the history of past reputation and indeed by the effectiveness of current marketing.

Classification is problematic for consumers. Unless the classification is current and comprehensive, you have to ask whether its main effect isn't to fool the consumer. (And when the same terms have different meanings in different appellations, it's easy enough to be fooled.) But if the classification is totally current and does no more than ratify last year's price hierarchy, what purpose would it serve? To offer some guidance that goes beyond prices per se requires a delicate balance in reconciling past accomplishments with present performance. It may be a laudable aim to reflect a longer term view of underlying quality than any one year's prices can provide, but is it practical or useful to the consumer faced with the need to choose a bottle now?

Do any of the existing classifications really make a useful difference? Faced with a list of unknown wines, is it easier to distinguish one from the Médoc or from St. Emilion on the basis of its classification, compared with one from unclassified Pomerol? Well, yes, but the price you pay for this guidance is that you may be fooled. And whether a classification as outdated as that of 1855 does more harm or good (and to whom) is a matter for individual judgment.

With several hundred châteaux in the Médoc, for example, it is useful to see on the label of an unknown château "Grand Cru Classé" or "Cru Bourgeois" to give some rough indication of level, and to distinguish them from the crowd. But of course guidance goes only so far if the classification is not up to date. The 1855 classification shows how extremely detailed mapping of a few châteaux into several levels can lose credibility as time passes. Better credibility is achieved in Saint Emilion, where on balance the Premier Grand Cru Classés are the best of the appellation and the Grand Cru Classés are mostly better than the Grand Crus. The flaw here is the omission of many of the better châteaux from the classification, thus undercutting its purpose altogether. And does the range of variation become so broad as to lose utility when a class is as large as the 46 Grand Cru Classés?

Any useful classification needs to bring something else to bear in providing an alternative light in which to regard, or independently validate, prices. Burgundy accomplishes this by classifying the terroir: you can assess how the market regards a particular producer by viewing his price for a given appellation against the range of other producers for that appellation. Classification by price immediately places you on the uncomfortable horns of the dilemma: accepting last year's prices does no more than repeat the judgment of the market; but diverging from current pricing questions whether the classification is relevant. And the increasing pace of change means that classifications can become rapidly outdated: is this detrimental in protecting those who should be demoted and suppressing those who should be promoted?

Perhaps you can't buck the market, but there is no denying the effect of classifications on prices. The endurance of the 1855 classification, and its emulation by other regions in Bordeaux, is a tribute to its effectiveness as a marketing ploy. But as they say in criminal cases: cui bono (who benefits)? There's no doubt that the classification is great for those included, especially at the top and at the bottom. Producers who have been excluded, or classified at a lower level than they now deserve, may feel less sanguine. Of course, the consumer is on the other end of the see-saw. Consumers have certainly overpaid in the past for châteaux failing to perform up to the standard of their classification, but the counterweight is that there are also bargains to be had among the over-performers.

Under more intensive scrutiny than ever before, with instant assessment provided by innumerable experts, with increasing competition from the varietal-labeled wines of the new world, Bordeaux has the same need as other wine-producing regions to make itself stand out from the crowd. Its unique classification system could have that effect, but runs the risk of falling into irrelevance if it is massively out of date or fails to include some of the best wines. With the 1855 classification showing only partial connection to reality, and the Cru Bourgeois and St. Emilion classifications suspended by court order, there is no time to be lost for Bordeaux to put its house into order.

Bibliography

Brook, Stephen. *Bordeaux. People, Power and Politics* (Mitchell Beazley, London, 2001).

Brook, Stephen. *The Complete Bordeaux* (Mitchell Beazley, London, 2007).

Cocks, Charles & Edouard Féret. *Bordeaux Et Ses Vins Classés Par Ordre De Mérite* (Editions Féret, Bordeaux, 1868, 1908, 1929, 1949, 1969, 1982, 2001, 2004, 2007).

Dion, Roger. *La Création du Vignoble Bordelais* (Editions de l'Ouest, Angers, 1952).

Dion, Roger. *Histoire de la Vigne et du Vin en France. Des Origines aux XIX Siècle* (Imprimerie Cevin et cie, Paris, 1959).

Enjalbert, Henri. *Les Grands Vins De Saint-Emilion, Pomerol, Fronsac* (Editions Bardi, Paris, 1983).

Enjalbert, Henri. *Histoire De La Vigne Et Du Vin, L'avènement De La Qualité, 2nd edition* (Bordas, Paris, 1987).

Faith, Nicholas. *The Winemasters of Bordeaux, 2nd edition* (Prion Books, London, 1999).

Faugère, Pierre & Eric Lillet. *Les Bordeaux Rive Gauche* (Editions 33 sur vin, Bordeaux, 1990).

Franck, William. *Traité Sur Les Vins Du Médoc Et Les Autres Vins Rouges Et Blancs Du Département De La Gironde* (Chaumas, Bordeaux, 1864).

Jefford, Andrew. *The New France* (Mitchell Beazley, London, 2002).

Lafforgue, Germain. *Le Vignoble Girondin* (Louis Larmat, Paris, 1947).

Lavaud, Sandrine. *Bordeaux Et Le Vin Au Moyen Age* (Editions Sud Ouest, Bordeaux, 2003).

Lichine, Alexis. *Encyclopedia of Wines and Spirits,* (Knopf, New York, 1967, 1974).

Markham, Dewey. *A History of the Bordeaux Classification* (John Wiley & Sons, New York, 1997).

Penning-Rowsell, Edmund. *The Wines of Bordeaux* (Wine Appreciation Guild, San Francisco, 1985, 1989).

Peppercorn, David. *Bordeaux,* (Faber & Faber, London, 1982, 1991).

Pijassou, René. *Le Médoc: Un Grand Vignoble De Qualité: Tomes I & II* (Tallandier, Paris, 1978).

Ray, Cyril. *Mouton-Rothschild: the Wine, the Family, the Museum* (Christie's Wine Publications,, 1974).

Réjalot, Michel. *Les Logiques du Château* (Bordeaux University Press, Bordeaux, 2007).

Roudié, Philippe. *Le Vignoble Bordelais* (Privat, Toulouse, 1973).

Roudié, Philippe. *Vignobles et Vignerons du Bordelais 1850-1980, 2nd edition* (Presses Universitaires, Bordeaux, 1994).

Shaw, Thomas George. *Wine, the Vine, and the Cellar, 2nd edition* (Longman, London, 1864).

Thiney, Marie-José. *Fascinant Médoc* (Editions Sud Ouest, Bordeaux, 2003).

Wilson, James. *Terroir* (Wine Appreciation Guild, San Francisco, 1998).

Wine and Spirit Trade Record, *Clarets and Sauternes: Classed Growths of the Médoc* (London, 1920).

Notes

References given in full in the bibliography are cited in the notes by author and short title only, with specific page numbers where appropriate. Other references are given in full when first cited in the individual notes. Organizations that are abbreviated by initials are: *CIVB* - Le Conseil Interprofessionnel du Vin de Bordeaux; *FGVB* - La Fédération des Grands Vins de Bordeaux; *INAO* - Institut National des Appellations d'Origine.

Chapter 1 Terroir and Typicité

[1] Patrick E. McGovern, *Ancient Wine : The Search for the Origins of Viniculture* (Princeton: Princeton University Press, 2003), p 72.

[2] Ibid., p 71. The resins inhibit the bacteria that convert wine to vinegar.

[3] Pliny the Elder (70 C.E.). The 14th book of the history of nature. Containing the Treatise of Trees bearing fruit. Chapter VI.

[4] Products, including bread, cookies, and still wine—all absolutely nothing to do with sparkling wine— that have been labeled for more than 1000 years with the name of the town of Champagne in the Vaud region of Switzerland had to stop using the name after a court case brought by the champagne producers in 2008. (John Tagliabue, *Champagne, Switzerland, can't use its own name* [International Herald Tribune, April 27, 2008].)

[5] Formally defined by the European Union as QWPSR (Quality Wine Produced in a Specific Region).

[6] INAO: Superficie et récolte revendiquées pour la campagne 2005-2006.

[7] It's a basic principle of the AOC system that wine from higher-level appellations can always be declassified to the lower level appellations that contain them. So if a producer decides that wine produced from a district vineyard isn't really good enough (or if in the past the authorities decided he had produced too much wine), the wine can be sold instead under the regional appellation. So any wine produced in Graves could be sold as AOC Bordeaux.

[8] Aerial view from Google Earth.

[9] Based upon classification of land areas by the AOC. Both pyramids would be sharper in terms of quantities of wine produced, since higher levels of classification produce less wine per unit area.

[10] About 16% of generic AOC Bordeaux makes the grade as Supérieur. (CIVB, 2006.)

[11] Aerial view from Google Earth.

[12] The figure shows typical base levels. For red wine, Bourgogne AOC is 55 hl/ha, some districts are 50 hl/ha, communes are typically 40 hl/ha, premier and grand crus are usually 37 hl/ha and 35 hl/ha respectively. Generic Bordeaux AOC is 55 hl/ha, Bordeaux Supérieur is 50 hl/ha, the Côtes, Médoc, and Graves

are also 50 hl/ha, Haut-Médoc is 48 hl/ha, communes in the Haut-Médoc are 45 hl/ha, some of the AOCs in the Libournais are 42 hl/ha.

[13] According to the latest regulations from INAO, published November 19, 2008, and applying to the 2008 vintage, for example, Bourgogne AOC was 61 hl/ha, communes 48-50 hl/ha, premier and grand crus mostly 42-45 hl/ha. In Bordeaux. the Haut-Médoc was increased to 55 hl/ha, the same as Bordeaux, and *higher* than Bordeaux Supérieur which was 53 hl/ha. The communes were even higher yet at 57 hl/ha!

[14]   INAO lists Cabernet Sauvignon, Cabernet Franc, Merlot, Malbec, Carmenère, and Petit Verdot as the only permitted black varieties. Sémillon, Sauvignon Blanc, Sauvignon Gris, and Muscadelle are listed as "principal" white varieties, with the lower quality varieties Colombard, Merlot Blanc, and Ugni Blanc listed as "accessory" varieties. (CDC Bordeaux Homologation, June 11, 2008.)

[15] See Figure 85 in Chapter 10.

[16] According to the agricultural census of 2000, 25% of the producers of AOC wines also produced a Vin de Pays wine. (Jean Strohl et al., January 2005, Agreste #157: La Statistique Agricole, Service Central des Enquêtes et Études Statistiques, Paris.)

[17] This is a growing trend nationally. In the 2000 vintage, 10% of wines that could have been labeled AOC were in fact labeled as Vin de Pays, largely in the various appellations of the south. Ibid.

[18] The Meritage Association was formed in 1988 by a group of American producers to identify wines blended from the traditional Bordeaux varieties, including Cabernet Sauvignon, Merlot, Cabernet Franc, Petit Verdot and Malbec. (see http://www.meritagewine.org/).

[19] Bloomberg news, April 26, 2006; see
http://www.bloomberg.com/apps/news?pid=10000088&sid=aQHKwfEfQVNY

[20] BBC news, August 10, 2006;
  see http://news.bbc.co.uk/2/hi/europe/5253006.stm

[21] Bordeaux is an exception where there is almost no declassification of AOC wine. In 2000, 99% of the potential AOC wines were labeled as such, by contrast with the national situation. (Jean Strohl et al., January 2005, Agreste #157: La Statistique Agricole, Service Central des Enquêtes et Études Statistiques, Paris.)

[22] Peppercorn, *Bordeaux*, 1991, p. 702; CIVB Memorandum (2006). See Figure 107 for a more detailed account.

Chapter 2 A Sense of Place

[1] The first evidence for vineyards comes from a mention in Pliny's Natural History in C.E. 71.

[2] Dion, *Histoire de la Vigne*, p. 367.

[3] Ibid., p. 121.

[4] For ancient varieties known to the Greeks and Romans see Andrew Dalby, *Food in the Ancient World from A to Z*. (Routledge, 2003), pp. 164-166.

[5] Pijassou, *Le Médoc*, pp. 290-293; Dion, *Histoire de la Vigne*, pp. 121-126.

[6] Biturica (or Biturigiaca) was described by Columella (DA 3.2.28) and Pliny (NH 14.27) as robust and high in yield.

[7] We now know that Cabernet Sauvignon derives from a chance cross between Cabernet Franc and Sauvignon Blanc, probably some 600 years ago. There is no information about the origins of these two varieties or the other Bordeaux varieties. (John E. Bowers & Carole P. Meredith, *The Parentage of a Classic Wine Grape, Cabernet Sauvignon* [Nature Genetics, 16, p. 84, 1997].)

[8] Dion, *Histoire de la Vigne*, p. 130.

[9] Tim Unwin, *Wine and the Vine: An Historical Geography of Viticulture and the Wine Trade* (London: Routledge, 1996), p. 123.

[10] This is an inference based on lack of references to activity rather than due to direct information. See Pijassou, *Le Médoc*, p. 294.

[11] Dion, *Histoire de la Vigne*, p. 367.

[12] Ibid., p. 365.

[13] There was also a lesser trade in older wines that were kept on the lees until the following Spring. (Margery Kirkbride James, *Studies in the Medieval Wine Trade* [Oxford: Clarendon Press, 1971], pp. xvi, 17.)

[14] Dion, *Histoire de la Vigne*, p. 386.

[16] Unwin, *Wine and the Vine* , pp. 197-202.

[16] Kirkbride James, *Studies in the Medieval Wine Trade* , pp. 10-11.

[17] A. D. Francis, *The Wine Trade* [London: Adams & Charles Black, 1972], p 9.

[18] At the start of the 14th century, Bordeaux wines accounted for only 120,000 hl out of a total exported of 850,000 hl. See Pijassou, *Le Médoc*, p. 307 and ref 16 below, p. 32.

[19] Lavaud, *Bordeaux et le Vin*, p. 169

[20] Dion, *Histoire de la Vigne*, p. 384.

[21] Lavaud, *Bordeaux et le Vin*, p. 171

[22] Thiney, *Fascinant Médoc*, p. 159.

[23] Painting depicting the Battle of Castillon (1453) by the French painter Charles-Philippe Larivière (1798–1876). Painting is in the Galerie des Batailles, Château de Versailles.

[24] Dion, *Histoire de la Vigne*, p. 396.

[25] Ibid., p. 397.

[26] Ibid., p. 426.

[27] Farther to the north, in the Charente, the Dutch were instrumental in the development of Cognac. In fact, "brandy" comes from the Dutch "brandewijn," which means burned wine. The trade was important from the first half of the 17th century. (Nicholas Faith, *Cognac* [Boston: Godine, 1987], p. 29-33.) The first records of exports date from 1617 (Enjalbert, *Histoire de la vigne*, p. 37.)

[28] The blockade lasted from 1688-1697 and essentially brought exports to a halt. (Pijassou, *Le Médoc*. pp. 347-350.)

[29] A rough idea of the extent to which Portuguese wines replaced French is given by comparing the 15,000 tuns of French wine imported into London in 1687 before the blockade with the level of 9000 tuns imported from Portugal in 1694. (Data from A. D. Francis, *The Wine Trade* [London: Adams & Charles Black, 1972], pp, 99, 107.)

[30] Pijassou, *Le Médoc*, pp. 364, 368.

[31] Hugh Johnson, *The Story of Wine* (London: Mitchell Beazley, 2005), p. 111.

[32] In 1717, Holland took 67% of Bordeaux exports, while England took only 12%. (Penning-Rowsell, *Bordeaux*, 1989, p. 98.)

[33] In 1713, Portugal provided 39% of imports, Spain was 26%, and France was 16%. (Francis, *The Wine Trade*, p. 320.)

[34] Vincent John Nye, *War, Wine, and Taxes: The Political Economy of Anglo-French Trade, 1689-1900* (Princeton: Princeton University Press, 2007), p. 50.

[35] One illustration is the discrepancy between volume and value of exports to England. From 1751 to 1789, England took about 6% of Bordeaux's exports; but in 1787 it accounted for 26% of the value. (Penning-Rowsell, *Bordeaux*, 1989, p. 98).

[36] Lavaud, *Bordeaux et le Vin*, p. 18

[37] "Thin and infertile countryside" was a description used in 1416 and repeated in 1524 by the local authorities. (Pijassou, *Le Médoc*, p. 314.)

[38] Pijassou, *Le Médoc*, p. 304; Thiney, *Fascinant Médoc*, pp. 166-168.

[39] Pijassou *Le Médoc*, p. 323.

[40] It's not entirely clear whether the trigger was concern about excessive wine production, possible disruption to production of corn, or simple protectionism. (Société Académique d'Agen (1908). *Recueil des Travaux*, pp. 342-344; Alan I. Forrest, *The Revolution in Provincial France: Aquitaine, 1789-1799.* [Oxford: Oxford University Press, 1996], p. 125.)

[41] Pijassou, *Le Médoc*, p. 421.

[42] see Atlas de la Gironde (France: L'Association, France).

[43] Masse Carte du Médoc (1709-1723) was at a scale of 1/28,800. The Carte de Belleyme (1761-1813) covered the region in 35 pages at a scale of 1/43,200.

[44] By 1755, the Médoc accounted for almost 25% of production by major owners in the Bordeaux region, while the Graves accounted for 18%. Within the Médoc, 75-80% of production was in the Haut-Médoc. (Gérard Aubin, *La seigneurie en Bordelais au 18e siècle d'après la pratique notariale*, 1715-1789 [Rouen: Université de Rouen, 1989], p. 387.)

[45] Pijassou, *Le Médoc*, p. 477.

[67] Philippe Courrian & Michel Creignou, *Vigneron du Médoc* (Paris: Editions Payot & Rivages, 1996), p. 17.

[47] Kirkbride James, *Studies in the Medieval Wine Trade,* p. 60.

[48] Pijassou, *Le Médoc*, p. 327.

[49] Pijassou, *Le Médoc*, p. 327.

[50] In the second half of the 16th century, the wines of the graves inland were consistently higher priced than those of the palus close to the river. For example,

the wines of Taillan (inland) priced consistently higher by roughly 20% than the wines of nearby Blanquefort (a marshy area). (Jean Cavignac, *La Vigne en Haut-Médoc au Seizième Siècle*, p. 89-90, in Vignobles et Vins d'Aquitaine [Bordeaux: Fédération Historique du Sud-Ouest, 1970].)

51 By the end of the century, there was demand for wines with origins in specific places, especially from English merchants. (Pijassou, *Le Médoc*. p. 328).

52 Dion, *Histoire de la Vigne*, p. 426.

53 Palus were planted on both left and right banks, often with Petit Verdot which adapted well to the conditions.) Henri Enjalbert, *La naissance des grands vins et la formation du vignoble moderne de Bordeaux*: 1647-1767, in *Géographie historique des vignobles*, (Ed.) Huetz de Lemps [Paris: Actes du Colloque de Bordeaux, CNRS, 1978. p. 65].)

54 Enjalbert, *Histoire de la vigne*, p. 68.

55 Prior to Prohibition, in 1919, California had 4 times more Zinfandel (a fine wine grape) than Alicante (a thick-skinned bulk wine grape). New plantings and replanting reversed their proportions so that Alicante outsold Zinfandel by 2.5 to 4 times over the period from 1925 to the end of Prohibition after 1932. (Charles L. Sullivan, *Zinfandel : A History of a Grape and Its Wine* [Berkeley: University of California Press, 2003].)

56 Soon after the start of Prohibition, in 1920, the price of Alicante grapes was $180/ton compared with $130/ton for Zinfandel. (New York Times, *Home Wine Making Saves Grape Growers*, October 30, 1921, p. 38.)

57 Prices in livres/tonneau were: palus, 90; Sauternes/Barsac, 84; Graves/Médoc, 78. (Pijassou, *Le Médoc*, p. 329; Markham, *A History of the Bordeaux Classification*, p. 211.)

58 Prices in livres/tonneau were: Médoc, 386; Graves, 298; palus, 257. (Pijassou, *Le Médoc*. p. 511.)

59 Diary of Samuel Pepys (London: Bell Publisher, 1900), p. 83.

60 Guildhall Library, *A Descriptive Catalogue of the London Traders, Tavern, and Coffee-house Tokens Current in the 17th Century* (London: Corporation of the City of London, 1855).

61 Pontack's was built on the site in Abchurch Lane (just off Lombard Street) where the White Bear Taven had burned down in the great fire of 1666. It stayed in business until the building was demolished in 1780. Some consider it to have been London's first restaurant. Prices were extremely high, with Haut Brion at 7 shillings/bottle compared to 2 shillings/bottle for other quality wine.

62 John Locke, *The Works of John Locke*, (Letters and Misc. Works, 1685) , vol 9, paragraph 1073.

63 The soil is in fact Günz gravel.

64 Thiney, *Fascinant Médoc*, p.170.

65 Pijassou, *Le Médoc*, p. 371.

66 Pijassou, *Le Médoc*, p. 397.

67 Markham, *A History of the Bordeaux Classification*, p. 47; Thiney, *Fascinant Médoc*, p. 182.

---

[68] Pijassou, *Le Médoc*, p. 1408.

[69] Pijassou, *Le Médoc*, p. 321.

[70] "Châteaux" multiplied quite quickly after the classification; by the 1868 edition of Cocks & Féret there were just over 300, including all the first growths of the Médoc and a quarter of the Grand Cru Classés overall.

[71] Strictly speaking this refers to wines of the left bank.

[72] "Clairet" remains an official description for wine style in Bordeaux, in addition to red, white, and rosé. AOC Bordeaux Clairet is like a much darker rosé or a very lightly colored red. It may be quite like "claret" of the 18th century. Clairet and rosé together account for about 1% of Bordeaux production, with clairet about one third of this. Specifications for clairet production are at www.inao.gouv.fr; statistics for production are from the CIVB for the 2006 vintage.

[73] The proverb came to mean: there is no drawing back. It was famously used to stiffen Louis XIV's courage at a battle in 1710. (Alphonse Mariette, *French and English Idioms and Proverbs with Critical and Historical Notes* [Paris: Hachette, 1896], p. 43.)

[74] A contemporary view in 1751 of the merits of wine of different ages noted, "wine begins to degenerate as it enters its second year." (L'Encyclopédie de Diderot et d'Alembert, 1751, tome 17, p. 290.)

[75] Cited in advertisements in the *London Gazette* after 1703. (Pijassou, *Le Médoc*. p. 372.)

[76] Pijassou, *Le Médoc*; p. 373; Faith, *The Winemasters of Bordeaux*, p. 26.

[77] "New French Claret" accounted for 70% of French wines sold in London during this period, which might argue that "new" means "fresh" rather than "grand". The fact that they were of the latest vintage was sometimes stated also. On the other hand, there seems also to have been an explicit association with grand vins. (Pijassou, *Le Médoc*. p. 377-378.)

[78] Pijassou, *Le Médoc*, p. 494.

[79] By the last decade of the 18th century, with the techniques for aging in cask developed, Château Latour was keeping the proprietor's reserve in a special "chai de conserve" for a longer period. In the period 1820-1825, the château rented cellars in Bordeaux to mature older wines, although it's not entirely clear to what degree this was to mature the wines or was forced upon the château by the need to preserve unsold wines. (Pijassou, *Le Médoc*, pp. 579-580.)

[80] Penning-Rowsell, *Bordeaux*, 1989, p. 158.

[81] Tim Unwin, *Wine and the Vine: An Historical Geography of Viticulture and the Wine Trade* (London: Routledge, 1996), p. 266.

[82] Pijassou, *Le Médoc*, p 597.

[83] More than 90% at the end of the century. (Cocks & Féret, *Bordeaux*, 1908, p. 87).

[84] John Vincent Nye, *The Myth of Free-Trade Britain and Fortress France: Tariffs and Trade in the Nineteenth Century* (Journal of Economic History, 51: 23-46, 1991), p 37.

85 Pijassou, *Le Médoc*, p. 345.

86 Grand Vins were first mentioned in official documents in 1730. (Henri Enjalbert, *La naissance des grands vins et la formation du vignoble moderne de Bordeaux*: 1647-1767, in *Géographie historique des vignobles*, (Ed.) Huetz de Lemps [Paris: Actes du Colloque de Bordeaux, CNRS, 1978. p. 81].)

87 Initially no distinction was made among the four first growths with regards to price. For the vintages of 1784-1786, all sold at the same price on the Bordeaux market. (Pijassou, *Le Médoc*. p. 537.)

88 The Writings of Thomas Jefferson (1905). Issued under the auspices of the Thomas Jefferson Memorial Association of the United States.

89 Pijassou, *Le Médoc*, p 537.

90 There were some occasional reports early in the century that wines forgotten in a cellar might taste better than the current vintage; but this was clearly contrary to expectation. (Asa Briggs, *Haut-Brion* [(London: Faber & Faber, 1994], p. 5.)

91 Paul Butel, *Les Dynasties Bordelaises de Colbert à Chaban* (Paris: Librairie Academique Perrin, 1991), p. 179.

92 The proportion was still only 9% for Bordeaux wine in 1877, and was less for wines of other origins exported from the port, perhaps reflecting the fact that "Bordeaux" was the highest quality. (San Francisco Chamber of Commerce, *Franco-American Commerce: Statements and Arguments in Behalf of American Industries Against the Proposed Franco-American Commercial Treaty* [Alta California Book and Job Printing House, 1879], p. 87.)

93 Berry Bros bottlings have generally sold for about two thirds the price of château bottlings on the auction market; other bottlings sell for less. But Berry Bros knew its cuves: for example, although half the crop of the 1945 Cheval Blanc was piqué (showed excess volatile acidity), examples from Berry Bros a few years ago were impeccable.

94 The tax in 1860 was reduced from 5s 9d to 1s, i.e. by 83%. Imports of French wine increased 6-fold, and from 8% of the market to 40%. (James Simpson, *Selling to Reluctant Drinkers: The British Wine Market, 1860-1914* [Economic History Review, vol. 57, pp. 80-108, 2004].)

95 Ibid.

96 Cocks & Féret, *Bordeaux*, 1908, p. 87.

97 England, Argentina, and Germany were of major (and almost equal) importance, followed by the United States, Holland, Uruguay, and Belgium. (Consular Reports, United States Dept. of State, State Dept, Statistics Bureau, 1883. p. 870.)

98 Philippe Roudié, *Vignobles et vignerons du Bordelais*, pp. 119, 210.

99 In detail 30% by value overall, but including 41% of fine wines. (CIVB Memorandum, 2005.)

100 See Figure 20.

101 "The cépages [in Entre-deux-Mers] are essentially the same as those of the palus; but the wines are better. However, they do not rise above the ordinary."

(Joachin Du Plessis de Grénadan. *Géographie agricole de la France at du monde.* [Massum et cie, 1903], p. 168.)

102 Several versions of this map can be found in literature around the turn of the century. It was based on an original from Dubois and Seurin. Ibid.

103 Data from the FGVB and CIVB.

104 Average holding was 6 ha in 1979, 8 ha in 1988, 13.5 ha in 2000. The number of growers declined from 21,273 in 1985 to 10,239 in 2005. (CIVB Memorandum, 2005.)

Chapter 3 The Importance of Being Classified

1 Markham, *A History of the Bordeaux Classification,* presents an extensive history of the classification on which I have drawn in this chapter.

2 The Chamber of Commerce requested the classification on April 5 and received the response on April 18. (Ibid., p. 98, 106.)

3 Markham, *A History of the Bordeaux Classification*, pp. 211-304.

4 The original documents concerning the 1855 classification were reproduced in "Les Grands Crus du Médoc classés en 1855," Chambre de Commerce de Bordeaux (1964).

5 Data from Markham, *A History of the Bordeaux Classification*, pp. 376-499.

6 André Jullien, *Topographie de tous les vignobles connus* (Paris, 1816).

7 Shaw, *Wine, the Vine, and the Cellar*, p. 268.

8 This included two of the first growths, Châteaux Margaux and Latour. (Pijassou, *Le Médoc.* p. 664.)

9 Châteaux are given their modern names where appropriate. Haut Brion is missing because of lack of data. Data may be biased by a series of years in which some châteaux sold their production in advance at a standard "subscription" price. (Markham, *A History of the Bordeaux Classification.*)

10 Markham, *A History of the Bordeaux Classification,* pp. 160-161.

11 For example, Christies Auction catalogs New York (September 16, 2006), Los Angeles (November 3, 2007), Amsterdam (December 11, 2007).

12 http://www.pauillac-medoc.com/default.asp?IDPAGE=153.

13 Personal communication to the author, August 2, 2007.

14 Quoted by Markham, *A History of the Bordeaux Classification,* p. 167.

15 The classification of the red wines of the Médoc was presented unchanged in *Bordeaux et ses Vins,* and indeed in other books on the subject. It was not until well into the twentieth century that the authors were to feel the need to present notes reflecting changes in status since the classification.

16 Décret of the Ministry of Agriculture #49-1369 of September 30, 1949; published in the Journal Officiel de la Republique Français, October 5, 1949.

17 A further provision was added that "cru classé" could also be used for wines of Bordeaux selected on the basis of merit by a "concours public" organized by the appropriate authorities and approved by the Ministry of

Agriculture. Décret of the Ministry of Agriculture #64-668 of June 27, 1964; published in the Journal Officiel de la Republique Français, July 4, 1964.

[18] The previous laws are repeated, using the same wording, in the Code du Vin, which governs wine production in France, under a section dealing with the prevention of terms on labels that would cause confusion. Article 284. *Interdiction de toutes marques sur les* étiquettes, récipients et papiers de commerce susceptibles de prêter à confusion.

[19] Edward Lewine, *Classified Matters* (New York Times magazine, August 17, 2008).

[20] Markham, *A History of the Bordeaux Classification,* p. 200.

[21] The Cru Bourgeois classification was drawn up in 1932 by the Bordeaux wine brokers, under the authority of the Chamber of Commerce and the Chamber of Agriculture. 444 châteaux were ranked into three levels of Cru Bourgeois. The list was never made official but was used for more than 50 years. The Syndicat des Crus Bourgeois du Médoc was established in 1962, and was authorized by a ministerial decree in 2000 to reclassify the Cru Bourgeois. This led to a classification that was published in 2003, with the intention of being revised every 12 years.

[22] The Cru Artisan classification, originally intended to describe wines made by artisans of the village, had fallen into disuse, but was revived in 2006, when 44 out of 59 applicants were approved for the qualification.

[23] The appellations take the names of individual villages, except for Margaux, which includes five communes, so wines in any of Arsac, Cantenac, Labarde, Margaux and Soussans can state "Appellation Margaux Contrôlée."

[24] It included 13 châteaux, all located in Pessac-Léognan (which subsequently separated from the Graves, in 1974).

[25] The 9 châteaux classified for white wine 7 of the original 13 classified châteaux plus an additional two that are classified only for white wine.

[26] See notes 24 and 25 in Chapter 5.

[27] Markham, *A History of the Bordeaux Classification.*

[28] Pijassou, *Le Médoc,* p. 1066

Chapter 4 Wine in the Time of Classification

[1] Yields fluctuated from 8 hl/ha to 35 hl/ha between 1840 and 1880. Calculated from data in Cocks & Féret, *Bordeaux,* 1908.

[2] Archives of N. Johnston in Bordeaux, undated but between 1765 and the Revolution, quoted by Pijassou, *Le Médoc,* p. 500.

[3] Blending was more important in poor years than in good years. A side light on its use to improve the wine is cast by recent experiments at Château Palmer. In 2004 and 2006 the château produced 100 cases of a wine by blending 85% of its own production with 15% of Syrah from the Rhône. This was sold as a table wine under the name "Historical XIXth Century Blend," with the vintage indicated only by the lot number (L20.04 or L20.06), at roughly the same price as the wine

of the vintage. The same experiment was not performed with the (much better) 2005 vintage because "In 2004 it worked very well. In 2005 with 15 percent of Syrah, it doesn't really change," according to the winemaker. (Eric Arnold, *Bordeaux Blended With Syrah* [Wine Spectator online, May 17, 2007].])

4 Quoted by Pijassou, *Le Médoc*, p. 591.

5 Franck, *Traité sur les vins du Médoc*, Tableau 1.

6 Shaw, *Wine, the Vine, and the Cellar*, p. 280.

7 The discrepancy actually suggests more intervention than merely adding 15% of a stronger wine.

8 Pijassou, *Le Médoc*, p. 835.

9 Commenting on the custom of blending, one contemporary writer said: "Hence we need not wonder at the statement of a gentleman who, after living twenty years in Bordeaux, doubted whether he had tasted, more than *three times,* any pure wine of the first quality." (John Ramsey McCulloch, *A dictionary, geographical, statistical, and historical, of the various countries, places, and principal natural objects in the world* [London: Longman, Brown, Green & Longmans, 1851], p. 902.)

10 Analytical data for 1855 obtained from Franck, *Traité sur les vins du Médoc* .

11 The best oak came from Stettin. (Pijassou, *Le Médoc*. p. 572.)

12 Charles Higounet, *La Seigneurie et le Vignoble de Château Latour* (Bordeaux: Federation Historique de Sud Ouest, 1974), p. 397.

13 Shaw, *Wine, the Vine, and the Cellar*, p. 263.

14 Cocks & Féret, Bordeaux, 1868-2007; Lichine, *Encyclopedia of Wines*, 1967, 1974; Faugère, *Les Bordeaux Rive Gauche;*; Hubrecht Duijker, *The Bordeaux Atlas and Encyclopedia of Château* (London: Ebury Press, 1997).

15 Pijassou, *Le Médoc*, p. 46.

16 Lichine, *Encyclopedia of Wines*, 1974.

17 Cocks & Féret, *Bordeaux*, 2007.

18 Jérôme Baudouin, *Des Crus Classés à Géométrie Variable* (La Revue du Vin de France, issue 506, November, 2006), pp. 28-34.

19 Data for 1855 from Shaw, *Wine, the Vine, and the Cellar;* current data from Cocks & Féret, *Bordeaux*, 2007.

20 Jérôme Baudouin, , *Des Crus Classés à Géométrie Variable.*

21 Pijassou, *Le Médoc*, p. 931, figure 144.

22 Conseil des Vins du Médoc.

23 Pijassou, *Le Médoc*, p. 1007.

24 John Hailman, *Thomas Jefferson on Wine* (University of Missisipi Press, 2006), p. 516.

25 Production figures are taken from Cocks & Féret, Bordeaux, 1868, 2007, but note that figures given by Franck, *Traité sur les vins du Médoc,* are much lower than those of Cocks & Féret, *Bordeaux*, 1868, in which case the increase in production would be even greater than shown.

[26] Data for 1835-1855 from Markham, *A History of the Bordeaux Classification*. Data for 1985-2005 obtained by the author from negociants' records for en primeur prices on the Place de Bordeaux.

[27] The average for the Médoc is a vineyard holding of 11.5 ha. Calculated from Cocks & Féret, *Bordeaux*, 2007.

[28] Data from CIVB and Association of Crus Bourgeois. Estimates for the 2004 vintage. Revenues include second wines as well as grand vins in each class. The economic share of Grand Cru Classés increased in 2005 and 2006.

Chapter 5 The Land and the Brand

[1] Gaston Marchou, *Le Vin de Bordeaux, cet Inconnu* (Montpellier: Causse et Cie, 1973).

[2] In Bordeaux the term palu is feminine and specifically means the band of alluvial territory along the banks of the Garonne and Dordogne rivers. Elsewhere the term is masculine and used generally to mean marshlands.

[3] Paul Massé, *Le Dessèchement des Marais du Bas-Médoc*. In Revue historique de Bordeaux et du Département de la Gironde (No. 1 p. 1-44, 1957); Henri Enjalbert, *Les Pays Aquitains*. (Bordeaux: Biere, Bordeaux, Tome I, 1960, p.171).

[4] Based on data from references in note 3 above.

[5] Lavaud, *Bordeaux et le vin*.

[6] For example, the community of Blanquefort brought an action against Conrad Gaussen in February 1600 on the grounds that drainage of the palu deprived them of their rights (but it failed). (Sandrine Lavaud, *La palu de Bordeaux aux XVᵉ et XVIᵉ siècles* [Annales Du Midi, t. 114, janv-mars 2002], p. 43.)

[7] Sandrine Lavaud, *La palu de Bordeaux aux XVᵉ et XVIᵉ siècles* (Annales Du Midi, t. 114, janv-mars 2002), p. 25-44.

[8] Ibid., p. 32.

[9] Aerial view from Google Earth.

[10] Philippe Roudié, *Vignobles et vignerons*, p. 89.

[11] Marcel Lachiver, *Vins, Vignes et Vignerons. Histoire de Vignoble Français* (Paris: Fayard, 1988), p. 357.

[12] Personal communication to the author at Château d'Yquem, April, 2006.

[13] Gérard Seguin, *Influence des facteurs naturels sur les caractères des vins. In Traité d'ampélologie*, (Paris: Bordas. Sciences et Technique de la vigne, 1980); Wilson, *Terroir*, p. 188.

[14] Aerial view from Google Earth.

[15] Aerial views from Google Earth.

[16] Wilson, *Terroir*, pp. 187-191.

[17] Pijassou, *Le Médoc*, p 1355-1361; Wilson, *Terroir*, p. 195.

[18] Wilson, *Terroir*, pp. 194-198.

[19] Ibid., p. 197.

[20] Ibid., pp. 198-199.

[21] Personal communication to the author (July 11, 2007).

[22] Château St. Pierre was classified as a single quatrième cru classé in 1855, although actually the château had been split into two parts, called Château St. Pierre Sevaistre and Château St. Pierre Bontemps, in 1832. However, in 1923 they were recombined.

[23] Batailley was split as recently as 1942 into Batailley and Haut Batailley (for reasons of inheritance). Haut Batailley is much the smaller part, but like Batailley, retains the right to use the Cinquième Grand Cru Classé designation.

[24] Châteaux Boyd Cantenac and Cantenac Brown were under common ownership in 1855, and were classified as a single troisième Grand Cru Classé. However, subsequently they split apart, with both châteaux demanding the rights to the description of third growth. It took a legal action toward the end of the 19th century for Cantenac Brown to be allowed to use the description of third growth (which is also used by Boyd Cantenac).

[25] An illustration of the pulling power of the classification comes from the history of Château Clerc Milon. Just before Jean Baptiste Clerc, the owner of the château, died in 1863, he sold part of the estate to a M. Lamena, who then sold it to Jacques Mondon. M. Mondon went to court for the right to use the name of Clerc Milon, and correspondingly to describe his wine as Grand Cru Classé. He won, although in fact he owned only the smaller part of the original estate. His château became known as Clerc-Milon-Mondon.

[26] Gruaud Larose split into two separate châteaux, called Gruaud Larose Sarget and Gruaud Larose Bethman in 1917, but they were recombined into a single château in 1935.

[27] Robert Daley, *The Miracle of Château Gloria* (New York Times, November 14, 1976).

[28] Peppercorn, *Bordeaux*, 1991, p. 266.

[29] Lichine describes the process of acquisition in his *New Encyclopedia of Wines and Spirits* (New York: Knopf, 1977), p. 382.

[30] Clive Coates, *The Wines of Bordeaux: Vintages and Tasting Notes 1952-2003* (Berkeley: University of California Press, 2004), p. 156.

[31] Interview with the author, April 2008.

[32] Quoted in Robert C. Ulin, *Invention and Representation as Cultural Capital: Southwest French Winegrowing History* (American Anthropologist, New Series, 97: 519-527, 1995).

[33] Frank Prial, *Wine Talk* (New York Times, November 15, 1995).

[34] Cour administrative d'appel de Bordeaux 6ème chambre (formation à 3) 20 mars 2007 n°05BX00262. See http://www.lexeek.com/jus-luminum/decision-caa-bordeaux-6eme-ch-20-03-2007-05bx00262,307095.htm

[35] Journal Officiel, October 3, 2007. Décret no 2007-1412 du 1er octobre 2007 modifiant le décret du 10 août 1954 modifié définissant l'appellation d'origine contrôlée "Margaux" No. AGRP0754332D.

[36] Real estate agents in St. Emilion give an average for St. Emilion Grand Cru (essentially unclassified) vineyards of €230,000 per hectare in 2006. Grand Cru vineyards for sale at various agents in 2008 averaged €300,000/ha. Given the

relatively small number of classified châteaux, numbers of sales are low and averages not very reliable, but €1 million/hectare is a conservative estimate for Grand Cru Classé vineyards based on reported sales since 2006.

[37] Average house prices quoted by estate agents in Libourne in 2008 show €300,000 for an area of 300 m², which is equivalent to €10 million/hectare. Château Quinault, which is within the town and surrounded by housing, was sold during 2008 for a price thought to have been €8-10 million (Decanter.com web site, September 4, 2008.) This prices the sale at €600,00/ha, above most unclassified châteaux but below Grand Cru Classé. The new proprietors, Bernard Arnault and Albert Frère, who already own Château Cheval Blanc, are among the richest men in France.

Chapter 6 Crisis and Prosperity

[1] The twenties were quite decent, the thirties were terrible, the forties and fifties about average, the sixties quite good, and the seventies somewhat difficult, until the eighties ushered in an era with more frequent good vintages.

[2] Gilbert Garrier, Le Phylloxéra. Une Guerre de Trente Ans 1870-1900 (Paris: Albin Michel, 1989).

[3] Florence Mothe, Toutes Hontes Bues. Une siècle de vin et de negoce à Bordeaux (Paris: Albin Michel, 1992), p. 53.

[4] An account of its development by the inventor can be found in Alexis Millardet, Notes sur les vignes americaines et opuscules divers sur le même sujet (Ser. I-III, University of California Press, p. 19-20, 1881).

[5] Jean Augustin Barral and Henry Sagnier, Dictionnaire d'agriculture, encyclopédie agricole complète (Paris: Hachette et cie, Paris, 1889), p. 74.

[6] For vintages 1840-1949 see Germain Lafforgue, Cent cinquante ans de production viticole en Gironde (Bulletin Technique d'Information des Ingenieurs des Services Agricoles, pp. 293-301, 1954). For subsequent vintages see Cocks & Féret, Bordeaux, 1969-2007, and CIVB.

[7] Data for the 19th century are not entirely reliable because different sources give different values for vineyard areas. Data for the 20th century from Cocks & Féret, Bordeaux (various editions) and the CIVB.

[8] Yields increased all over France. They increased less in the Gironde because a large proportion of production is AOC, and yields are therefore limited by appellation rules.

[9] Yields calculated by comparing average production for 5 year periods with the average area of vineyards. Data from Cocks & Féret, Bordeaux, 1949, and the CIVB.

[10] Data from Pijassou, Le Médoc, pp. 1412-1415.

[11] Data from Pijassou, Le Médoc, pp. 1437-1443.

[12] En primeur prices on the Place de Bordeaux obtained by the author from negociants' archives.

[13] Robert Forster, *The Noble Wine Producers of the Bordelais in the Eighteenth Century* (The Economic History Review, New Series, Vol. 14, No. 1, pp. 18-33, 1961), p 21.

[14] Gérard Aubin, *La seigneurie en Bordelais au 18e siècle d'après la pratique notariale*, 1715-1789 (Rouen: Université de Rouen, 1989), p. 275.

[15] Forster, *The Noble Wine Producers*, p 29.

[16] Aubin, *La seigneurie en Bordelais*, p. 390.

[17] In 1852 the English banker Charles Cecil Martyns purchased Châteaux Cos d'Estournel and Cos Labory when the founder of Cos d'Estournel, Louis Gaspard d'Estournel, ran into financial difficulties. Two wine merchants of foreign origin bought châteaux; Sebastian Jurine (Swiss) bought Lynch Bages in 1824, and Halvorous Sollberg (Swedish) bought Marquis de Terme in 1845. Previously the Irish influx had led to purchases of some estates, most notably Léoville Barton and Langoa Barton, where the influence remains strong to this day. And the English Major General Palmer had founded Château Palmer, although by 1853 it had been sold to the French Péreire banking family.

[18] Ray, *Mouton-Rothschild*, p. 28.

[19] Based on a survey of châteaux whose balance sheets are available through the Registre National du Commerce et des Sociétés at www.euridile.com.

[20] Upto one third of châteaux reported a negative balance after allowing for interest payments.

[21] The average price for the 2005 vintage en primeur on the Place de Bordeaux for the châteaux in this survey was 1.8 times the price of the 2004 vintage. (En primeur prices on the Place de Bordeaux obtained by the author from negociants' archives.)

[22] Because of delays before receipts are booked from a given vintage, and with variations in the fiscal year, the results are mostly seen as a dramatic improvement on the balance sheet for the fiscal 2007 year.

[23] Average profits in fiscal 2007 were 2.4 times those of fiscal 2006. The average *increase* in profits in 2007 compared with the preceding three years is equivalent to 24% of cash flow, but the range is of course extremely wide. Based on a survey of châteaux whose results are available from the Registre National du Commerce et des Sociétés at www.infogreffe.fr.

[24] This and subsequent figures and tables are based on stated ownership of each Grand Cru Classé in 2008.

[25] The wealthiest investors focus on the top end of the market; for example, luxury goods companies or those associated with them own several Grand Cru Classés and their right bank equivalents, but their purchases overall in the period 1976 to 2003 amount to only 5% of the Bordeaux market. Banks and insurance companies account for more than 40% of all purchases in this period. Foreign investors accounted for roughly one third of all purchases in this period (Réjalot, *Les Logiques du Château*, pp. 228, 232.)

[26] In some cases members of the family still own châteaux, but independently of the negociant firm itself.

27 Challenge magazine: see
http://www.challenges.fr/classements/fortune.php

Chapter 7 *Winners and Losers*

1 César Compadre (Sud Ouest, December 13, 2005).

2 Alain Vironneau, Annual general assembly of the Syndicat des Vins de Bordeaux, 2005.

3 Quoted in The Independent, London, December 2, 2005.

4 Quoted in Jane Anson, Wine and Spirits Magazine, 2006. See http://www.newbordeaux.com/documents/bordeaux_property_prices.html

5 Jane Anson, *Bordeaux Regional Analysis*, (Neustadt, Germany: Meininger's Wine Business International, February 2008).

6 CIVB Memorandum (2006).

7 Although it should be said that much of the decline was due to forcing out poor, old-fashioned producers; the standard of what is left is much improved.

8 The basic problem remains that its low reputation makes it impossible to get an economic price. In 1991, much of the market was lost when prices were forced up to uncompetitive levels by low yields. The same could happen with the 2008 vintage, where yields are down about 40% on the previous year.

9 In 1990, Bordeaux dominated the wine export market, with exports about 5 times those of Australia. Today, Bordeaux's exports are about one third of those of Australia, which are roughly comparable to total production in Bordeaux.

10 CIVB Memorandum (2006).

11 €300 million were requested in 2004. By 2006, the equivalent of 4 million cases was being distilled. CIVB (2008). See
http://www.bordeaux.com/Data/media/DP08_FR_VinsDeBdxChiffres.pdf

12 Grants of €15,000 per hectare were offered (L'Express, May 15, 2007). This was the limit set by the Ministère de l'Économie, as stated in the Journal Officiel of September 9, 2006, p. 2490.

13 Between 2005 and 2007, less than 3000 ha were uprooted; see CIVB report (2008).

14 Deuxième Grand Cru Classés increased from 8500 Francs/tonneau to 35,000 Francs/tonneau between the 1970 and 1972 vintages; generic Bordeaux increased from 1200 to 3750 francs/tonneau. (Le Figaro, May 22, 1973, p. 30.)

15 52 cooperatives account for 25% of all production. CIVB: see http://www.bordeaux.com/Economie-Et-Metiers/default.aspx?culture=fr-FR&country=FR

16 Quoted in Réjalot, *Les Logiques du Château*, p. 281.

17 Jane Anson, *Bordeaux Regional Analysis,* (Neustadt, Germany: Meininger's Wine Business International, February 2008).

18 The profession of courtier is now regulated by a décret (legal proclamation) of May 30, 1997 (décret 95/591). The professional organization, the Fedération

Nationale des Syndicats de Courtiers en Vins et Spiritueux de France, has about 600 registered members. See www.courtiersenvin.com.

[19] Today there are less than 20 negociants in the vicinity of the Quai des Chartrons. In 1950, there were close to 200. (Réjalot, *Les Logiques du Château*, p. 143.)

[20] Quoted in Pijassou, *Le Médoc*, p. 610.

[21] Quoted in Pierre Bert, *In Vino Veritas. L'Affaire des Vins de Bordeaux* (Paris: Albin Michel, 1975), p. 87.

[22] Florence Mothe, *Toutes Hontes Bues. Une siècle de vin et de negoce à Bordeaux* (Paris: Albin Michel, 1992), p. 181.

[23]Philippe Courrian & Michel Creignou, *Vigneron du Médoc* (Paris: Editions Payot & Rivages, 1996) p. 56.

[24] Union des Maisons de Bordeaux (2008). *L'economie du vin.*

http://www.vins-bordeaux-negoce.com/economie.asp

[25] In 2005, 42% was bottled by the château for sale under its label, and a further 12% was bottled at the property by a negociant. C.I.V.B. (2006). Memento Économique du Vin de Bordeaux.

[26] Quoted in Alexis Bespaloff (New York magazine, vol 19, no. 17, April issue, 1986), pp. 98-100.

[27] Réjalot, *Les Logiques du Château*, pp. 241 & 249.

[28] Ibid., p. 267.

[29] Ibid., p. 253.

[30] CIVB: see http://www.bordeaux.com/Economie-Et-Metiers/Les-Chiffres-Cles-De-La-Filieres.aspx?culture=fr-FR&country=FR

[31] Réjalot, *Les Logiques du Château*, p. 257.

[32] Ibid., p. 255.

[33] Jane Anson, *The Place de Bordeaux* (Neustadt, Germany: Meininger's Wine Business International, April 13, 2007), p 58.

[34] Ibid., p 61.

[35] Réjalot, *Les Logiques du Château*, p. 26 and p.42.

[36] In the United States market, Yellow Tail spends about $9 million per year on advertising; Turning Leaf or Woodbridge brands spend about $8 million per year. (Adams Wine Handbook [New York: Adams Media Inc, 2007].)

[37] En primeur sales via the Place may use the 10-40-50 basis, which means that 10% is paid immediately, 40% at the end of the year, and 50% the June following. However, the bill of sale can be used to get cash from the bank immediately (albeit with a charge).

[38] On both sides of the Atlantic, 1966 appears to have been the first year when Bordeaux was offered en primeur to the consumer. I am indebted to Hugo Rose MW for the information that Lay & Wheeler in London first offered Bordeaux en primeur at this time, and to Jeremy Noyes for information about the offering at Zachys at the same time.

[39] One indication of the transition occurring during the 1970s may be that prices were quoted on the Place de Bordeaux in tonneaux (barrels of 900 liters) until 1978, when most quotations changed to a price per bottle.

[40] Zachys offered about 30 wines en primeur in 1966 compared with roughly 300 in 2005. Personal communication: Jeremy Noyes.

[41] When a château also has a second wine, assemblage is the point of decision for which barrels are used for the grand vin and which are relegated to the second wine.

[42] A survey undertaken by the author in 2008 showed that 70% of châteaux take the decision before starting the maturation in barrel, so the blend accurately represents the final planned wine. In other cases, the sample shown en primeur is more of an estimate of what the final wine will look like.

[43] The Bordelais claim this is rare, because any regular discrepancy in quality between en primeur samples and final bottled wine would be counter-productive. "We are always on patrol to spot the offenders," one negociant said to me in August 2008. But others are not so sure. Jeffords entitled a section on the system, "Great Bordeaux is sold fraudulently," in his book *The New France*, p. 175.

[44] One Grand Cru Classé uses a tiny amount of American oak (<1%) in its final blend, but bumps this up to 8% for the sample that is shown en primeur. The winemaker claims that this merely gives the inexperienced taster a better view of what the wine will look like at maturity. Personal communication to the author at the château in March 2006.

[45] Peppercorn, *Bordeaux*, 1991, p. 267.

[46] Personal communication from Daniel Lawton.

[47] Cocks & Féret, *Bordeaux*, 1908, lists 62 châteaux in the Médoc that were under abonnement in 1907, including 13 of the Grand Cru Classés (and all of the first growths).

[48] Faith, *The Winemasters of Bordeaux*, p. 63.

[49] Things can go the other way, of course. In 1866-1867 hot summers seemed to promise good vintage, but then there was heavy rain. Most of the crop had been sold sur souche; this time it was the negociants who took a beating.

[50] François Mauriac, *Préséances*. (Paris: Flammarion, 1928).

[51] Florence Mothe, *Toutes Hontes Bues. Une siècle de vin et de negoce à Bordeaux* (Paris: Albin Michel, 1992), p. 259.

[52] Stephen Brook, *Bordeaux. People, Power and Politics*, p. 58.

[53] Quoted in Revue du Vin de France, August 2008, p. 10. *Tensions entre Latour et le négoce bordelais.*

[54] César Compadre, Sud Ouest, July 3, 2007, p. 10.

[55] When the en primeurs are first released, their relative prices in all consumer markets closely reflect the initial release price, partly due to an unwritten understanding on margins. As the initial supply is sold, and once the initial period of honoring the margins passes, readjustment occurs, especially with increased markup of wines that have been perceived as too cheap.

[56] Quoted in Faith, *The Winemasters*, p. 249.

[57] François Renard, Le Monde, October 16, 1990.

[58] Pierre Cherruau, Le Monde, August 24, 1997.

[59] John Hess, New York Times, November 26, 1970.

[60] Robert Alden, New York Times, November 22, 1961.

[61] Prices obtained by the author from negociants' archives. Vintage ratings from The Wine Advocate, Baltimore.

[62] Pijassou, *Le Médoc*, p. 1454.

[63] Data from the Syndicat of Courtiers in Bordeaux as quoted by Pijassou, *Le Médoc*, p. 1454.

[64] Jean-Claude Guillebaud, Le Monde, September 13, 1972.

[65] The price of Lafite Rothschild fell from 120,000 to 70,000 Ff per tonneau from the first to the second tranche for the 1973 vintage.

[66] One major negociant started 1974 with 110 million Ff of claret, and in a 3-week period its value dropped to 58 million.

[67] Le Point (May 5, 2000, #1442).

[68] Sud-Ouest, Bordeaux, April 19, 2004 and June 22, 2004.

[69] http://www.jancisrobinson.com/articles/20070410_3.

[70] Réjalot, *Les Logiques du Château*, p. 99.

[71] Paul Butel, *Les Dynasties Bordelaises de Colbert a Chaban* (Paris: Libraire Academique Perrin, 1991). p. 378. Proportion of negociant business as shown in records of Tastet & Lawton.

[72] Faith, *The Winemasters of Bordeaux*, p. 113.

[73] Florence Mothe, *Toutes Hontes Bues. Une siècle de vin et de negoce à Bordeaux* (Paris: Albin Michel, 1992), p. 260.

[74] Data from Réjalot, *Les Logiques du Château*, p. 234, updated from public records and allowing for subsequent mergers and acquisitions.

Chapter 8 The Price of Reputation

[1] This has been attributed by Jonathan Fenby, *On the Brink* (New York: Arcade Publishing, 1999) to a recollection by U.S. Secretary of State Madelaine Albright of a French response to a proposal for European cooperation.

[2] Decanter magazine (U.K.) was founded in 1975, Finigan's Private Guide to Wines (U.S.) became national in 1977, The Wine Advocate (U.S.) was founded in 1978, and The Wine Spectator (U.S.) in its present form dates from 1979.

[3] The Private Guide finally ceased publication in 1990.

[4] Comment to the author by a château proprietor in Margaux, March 2009.

[5] Robert Parker, *The Wine Advocate*, issue 140, 2002, p. 36.

[6] Quoted in Elin McCoy, *The Emperor of Wine: The Rise of Robert M. Parker, Jr. and the Reign of American Taste* (Ecco, 2005), p. 288.

[7] Jancis Robinson, (2003). http://www.jancisrobinson.com/jr7046.

[8] Hanna Agostini, *Robert Parker. Anatomie d'un Mythe* (Paris: Editions Scali, 2007).

[9] Elin McCoy, *The Emperor of Wine*.

[10] Hadj Ali, Lecocq, and Visser (2005).

http://www.inra.fr/Internet/Departements/ESR/UR/lea/documents/wp/wp0507.pdf. Interestingly, an earlier paper including some of the same authors did not include critics' ratings as a factor to analyze in price (P. Combris, S. Lecocq and M. Visser, *Estimation of a hedonic price equation for Bordeaux wine; does quality matter?* [The Economic Journal, 107, pp. 390-402, 1997].)

[11] Colin Hay, *Globalisation and the Institutional Re-embedding of Markets: The Political Economy of Price Formation in the Bordeaux En Primeur Market* (New Political Economy, Vol. 12, pp 185-209, 207. Routledge, London).

[12] Critics' ratings taken from their publications; en primeur prices on the Place de Bordeaux obtained by the author from negociants' archives.

[13] En primeur prices on the Place de Bordeaux obtained by the author from negociants' archives.

[14] Based on ratings in the April issues of The Wine Advocate for wines tasted in barrel.

[15] The same analysis shown in Table 12 was performed separately for the left bank and right bank.

[16] Personal communication from Christian Seely; April 28, 2008.

[17] En primeur prices on the Place de Bordeaux obtained by the author from negociants' archives.

[18] Survey based on prices in U.S.A., U.K., France as reported on www.wine-searcher.com.

[19] En primeur prices on the Place de Bordeaux obtained by the author from negociants' archives.

[20] From the auction price database at www.vines.org.

[21] David Peppercorn, *Bordeaux, 1st edition* (London: Faber & Faber, 1982), p. 84; Michael Broadbent, *The Great Vintage Wine Book, 1st edition* (New York: Knopf, 1980), p. 90.

[22] Prix de sortie obtained from the châteaux, auction prices from the archives at Christies.

[23] Auction prices obtained by the author from archives at Christies, London.

[24] En primeur prices on the Place de Bordeaux obtained by the author from negociants' archives.

[25] A Christies auction in New York on November 21, 2008 sold only 65 lots out of 230. Most of those that sold were well below their low estimates. Although the art auctions showed a similar drop in price, they did better in selling ~65% of the lots.

[26] Wine prices from the www.vines.org auction database, art prices from Christies and Sothebys for New York auctions.

[27] Observation by the author.

[28] En primeur prices on the Place de Bordeaux obtained by the author from negociants' archives.

[29] Its best year was 1997 (a relatively poor vintage with unreasonably high prices). Prices on the Place de Bordeaux were as follows. Léoville Las Cases was

quoted at 68.60 compared with 76.22 for the Médoc first growths. Its second wine, Clos du Marquis, was quoted at 18.29, in the middle of the prices for second wines of the first growths (Forts de Latour 22.87, Pavillon Rouge de Margaux 19.51, Carruades de Lafite 16.01 €/bottle.) En primeur prices on the Place de Bordeaux obtained by the author from negociants' archives. Fluctuations in prices during the en primeur campaign might explain reports that Léoville Las Cases equaled first growth prices that year, and that its second wine placed higher than the second wines of the first growths.

[30] The Wine Advocate, Baltimore. Prices from April issues reporting on the en primeur wines.

Chapter 9 The Rise of the Right Bank

[1] Hugh Johnson, *The Story of Wine* (London: Mitchell Beazley, 2005), p. 201.

[2] Data from Penning-Rowsell, *Bordeaux*, 1989, p. 592.

[3] Syndicate Viticole de Saint Emilion (2008).

[4] Ibid., p. 515; Ministry of agriculture viticultural census (1968, 1988, 2000); Cocks & Féret, *Bordeaux*, 1969.

[5] Henri Enjalbert, *Les grands vins de Saint-Emilion, Pomerol, Fronsac* (Paris: Editions Bardi, 1983) , p. 514.

[6] Henri Enjalbert, *Les grands vins de Saint-Emilion.*

[7] Frédéric Durand-Bazin, Le Figaro, September 9, 2008.

[8] Sophie Kevany, Decanter, August 15, 2008. See http://www.decanter.com/news/265596.html

[9] Quoted in New York Times, July 24, 2008. *Ruling Turns a Village of Winemakers on Itself.*

[10] Interview with the author, April 9, 2008.

[11] En primeur prices on the Place de Bordeaux obtained by the author from negociants' archives.

[12] Frank Prial, *Wine Talk: $1,000 Wines You Never Heard Of* (The New York Times, October 25, 2000).

[13] Based on a survey by the author. But note that identification of a garage wine can be subjective.

[14] Decanter magazine (2005), review of 2004 en primeurs.

[15] Interview with the author, April 9, 2008.

[16] Interview with the author, April 10, 2008.

[17] Magnum of Le Pin 1982 sold as lot 23 for $23,500 at Christies New York, March 2, 2006. Double magnum of Pétrus 1982 sold as lot 3 at Sothebys London, April 11, 2007 for £17,250. This is equivalent to $11,750/ bottle for Le Pin and $8,500/bottle for Pétrus.

[18] www.vines.org auction database.

[19] En primeur prices on the Place de Bordeaux obtained by the author from negociants' archives.

[20] Ibid.

21 Based on a survey by the author of prices at leading stores in the U.S.A. and U.K.

22 En primeur prices on the Place de Bordeaux obtained by the author from negociants' archives.

Chapter 10 The New Bordeaux

1 The great oenologist Emile Peynaud pointed out that the 1982s actually had more tannin than the 1978s or 1975s but the tannins were less evident because they were hidden by fruit. (Alexis Bespaloff, *Waiting for Bordeaux*, New York Magazine, October 3, 1983.)

2 The Writings of Thomas Jefferson (1905). Issued under the auspices of the Thomas Jefferson Memorial Association of the United States.

3 The proprietors of the first growths believed Jefferson may have been drinking his wines too young. (James M. Gabler, *Passions: The Wines and Travels of Thomas Jefferson* [Bacchus Press, 1995], pp. 118-119).)

4 George Saintsbury, *Notes on a Cellar Book* (London: MacMillan, 1931), pp. 48, 51.

5 "The highest grades of claret will keep for from fifteen to eighteen years, constantly improving in delicacy. After that time they rapidly deteriorate." (Henry Wolsmar Ruaff, *The Century Book of Facts* [The King-Richardson Company, 1900], p. 425.)

6 "The Gironde red wines have sufficient body and alcohol to ensure stability without being heavy or fiery. At the same time, their acidity is very low and their bouquet characteristically delicate and elegant. It is to this relatively large amount of body and absence of an excess of acid and of tannin that the peculiarly soft effect of the Bordeaux wines on the palate is due." (The Encyclopedia Britannica, 11th edition, 1911, entry for *Wine*, p. 722.)

7 This conclusion is supported by the fact that there seems to have been relatively little technical change in the wine between 1860 and the early 20th century. Technical analyses of Château Lafite for vintages from 1865 to 1905 showed a small range of variation in alcohol around an average of 11%, and equally low variation in acidity or solid extract. (see note 6 above). The properties of Bordeaux wine were described in 1916 as having 10.5% alcohol and 0.175% tannin, not very different from those of 1855. (New International Encyclopedia, Dodd Mead, 1907. vol 23, p. 697).

8 "Even an ordinary Claret should not be drunk until it has been two years in bottle, and it is a shame to drink finer Bordeaux until they have a bottle-age of eight or ten years at least." (H Warner Allen, *The Wines of France* [London : Fisher Unwin, 1924], p. 89.)

9 For the lesser wines, high acidity may be more of a problem than high tannins in poor vintages.

10 The Wine Advocate, April 2004.

[11] JancisRobinson.com purple pages; see jancisrobinson.com/articles/tasting0405/article_view.

[12] The Vine (London: Coates Publishing, June 2004).

[13] Denis Morélot, *Statistique de la Vigne dans de Departement de la Cote-d'Or* (Dijon: Ch. Brugnot, 1831), p. 250.

[14] Georges Bord, *Essai sur les variations de l'encépagement dans le vignoble Bordelais* (Bordeaux: Imprimerie de la Feuille Vinicole, 1932)

[15] The Abbé Rozier at Béziers collected plants from the Gironde and as far away as Bergerac in an attempt to make a definitive list, but abandoned the project in 1774 due to difficulties with the inconsistency of naming. (Bord, *Essai sur les variations,* p. 6.)

[16] The list was contained in a memoire by Baron de Secondat entitled *L'Histoire Naturelle Du Chêne*. It listed as "raisons à grains ronde," Carmenet (Petite Vigne dure), Grand Carmenet, Petit Verdot, Massoutet, Tarney (Coulant du Bas-Médoc), Amaroi, Pied-rouge, Malbeck (Luckens), Petit Bouchères, Ceruchinet (Doux-Same), Balouzet (Mourane), Petite Mérille, Martimous, Muscat rouge. (Bord, *Essai sur les variations,* p. 5.) (Carmenet is probably Cabernet.)

[17] A book entitled *l'Ampelographie Universelle* discussed all known quality cépages. The first edition (of several) was published in 1841, and described 6 leading varieties of the Gironde, 3 minor varieties, and 4 poor quality varieties. (Bord, *Essai sur les variations,* p. 7.)

[18] The proprietor of Domaine de Carbonnieux listed 919 known varieties and identified the best varieties of the Gironde. (Bord, *Essai sur les variations,* p. 8.)

[19] Edouard Féret, *Statistique Générale Topographique, Scientifique, Administrative, Industrielle, Commerciale, Agricole, Historique, Archéologique Et Biographique Du Département De La Gironde* (Bordeaux: Editions Féret, 1874)

[20] Pessac had 50% Cabernet, 25% Merlot and 25% Malbec.

[21] Lafforgue, *Le Vignoble Girondin*, p. 150.

[22] Mothe, *Toutes Hontes Bues*, p. 199.

[23] Henri Enjalbert, *Les grands vins de Saint-Emilion, Pomerol, Fronsac* (Paris: Editions Bardi, 1983), pp. 508-509.

[24] Ministry of agriculture viticultural census (1968, 1988, 2000); Cocks & Féret, *Bordeaux*, 1969.

[25] Australia produced 29% red wine in 1993, but had increased to 55% by year 2000. (Australian Bureau of Statistics, Australian Wine and Grape Industry, Report 1329.0.)

[26] Roudié, *Vignobles et vignerons du Bordelais* p. 329

[27] CIVB census (1988).

[28] See note 14 in Chapter 1.

[29] CIVB census (2000).

[30] Ibid.

[31] Ibid.

[32] From data of Cocks & Féret, *Bordeaux*, 2007.

[33] Ibid.

[34] Cocks & Féret, *Bordeaux*, 1985, 1991, 2004, 2007; Hubrecht Duijker, *The Bordeaux Atlas and Encyclopedia of Château* (London: Ebury Press, 1997).

[35] Provided by Pichon Lalande.

[36] Results obtained at the University of Bordeaux from a test plot harvested in the Médoc. Potential alcohol is calculated by assuming that 18 g/l of sugar in the grapes gives 1% alcohol in the wine.

[37] Discussion with the author in Bordeaux, March 2009.

[38] Chaptalization is permitted up to 13% alcohol.

[39] http://www.decanter.com/news/82851.html

[40] It is admittedly difficult to assess changes in tannins other than quantity, since the chemistry of how different tannins affect taste is not at all understood. Although not everyone would agree, majority opinion is that tannins change in quality as well as quantity with berry ripeness.

[41] One significant change preceding 1982 was the move to destem grapes before fermentation. The stalks contain harsher tannins than the skin, so this had a softening effect. This demonstrates the effect of the nature of the tannins. Because the stalks contain water, but not sugar, and absorb alcohol, this change also increased alcoholic strength by up to 0.5%. It was advocated by Peynaud in his book of 1970 (later translated as Emile Peynaud, *Knowing and Making Wine* [New York: Wiley-Interscience, 1984], p. 146).

[42] Gregory Jones, *Climate and Terroir: Impacts of Climate Variability and Change on Wine*. In Fine Wine and Terroir - The Geoscience Perspective. R. W. Macqueen & L. D. Meinert (eds.), Geoscience Canada Reprint Series Number 9, 2006, Geological Association of Canada, St. John's, Newfoundland.

[43] From weather stations at Dijon, Bordeaux, and Nimes as available from the Goddard Institute.

[44] Weather data: Goddard Institute; Harvest dates: FGVB.

[45] Data from Bordeaux and Napa weather stations available via Goddard Institute.

[46] Data from France metéo.

[47] Quoted in Frank Ward (New York: Connoisseur magazine, May issue, 1987).

[48] By 1959, Peynaud published a scientific paper showing that malolactic fermentation could be induced by inoculating wine with the appropriate bacteria. (CR Seances Acad. Agric, France, 45, p. 355.)

[49] According to châteaux identified on the web sites of the oenologists or oenologists identified on the web sites of the châteaux.

[50] Bill Blatch, *Preliminary 2000 Bordeaux Vintage Report* (San Rafael, California: Wines & Vines, January issue, 2001).

Chapter 11 Grand Vins and Second Wines

[1] Eric Conan, *Les Grands Crus Degriffés*. (L'Express, January 24, 2005, Paris.)

[2] Frank Prial, Wine Talk (New York Times, August 16, 1989).

[3] Benjamin Lewin, *The Role of Second Wines in Bordeaux* (London: Institute of Masters of Wine), p. 40.

[4] The first mention of second wines dates from 1735. (Marcel Lachiver. *Vins, vignes et vignerons. Histoire du vignoble Français.* [Paris: Fayard, 1988], p. 305.

[5] Quoted in Pijassou, *Le Médoc*, p. 552.

[6] Quoted in Pijassou, *Le Médoc*, p. 553.

[7] At Château Latour, the grand vin was matured in oak from Stettin, which was "stronger" than the oak from Lübeck used for used for the second wines. (Pijassou, *Le Médoc*. p. 572.)

[8] Pijassou, *Le Médoc*, p. 551.

[9] Butel, Paul. (1963) *Grands propriétaires et production des vins du Médoc au XVIIIe siècle.* (Revue historique de Bordeaux et du Département de la Gironde 12, p. 129-141.)

[10] Pijassou, *Le Médoc*, p. 1394.

[11] Pijassou, *Le Médoc*.

[12] René Pijassou, *Château Rauzan-Segla. La naissance d'un Grand Cru Classé* (Paris: Editions de la Martiniere, 2004)

[13] Lewin, *The Role of Second Wines in Bordeaux*, p. 5.

[14] The description refers more to the conditions of vinification in this vintage than to the usual selection of cuves, but shows that the term was in accepted usage. Because of hot conditions, ice was added to control the fermentation temperature of Château Lafite, but some barrels were kept aside and fermented without any ice; these were labeled as the second wine.

[15] Much of the information in this chapter is based on data in Benjamin Lewin, *The Role of Second Wines in Bordeaux* (London: Institute of Masters of Wine), as detailed in individual notes.

[16] Ibid., p. 14.

[17] Ibid., p. 10.

[18] Ibid., p. 15.

[19] Based on a survey by the author of wines available at retail in U.S.A. and U.K. in 2007.

[20] Lewin, *The Role of Second Wines*, p. 20

[21] Overall, 25% of second wines are made exclusively from young vines. (Lewin, *The Role of Second Wines, p. 20*.)

[22] Personal communication, Rémi Edange, Domaine de Chevalier, April 2008.

[23] Grand vin provided an average 69% of production compared to 31% for second wine. (Lewin, *The Role of Second Wines*, p. 32.)

[24] The proportion of second wines whose names can be easily related to the grand vin is 85%at the present time. (Lewin, *The Role of Second Wines*, p. 16).

[25] Since 1990 the law has restricted "château" to AOC or VDQS (a classification for regions awaiting promotion to AOC) wines on condition that the grapes are harvested solely from the château's own vineyards and are vinified on the premises. (Code du Vin, Article 6 of Règlement 3201/90, October 16, 1990.)

²⁶ Personal communication from Cécile Loqmane at Baron Philippe de Rothschild, October 2007.

²⁷ Based on a survey by the author of châteaux listed by the FGVB on the web site www.monaoc.com.

²⁸ Before one of its sales, the French supermarket Carrefour actually referred to "phantom châteaux" in its catalog, since the name to be used on the label was not yet known. (Réjalot, *Les Logiques du Château*, p. 49.)

²⁹ Réjalot, *Les Logiques du Château*, p. 46.

³⁰ Ibid., p. 55.

³¹ Philippe Pairault, proprietor of Château Teynac, St. Julien (2008).

³² The length of time spent in oak varies from 10-24 months for grand vins, and from 6-18 months for second wines. Most second wines are matured in old oak, but a minority of 10% see no oak at all. (Lewin, *The Role of Second Wines*, p. 25.)

³³ Lewin, *The Role of Second Wines*, p. 26.

³⁴ For the 2006 vintage.

³⁵ At Cru Classés, the average plantings of Cabernet Sauvignon decreased from 65% to 61.5% between 1985 and 2007. However, the average proportion of Cabernet Sauvignon in their grand vins in the 2006 vintage was 66.2%. (Lewin, *The Role of Second Wines*, p. 26.)

³⁶ François Mitjavile, interview with author, April 2008.

³⁷ Comments from proprietors in the Graves and in the Médoc to the author, November 2007.

³⁸ Lewin, *The Role of Second Wines*, p. 35.

³⁹ Bernard Ginestet, *Pauillac* (Paris: Jacques Legrand, 1984).

⁴⁰ Philippe Maurange, *Les Seconds Vins de Grands Crus* (Nanterre: La Revue de Vin de France, issue 439, 2000), p. 35.

⁴¹ Jefford, *The New France*, p. 176.

⁴² Lewin, *The Role of Second Wines*, Appendix 1.

⁴³ Sales of second wine therefore generate ~15% of total revenue for châteaux that have them. (Lewin, *The Role of Second Wines*, p. 29.)

⁴⁴ The total revenue from second wines amounts to more than €100 million for sales at the châteaux, corresponding to a retail value of €300 million (Lewin, *The Role of Second Wines* p. 33.) This compares with a total retail value for all Bordeaux wines of approximately €3 billion (CIVB, *Bordeaux wine economy* 2006.). This places second wines at roughly 10% of the market, with an economic importance greater than the sectors of either dry white or sweet wines.

⁴⁵ CIVB, *Bordeaux wine economy*, 2006.

Chapter 12 Plus Ça Change

¹ P. E. Schneider, *France's wine casks are in the red* (New York Times magazine, December 8, 1957).

---

[2] Leo A. Loubère, *The Wine Revolution in France* (Princeton: Princeton University Press, 1990).

[3] Pliny XXIII.1.

[4] Quoted in Francisque Michel Francisque, *Histoire du commerce et de la navigation à Bordeaux* (Bordeaux: Delmas, 1870).

[5] Blending or mixing wines from Crus of different qualities was banned by parliamentary decree of July 18, 1764, with a penalty of 10,000 livres; proprietors were ordered to identify their wines. (Patrice O'Reilly, *Histoire complète de Bordeaux* [Bordeaux: Delmas publisher, 1860], p. 296.)

[6] Quoted in Alain Huetz de Lemps, preface to M. Paguiere, *Classification et Description des Vins de Bordeaux*, reprinted by Societé des Bibliophiles de Guyenne, Bordeaux, 1977).

[7] Ibid.

[8] J. A. Cavoleau, *Oenologie Française, ou statistique de tous les vignobles et de toutes les boissons vineuses et spiriteuses de la France* (Paris, 1827).

[9] George Ripley, & Charles Anderson Dana, *The American Cyclopaedia: A Popular Dictionary of General Knowledge: France (Wines of)*, (Appleton, 1874), p. 412

[10] Archives of N. Johnston in Bordeaux, 1765, quoted by Pijassou, *Le Médoc*, p. 497.

[11] Quoted by Pijassou, *Le Médoc*, p. 592.

[12] Cyrus Redding, *A History and Description of Modern wines.* (London: Henry Bohn, 1833).

[13] James M. Gabler, *Passions: The Wines and Travels of Thomas Jefferson* (Bacchus Press, 1995), p. 133.

[14] Florence Mothe, *Toutes Hontes Bues. Une siècle de vin et de negoce à Bordeaux* (Paris: Albin Michel, 1992), p. 99.

[15] From 52 million hectoliters (580 million cases) to 25 million hectoliters (280 million cases) See Gilbert Garrier, *Le Phylloxéra* (Paris: Albin Michel, 1898), p. 175.

[16] From 3.39 million hl in 1870 to 1.66 million hl in 1880, with a low point the following year of 1.27 million hl. (Cocks & Féret, *Bordeaux*, 1908, p. 84.)

[17] New York Times, April 18, 1881.

[18] In the 1870s, exports stayed at $45-50 million, but imports rose from $1 million to $21 million. Ibid.

[19] Ibid.

[20] Albert Bonnet (proprietor of Château de Toujague at Soussans in 1896) "*La Chaudière*"; reprinted in Vignobles et Vins d'Aquitaine, (Bordeaux: Sud Ouest, 1970), p. 325.

[21] Quoted in Pijassou, *Le Médoc*, p. 820.

[22] Or even more. Production dropped from ~60 million hl in 1870 to a low of ~35 million hl after 1880. Exports dropped to 2 million hl, and imports increased to 7 million hl; this made the total amount of wine available as ~40 million hl. If consumption stayed steady, therefore, the gap of 20 million hl must have been filled by other means than authentic wine. This calculation was first made by

Armand Gautier, *La sophistication des vins: méthodes analytiques et procédés pour reconnaitre les fraudes* (Baillière, 1898), p. 3.

[23] Alessandro Stanziani, *La Falsification Du Vin En France, 1880-1905: Un Cas De Fraude Agro-Aliminetaire* (Revue d'Histoire Moderne et Contemporaine, v. 50, 2003), p. 154.

[24] Pijassou, *Le Médoc*, pp. 836-838.

[25] Ibid., p. 840.

[26] Ibid., p. 845.

[27] Quoted in Pijassou, *Le Médoc*, p. 899.

[28] See note 25 in Chapter 11.

[29] Le Figaro (1973), May 23, p. 4.

[30] An entertaining memoir of the scandal was published by its protagonist: Pierre Bert, *In Vino Veritas. L'Affaire des Vins de Bordeaux* (Paris: Albin Michel, 1975)

[31] An extensive account of the scandal is in Faith, *The Winemasters*, pp. 253-290.

[32] Bert, *In Vino Veritas,* p. 128.

[33] Quoted Bert, *In Vino Veritas*, p. 176.

[34] Faith, *The Winemasters*, p. 266.

[35] Quoted in Faith, *The Winemasters*, p. 290.

[36] Dominique Richard (Sud Ouest, February 18, 2002), p. 6.

[37] Dominique Richard (Sud Ouest, March 14, 2005), p. 11.

[38] Dominique De Laage (Sud Ouest, February 23, 2002).

[39] Dominique Richard (Sud Ouest, July 6, 2006, p. 10).

[40] Quoted in La Revue du Vin de France, April (2008), p10.

[41] Data from INAO.

[42] Lafforgue, *Le Vignoble Girondin*, p. 275.

[43] Michel Bettane, 2005, Forum Vinexpo. http://www.academie-amorim.com/us/rencontres/actes_vinexpo_gb.pdf.

[44] Cocks & Féret, *Bordeaux*, 1908, 1982; Lafforgue *Le Vignoble Girondin*; Philippe Roudié, *Vignobles et vignerons du Bordelais*, p. 349; CIVB.

[45] Kermit Lynch, *Adventures on the Wine Route* (New York: Noonday Press, 1988), p. 179.

[46] see www.quechoisir.org.

[47] There are reports from all over France of wines being refused the AOC agrément because they are not "typical". Sometimes, of course, they are indeed flawed, but there is a trend to exclude wines with originality, especially those made by completely natural means. "It is becoming increasingly difficult for the small minority of natural winemakers to continue to work in the context of the AOC because the AOCs want to enforce a uniform and mediocre style with no tolerance for originality and authenticity... [The] bureaucrats ... have flattened out, if not lowered quality and made many of France's best winemakers the

targets of an intolerant offensive." [Louis/Dressner Selections (2007); see http://louisdressner.com/basicsearch/?s=brun].

[48] Rudolph Chelminski, *I'll Drink to That: Beaujolais and the French Peasant Who Made It the World's Most Popular Wine* (New York: Gotham, 2007). p. 257.

[49] Everyone involved in this affair appears to feel sensitive about it. Christie's refused permission for reproduction of an original photograph of the bottle, as did its owner.

[50] Benjamin Wallace, *The Billionaire's Vinegar* (New York: Crown Publishing, 2008).

[51] Decanter, September 2008, London, p. 106.

[52] Patrick Keefe, *The Jefferson Bottles*. New Yorker, September 3, 2007.

Chapter 13 Rational Classification

[1] Franck Ferrand et al., *Bordeaux. Grands crus classés 1855-2005* (Paris: Flammarion, 2004).

[2] Eric Conan, *Tempête sur les grands crus* (L'Express, November , 2005).

[3] Berry Bros, 2008. http://www.bbr.com/US/wine-knowledge/classifications.lml

[4] Ronald Barton, *How the clarets were classified*. In The Compleat Imbiber, ed. Cyril Ray. Eriksson, New York, pp. 113-124, 1973.

[5] Faith, *The Winemasters*, p. 77.

[6] Kermit Lynch, *Adventures on the Wine Route* (New York: Noonday Press, 1988), p. 57.

[7] Lichine, *Encyclopedia of Wines and Spirits*, 1967, p. 146.

[8] Bernard Ginestet, *La Bouillie Bordelaise* (Paris: Flammarion, 1975), p. 41.

[9] Markham, *A History of the Bordeaux Classification*, p. 193.

[10] Pijassou, *Le Médoc*, p. 1408.

[11] Ibid., p. 515

[12] Ibid., p. 1408.

[13] Markham *A History of the Bordeaux Classification*.

[14] Ibid., p. 341

[15] Sud Ouest (1961), November 11.

[16] Lichine, *Encyclopedia of Wines and Spirits*, 1974.

[17] Pijassou, *Le Médoc*, p. 1065.

[18] Sud Ouest (1961), November 27

[19] Quoted in Pijassou, *Le Médoc*, p. 1065.

[20] Quoted in Pijassou, *Le Médoc*, p. 675.

[21] Cocks & Féret, *Bordeaux*, 1868.

[22] En primeur prices of Tastet & Lawton as quoted in Penning-Rowsell, *Bordeaux*, 1985.

[23] A book published in the British wine trade noted in 1920: "It is not surprising, therefore, that the Wines from Château Mouton-Rothschild, although still classed as "second growth," always sell at a price actually superior to those

of this class, and since some years have reached figures analogous to those of the Premier Crus; whilst it is worth recording that of the earlier vintages among the Château bottlings, the 1869, 1871 and 1875 Wines have been quoted wholesale on the London market at some of the highest figures ever known, especially the vintage last mentioned." (Claret and Sauternes, The Wine and Spirit Trade Record, London.)

24 Pijassou, *Le Médoc*, p. 1091.

25 Archives of the Chambre de Commerce et d'Industrie de Bordeaux.

26 The Journal Officiel (JO) publishes laws, décrets, and arrêtés on a daily basis.

27 Communication to the author from Jean Pascale in the Direction Commerciale Châteaux Baron Philippe Rothschild SA. May 24, 2007.

28 Archives of the Chambre de Commerce et d'Industrie de Bordeaux.

29 Communication to the author from the Centre de Documentation et d'Archivage de la Direction des Archives de France, June 2007.

30 Sud-Ouest, June 28, 1973, in the section "vie économique," p. 10.

31 In 1964, "cru classé" was qualified in the code by adding "whether or not preceded by an indication of hierarchy."

32 See notes 16-18 in Chapter 3.

33 French government archives.

34 En primeur prices on the Place de Bordeaux obtained by the author from negociants' archives.

35 Although Palmer was a third growth in the 1855 classification, and Lynch Bages was a fifth growth, they have priced with the best of the second growths for so long that they are usually considered part of the group of the super-seconds.

36 Prices are first tranche en primeur on the Place de Bordeaux obtained by the author from negociants' archives (converted to euros for years prior to 1996).

37 See note 28 in Chapter 8.

38 See note 35 above.

39 En primeur prices on the Place de Bordeaux obtained by the author from negociants' archives, augmented by retail prices for a small number of châteaux that are not quoted on the *Place*. Differences in the order of classified growths from Figure 34 show the changes that occur between ten-year and twenty-year assessment periods.

40 Interview by the author at Château Sociando-Mallet, April 7, 2008.

41 Based on retail prices for the period 2003-2005 as determined by the author from a survey of leading merchants in the U.S. and U.K. Price sets for individual producers were normalized and merged to give an overall hierarchy.

42 Based on retail prices for the period 2003-2005 as determined by the author from a survey of leading merchants in the U.S. and U.K.

Index